15-MINUTE INK LANDSCAPES

Simple, Striking, Soothing Lineart of Forests, Mountains, Beaches & More

ROSA HOEHN

Creator of Lines and Mountains

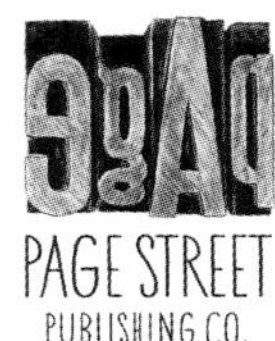

PAGE STREET PUBLISHING CO.

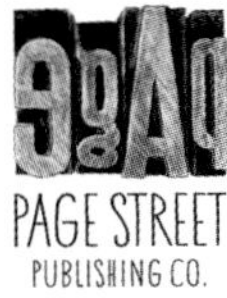

First published in 2022 by
Page Street Publishing Co.
27 Congress Street, Suite 1511
Salem, MA 01970
www.pagestreetpublishing.com

Distributed by Macmillan, sales in Canada by The Canadian Manda Group.

30 29 28 27 26 5 6 7 8 9

ISBN-13: 978-1-64567-697-3
ISBN-10: 1-64567-697-8

Library of Congress Control Number: 2022935163

Cover and book design by Emma Hardy for Page Street Publishing Co.
Illustrations by Rosa Hoehn

Printed and bound in China

Page Street Publishing protects our planet by donating to nonprofits like The Trustees, which focuses on local land conservation.

TO ALL THOSE WHO WANT TO START DRAWING BUT ASSUME THEY HAVE NO TALENT. GRAB A PEN AND SURPRISE YOURSELF WITH WHAT YOU CAN DO!

AND TO EVERYONE WHO NEEDS A TIMEOUT FROM A BUSY LIFE; MAY DRAWING DO FOR YOU WHAT IT DOES FOR ME, NAMELY BRING SOME RELAXATION AND SOME PEACEFUL “ME TIME”.

CONTENTS

Introduction 6
Materials 7

LINEWORK BASICS 8
Warm-Up Exercises 8
Outlines, Textures and Line Weight 10

TIPS FOR CREATIVITY 11
The Key to Getting Good at Drawing: Regular Drawing Practice 11
Tips for Tracking Progress and Holding Yourself Accountable 11
Small Tips for Making Your Work Look More Professional 12

DRAWING PROJECTS 14

MOUNTAINSCAPES 15
The Way to the Mountaintop 16
Cable Car over the Mountains 19
Van Life Night Scene 22
Winter Mountains with Ski Tracks 26
Circle Scene of a Forest Campground 29

BEACH SCENES 33
Surf Shack 34
Seagulls Flying over the Dock 37
The Lighthouse in the Dunes 40
Thunderstorm over the Sea 44
Sailing Around Tropical Islands 47
Chill-Out Hammock Between Palm Trees 50

UNDERWATER SEASCAPES 55
Baby Seals Playing in the Waves 56
Jellyfish Swarm 58
Diver Swimming Through a School of Fish 61
Whale with Small Fish Friends 64
Turtle Swimming over Seaweed 67

DESERT LANDSCAPES 71
Rock Formation Landscape 72
Cacti in the Desert 75
Adobe Houses and a Snake 78
Desert Night Sky 81
Linework Canyons 84

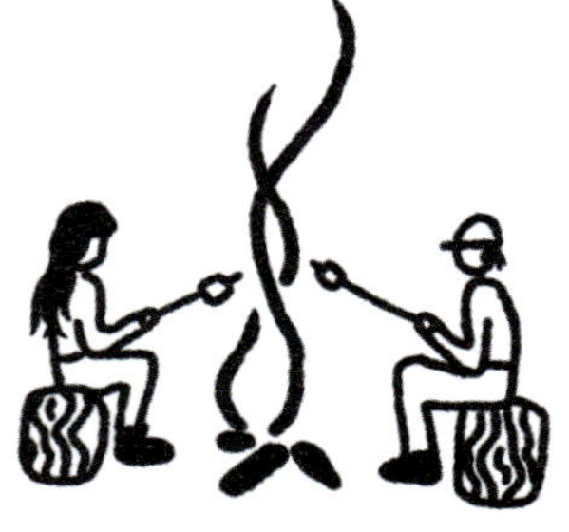

LAKES, RIVERS AND WATERFALLS 87

Small Wood Cabin on the Lake 88
Fishing on a Mountain Lake 91
Canoeing Along the River 93
High Waterfall 95
Bridge over a Small Forest Stream 98

FOREST SCENES 103

Cabin in the Woods 104
Wolf Howling at the Moon 106
Deer Family in a Forest Meadow 109
Misty Winter Forest 112

IN SPACE 115

Secret Planet Landscape 116
A Cloud of Planets 119
Galaxy in a Jar 122
Astronaut Floating Through Outer Space 125
The Astronaut and the Moon 127

COUNTRY LIFE 131

Windmills in the Country 132
Small Farm Scene 135
Flock of Birds Sitting on Power Lines 138
Hilly Landscape with Mushrooms 142

NIGHT AND DAY 145

Mountain Scene in Day and Night 146
Sun and Night Sky over a Cabin 151
Sun and Moon Reflection over the Sea 155

THE SEASONS 159

Base Drawing 160
Spring: Cabin Surrounded by Blooming Trees 162
Summer: Sunny Patch of Leafy Trees 164
Autumn: Trees and Falling Leaves 166
Winter: Snowy Treescape 168

WRAP-UP: DESIGN YOUR OWN MINI LANDSCAPES 170

Main Subject and Drawing Elements 171
References 171
Composition 171
Highlight Your Center of Interest 172
Displaying and Digitizing Your Work 173

Acknowledgments *174*
About the Author *175*
Index *176*

INTRODUCTION

Hi there! I'm Rosa. How exciting that you bought this book, which is the highlight of my personal art journey! What motivated you to start drawing? Curiosity? The need for a new hobby? Wanting to create something?

I started drawing because I liked creating. Back in high school, I took a lot of art classes, and I was considering going to university for graphic design. Because I lacked a clear direction for why I wanted this, I changed my mind and got a tourism degree instead. As life got busy, I forgot all about drawing.

Years later, in 2019, my job required lots of traveling. I was spending my days in hotels and airplanes and was beyond stressed. In the evenings, I would sit in my hotel room, too tired to do anything, yet my brain was too wired to relax. I tried working out in the hotel gym, yoga, meditation—all with mediocre results. One evening in London, I passed an art store and, on a whim, I went in and bought a set of pens and a sketchbook.

That's when drawing changed my life.

Mostly, it made me stop keeping an eye on the clock, and it helped my brain relax. I could get into that special flow state you might remember from your childhood: You were playing and hours went by, but it felt like minutes and your mum always called you in for dinner way too early. As adults, we rarely experience this, but drawing got me there. It's like meditation but without the, well, meditating.

Astonishingly, drawing also helped me clarify my journey and my goals. A finished drawing is the result of a series of unconscious decisions. What do I want to express, what elements do I want to include in my work, what style . . . and so on. To improve your drawings, you then reflect on these decisions and try to learn from them. As I did this more often, also unconsciously, I also got into the habit of applying this way of thinking to everyday life and made better decisions.

A couple of weeks after buying that sketchbook, I was hooked again and started my Instagram profile. It was initially meant as a visual journal for myself, then as a way to communicate with a group of people that shared the same interest, and ultimately helped me build my own business (thank you COVID-19 lockdowns). Most recently, it led to the amazing opportunity to write (and draw) this book.

In it, you will find dazzling line drawings of various landscapes from lakes and deserts to scenes set underwater and in space. Most of them are black and white, but some are in color and use minimalism to stunning effects. Notably, you'll be introduced to artistic concepts like negative space, monochromatic contrast and abstraction (which will help you suggest details and intricacy), as well as line weight and placing lines strategically to convey different perspectives.

As the title suggests, this collection of achievable projects takes no time at all, and if you are looking into learning how to draw, this book is a great way to start.

I hope these simple yet gorgeous projects do for you what art has done for me—namely, become a quick moment of relaxation that might just turn into a lifelong relationship with art. So, whether you are just starting out or have been drawing for a while, think about this before we start: Where do you want your art journey to take you?

Rosa

MATERIALS

Time to gather your drawing materials.

If you are only starting your art journey, you can use the supplies you already have at home. Pencils and pens, as well as printer paper or a notebook, can usually be found in every household.

For more experienced artists, I'm sure you have different art materials at home already. Line art doesn't require fancy stuff, so pick from your stash what works for you.

If you do want to invest in tools, I advise you to start with a good set of pens and good quality paper. Most important are black fineliner pens. Get three to four different sizes and a bigger nib or brush pen. Make sure they have waterproof ink. Some quality brands are Sakura® Micron®, Faber-Castell or Arteza®. For white pens, Sakura Gelly Rolls® or Uni-Ball® Signos™ work best.

With sketchbooks or drawing pads, look for the paper weight on the packaging. Aim for at least 120 to 150 grams per square meter (gsm), so the pens don't bleed through. A minimum of 250 gsm is needed if you want to add ink wash or watercolor. Sakura Micron® tends to have the best value for your money for sketchbook options. Hahnemüehle and Fabriano have beautiful paper but are generally more expensive.

I also recommend going to a store instead of shopping online. At the art store, you can touch the paper and try out the pens and also get advice from the staff. Most are artists themselves, and if you tell them about your project, they can help you pick suitable tools and materials.

I completed all drawings in this book with the following materials:

- Faber-Castell Pitt Artist Pen bullet nib in 1.5
- Sakura Pigma® Micron in 05 and 01
- Sakura Pigma Professional brush pen in MB
- White Sakura Gelly Roll® in 10 and 08
- Winsor & Newton® Black Indian Ink + small and medium round brushes
- Rohrer & Klingner® colored inks + small and medium round brushes
- Store-brand watercolor + small and medium round brushes
- Faber-Castell Pencils in F and 2B + kneadable eraser
- 300 gsm/140lbs Fabriano cold-pressed watercolor paper
- Ruler, circle stencil + compass

LINEWORK BASICS

After gathering your materials, you can dive right in. Working on basic drawing skills is fun if you pick a subject you like. Grab your ruler, pencil and pen and let's get started!

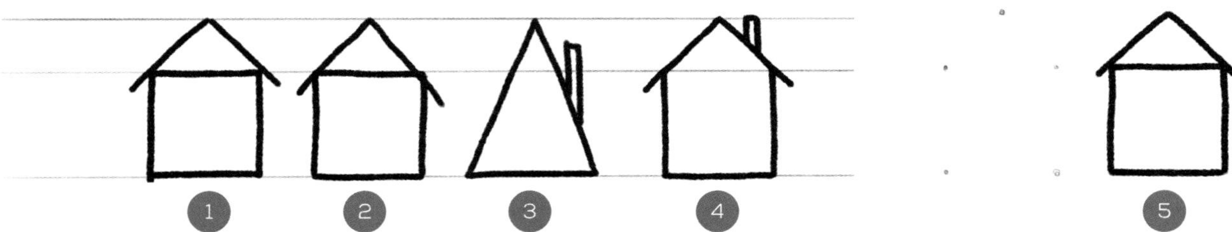

WARM-UP EXERCISES

Each time you start a drawing session, the first couple of lines come out a little wonky.

It's a bit like at the gym: You need to warm up your muscles first so you don't hurt yourself—or in this case, your beautiful drawing!

Before starting on any drawings, I usually do some basic linework to sharpen my skills and remind my fingers what drawing feels like. Some of the more traditional drawing books will tell you to draw lots of parallel lines of the same length, then move on to curved lines. The reason behind it is to have control of your stroke and be able to stop and start a line at a precise point.

All of this is important. I prefer to practice basic skills by drawing an actual subject.

First up: cabins to practice straight lines.

Use a ruler and draw three horizontal pencil lines on your paper. Then, do a simple cabin in pen—a square shape with a triangle for a roof.

Work slowly and make sure your lines are steady and straight and connect properly at the corners. Do as many as needed until you are comfortable with the lines and you get a nice result.

Try to avoid some of the small errors I made here when drawing the cabins: (1) the bottom left corner and the tip of the roof; (2) the roof alignment with the top right corner, the right side of the roof is a little too long; and (3) the top left corner of the chimney is uneven.

You can also vary the cabin to make it more interesting, like I did with (3) and (4). See how many variations you can come up with. For added difficulty, try this with just a couple of pencil dots as guidelines, like in (5), or with no pencil lines at all.

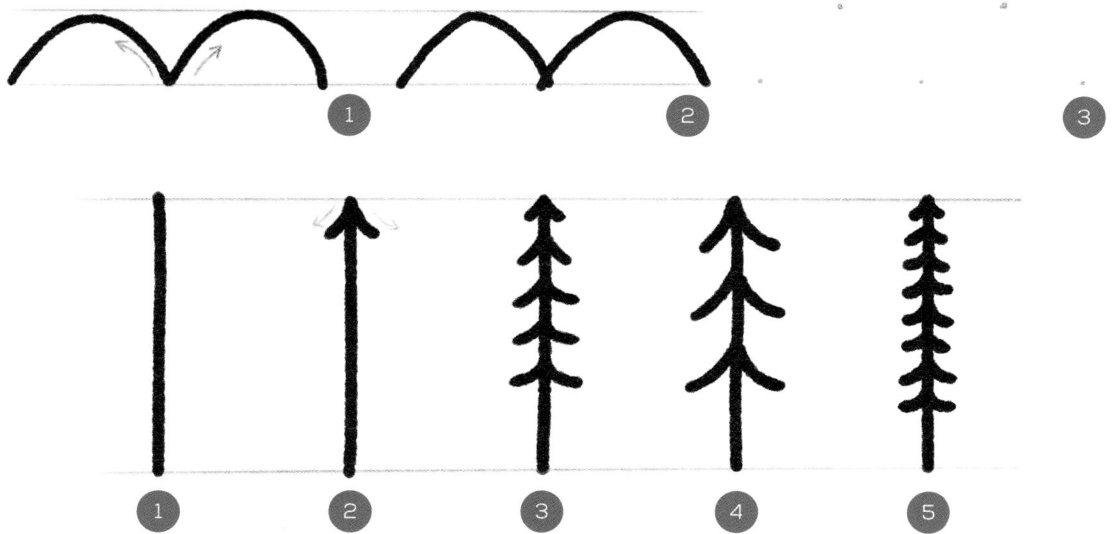

Next, let's draw flying birds and practice curved lines.

Use a ruler and draw two horizontal pencil lines on your paper. Then, draw the connected curves. Start from the middle and draw outward. Focus on getting both wings of the bird as symmetrical as possible, like in (1). Avoid a sloppy connection of both curves in the middle or an untidy, pointy curve, like the left wing in (2). When you've done a couple of birds with guidelines, make it more difficult by using just a couple of dots for guidance, like in (3) or draw on blank paper.

The last training step is combining straight and curved lines to make trees. Use your ruler again to draw two horizontal lines. Draw a vertical line with a pen—this is the tree trunk (1)—then, starting at the tip, angle a slightly curved line out to each side to draw the first pair of branches (2). Continue down the trunk with more branches (3). You can vary the size and the slope of the branches like in (4) and (5). Switch to just dots as guidance once drawing with guidelines becomes fairly easy.

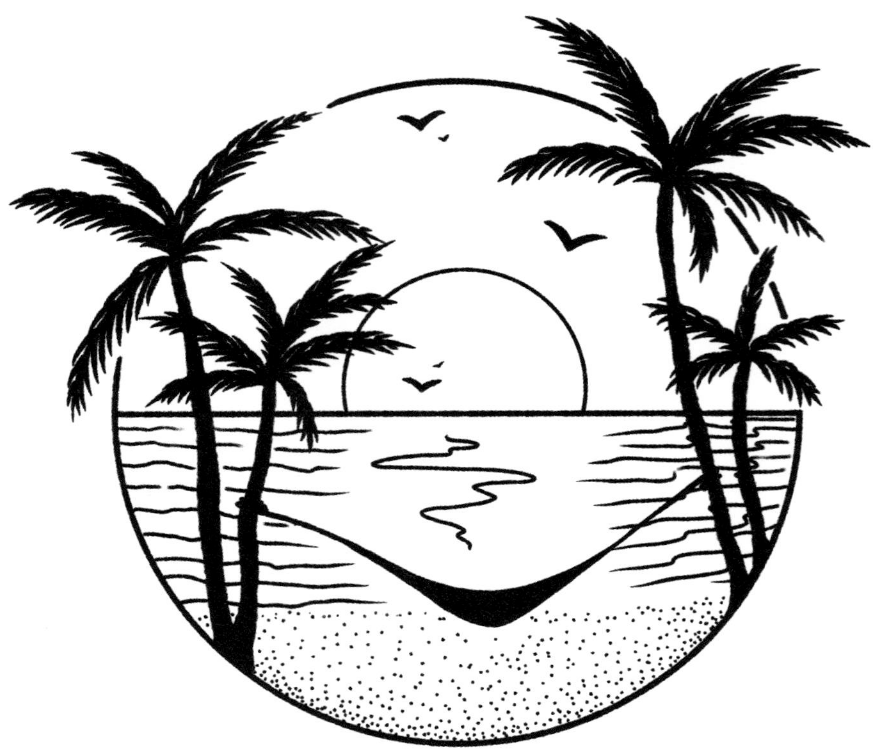

OUTLINES, TEXTURES AND LINE WEIGHT

When you draw the edges of an object to show its form, these are outlines. Look at the cabins, birds and trees in the previous exercises. All of them are created with outlines only.

To add some more details to our subject, we can use textures. A texture means we are giving more information about the surface area, and sometimes also how the light hits the surface. Examples are a wood texture on a cabin, sand on a beach or the rocky slopes of a mountain. For example, in the above drawing (see Chill-Out Hammock Between Palm Trees on page 50), there are two textures: the sandy texture of the beach, represented by lots of dots, and the sea surface on the sides of the setting sun. Irregular lines represent small waves and also show that this area of the sea does not reflect the light in the same way the water in front of the sun does.

Line weight means that a line varies in its thickness. This is very relevant when drawing with a brush (or any other pressure-sensitive medium) and also applies to angled or flat nibs. With regular fineliners, there is not a lot you can do as their nature is to provide a very steady line.

Still, you can get some variations. One I use often is a thinner start or end of the line. This means you lift or apply your pen gradually to the paper, changing the pressure. I find this is easier to do if you speed up your movement a little. In the beach drawing above, you can find this on the leaves of the palm trees, the birds' wings, the reflection of the sun on the water and the wave texture.

TIPS FOR CREATIVITY

THE KEY TO GETTING GOOD AT DRAWING: REGULAR DRAWING PRACTICE

I believe that drawing is more than 95 percent learned skill. Talent might help you in the beginning, as learning will feel more effortless, but in the end, it's your work ethic that will get you where you want to go and push you through that point where you feel you are standing still. Consistent practice will teach you how to translate what you see onto paper. For me, it changed my entire life and helped me build a small business.

Don't get discouraged if you are unhappy with your first drawings. It happens to all of us. Pick up your pen another time and try again.

Creating the habit of practicing my drawing skills on a regular basis was a game changer for me. Finding a couple of uninterrupted hours for drawing was hard, therefore I didn't do it enough. Then, I switched to 15 to 30 minutes each week. With the shorter and more regular sessions, I practiced way more and, of course, learned more. My progress motivated me so much that my weekly sessions soon increased to every other day and sometimes daily.

That's why this book is called *15-Minute Ink Landscapes*. It's entirely possible to draw one of them in about 15 minutes and have fun while improving your skills.

TIPS FOR TRACKING PROGRESS AND HOLDING YOURSELF ACCOUNTABLE

When drawing regularly, it's an important motivator to see how much progress you make. This is why I find it important not to put your work away in some drawer and forget about it, but to make it easily accessible. That way, you can go through the pieces and compare your most recent work with earlier drawings.

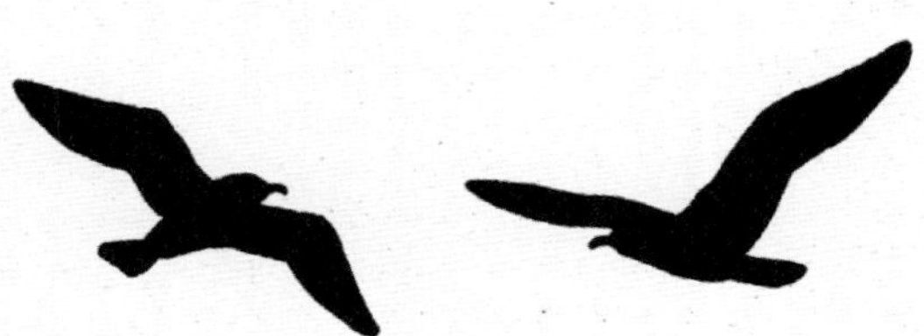

That was why I started my Instagram account @linesandmountains. It was meant as a visual journal of my art journey. You can also collect your drawings in one sketchbook or decorate your walls with your artwork (see the chapter Displaying and Digitizing Your Work on page 173 for ideas). Be creative. The only important thing is that you can see your work on a regular basis and be proud of your accomplishments.

As for holding yourself accountable, there are three steps to it: Set a goal for how often you want to draw, communicate that to someone else and schedule the time. I set the goal to post a new drawing on my Instagram account each week and communicated this. Of course, then I felt like I had to deliver on this promise. I scheduled time slots for drawing in my phone calendar in the beginning until it became a routine. And once I had connected with other artists, I became even more motivated to draw and post regularly because I suddenly got feedback on every single drawing I posted.

There are also other ways to include more drawing practice into a very busy day:

- You could draw your grocery shopping list—or your to-do list.
- For class notes or meeting notes, you could use the Sketch Notes technique.
- If you're keeping a journal, try drawing instead of writing.
- You could also keep a bullet journal; this technique combines artwork with elements from a day planner.

Every drawing you do is one baby step on your art journey—have fun with it!

SMALL TIPS FOR MAKING YOUR WORK LOOK MORE PROFESSIONAL

On Instagram, people often send me their drawings and ask for things to improve. The following tips are a list of the most common issues I see. They are quite easy to implement and will make your work look even nicer in an instant.

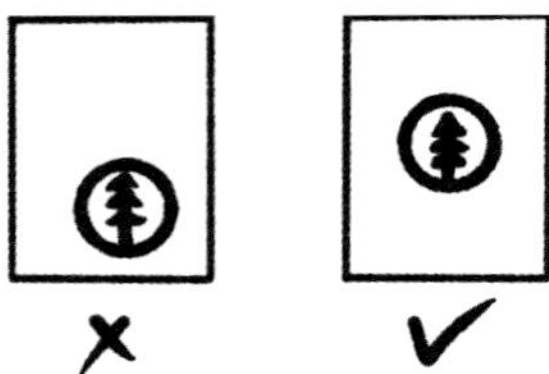

Before you start your drawing, take a minute to visualize where you will place the drawing on your paper. Choose the placement and size of your drawing intentionally, and don't just start somewhere on the page. That way, you can avoid running out of space on one end or accidentally creating an awkward page layout.

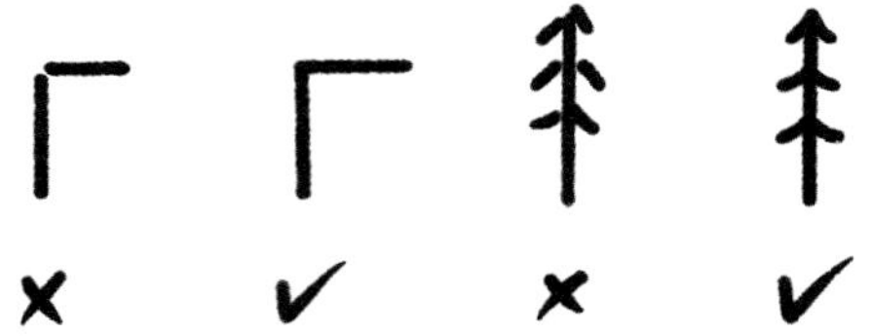

Concentrate on tidy lines and line connections. Subconsciously, sloppy linework will always make you think something is wrong with your drawing.

Draw in different line weights to create interest. This is easy when you use different-sized pen nibs. Drawings in just one line weight will seem more static and less interesting than one with more variations. The general rule is to draw the bigger shapes and objects in the foreground with thicker lines and details, and objects in the background with thinner lines.

Try to avoid covering a mistake with white paint. It will never have the same white as your paper and I find that draws the eye even more.

First, consider if your mistake is big and obvious enough to actually need fixing. Often, it's too small to be recognizable in the final drawing. If it needs fixing and it's small, it's best to gently scratch off the ink with a blade or some sandpaper. (Practice this before you use it on a drawing!)

If it's too big to scratch off, find a creative way to make it part of your drawing. Sometimes, mistakes are happy accidents that will make your work more interesting. The following progress drawings show you how I fixed slips of my pen by placing lines over the mark or using a black sky to cover an untidy line.

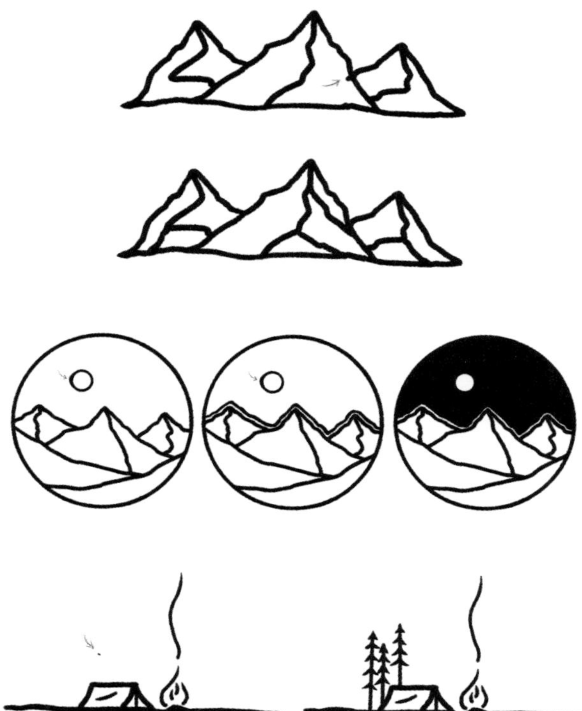

If you can't fix it, start over. I've had to redraw a lot of drawings and I was usually happy that I did because it improved the drawing. You can speed up the process by using a light box, a bright window or a glass table with a lamp underneath it to transfer your first try to a new sheet of paper.

DRAWING PROJECTS

Let's get drawing!

Get ready to experience all the wonders that ink pens can produce with projects that are as breathtaking as they are exciting. The projects start out with mountain scenes with pieces like Winter Mountains with Ski Tracks (page 26) before moving on to beaches. Chill-Out Hammock Between Palm Trees (page 50), anyone? Then continue with underwater seascapes (starting on page 55), deserts (from page 71), the countryside (page 131) and even space (page 115).

If you would like to try your hand at some bigger projects, you could dig into the night and day drawings (page 145)—where you can re-create the project on the cover, for example—or the section on the seasons (page 159).

All drawing projects are grouped by topic. Each category will feature different motifs and the projects will vary in difficulty. You can do one after the other or skip around to your liking.

For all drawings, you can do a full underdrawing in pencil that you ink afterward. To make the drawing process clearer for you to follow, this step is not always pictured.

Grab your pens and paper and dive in!

MOUNTAINSCAPES

Every part of the world has beautiful mountain ranges. And while their shapes, rock types, plants and animals may differ, one thing is the same everywhere: Mountains are fascinating and some even prefer them to the beach for vacationing.

I like mountains because I find them very relaxing. When you stand on top of a mountain, it puts things into perspective. You see that most of your problems are small and there is no use in obsessing over them so much. Drawing mountains is similarly relaxing to me. Focusing on the lines and rocky textures lets the rest of the world disappear for a while.

In the following projects, you can draw your way to the top of a mountain while practicing smooth curved lines. Your pens can take you on a road trip, camping or skiing, while you learn how to draw different tree types and the perfect crescent moon.

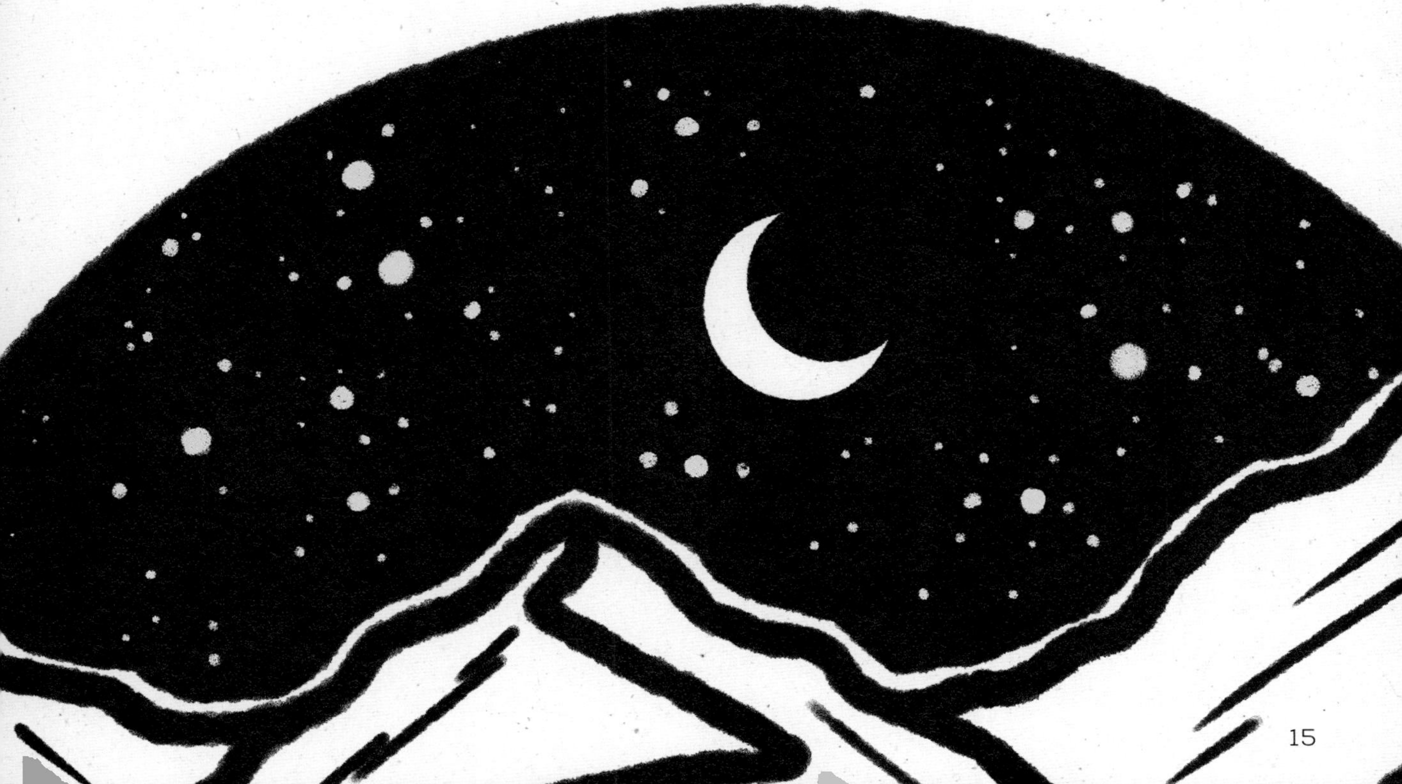

THE WAY TO THE MOUNTAINTOP

Hiking is one of my favorite outdoor activities. In the beginning, you are excited to have the trail in front of you. After miles and hours uphill, it's your legs, feet and lungs against your brain. They want to stop, but your brain wants to go to the top. I guess that's why it's the best feeling to reach it—because it's never easy. Finishing a drawing is the same, so we rush the process to get to that victorious feeling. As we work on the slowly curving shapes with our different-sized pens, try to go slow and lay down your lines deliberately. The overall quality of your drawing will be so much better for it and you'll avoid unnecessary mistakes.

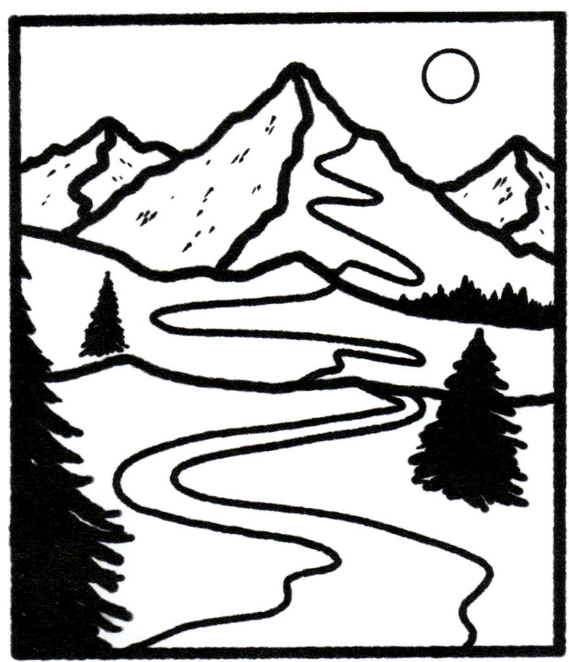

WHAT YOU NEED

Paper of your choice

Black pens in three sizes: 1.5, 05 and 01

Triangle ruler

Brush pen

Compass, circle tool or round object to trace

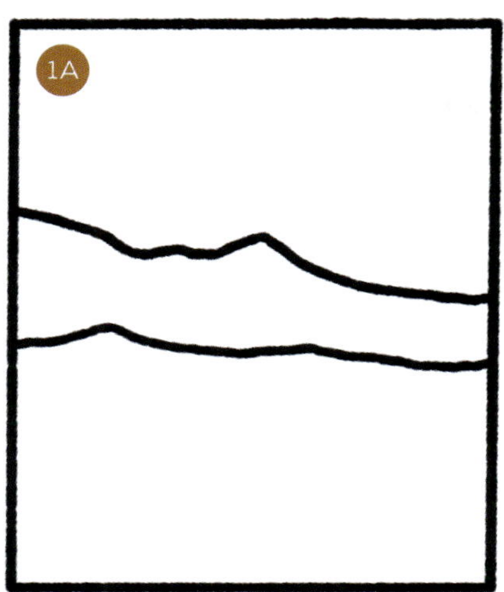

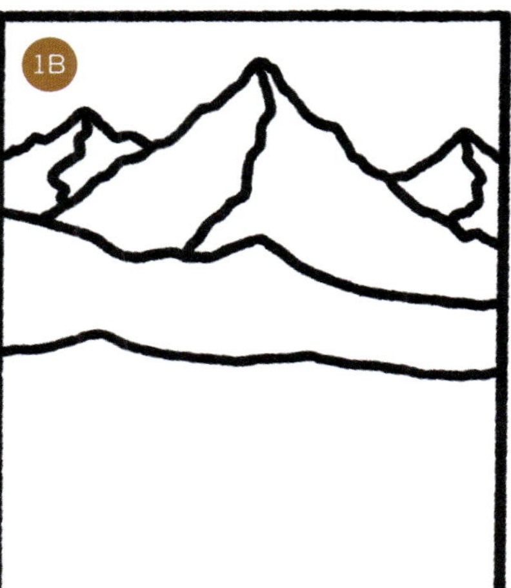

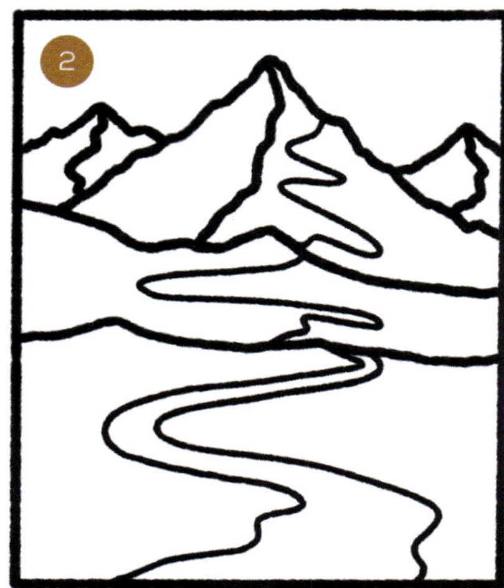

STEP 1

Draw the rectangle frame with your thickest (1.5) pen. Mine is around 3 x 4 inches (7.5 x 10 cm). Approximately in the middle of the rectangle, draw your first line. Mine is sloping toward the right and has some bumps. It's better if it's not perfectly level and straight as it will look more natural. A little way above that first line, draw a second line. There you can already include some smaller peaks.

Next, draw the mountains in the background. From the peaks, draw zigzag lines downward. These will make the mountains look somewhat three-dimensional and give the image more depth in the background.

STEP 2

Draw the path with a medium (05) pen in the fore-ground and your thin (01) pen in the background on the mountain itself. Try to do very smooth curves.

FUN FACT: For more stability, some artists hold their breath when drawing smooth curves or straight lines by hand. I also recommend controlling the movement with your whole arm, from the shoulder rather than just your wrist. It gives you a larger range of motion.

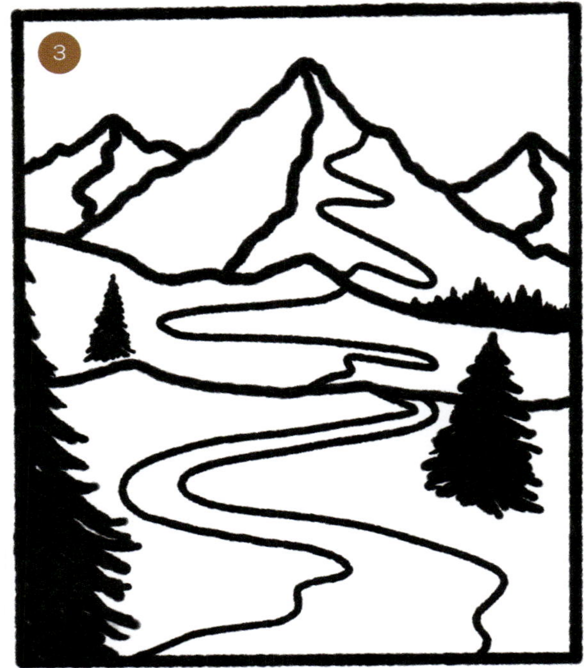

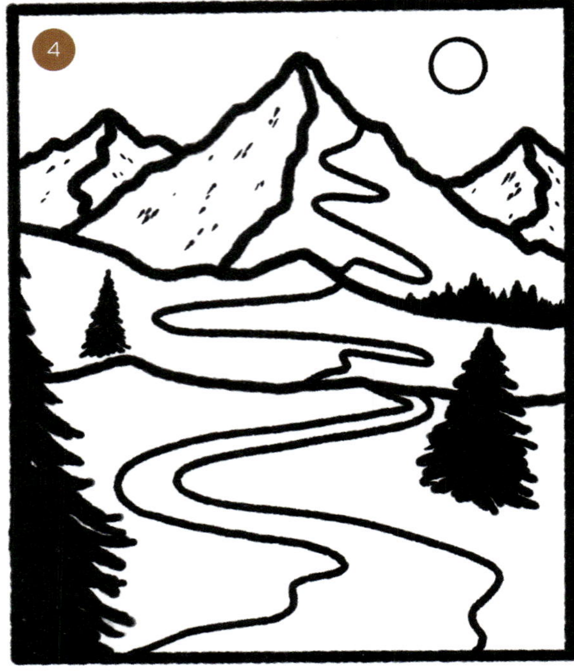

STEP 3

Next up are the trees. The bigger ones in the front can be done with a brush pen and your thick (1.5) pen. Toward the back as the trees get smaller, it's easier to use the medium (05) pen. The faraway trees just at the bottom of the background mountain are little more than an irregular zigzag line. As we want to give the impression that they are far away, no details are necessary. Use the thin (01) pen.

STEP 4

As finishing touches, add some small texture lines to the background mountains. This imitates rocky surfaces. Draw a circle for the sun with your medium (05) pen. If you want, you could also add some grass blades in the foreground.

CABLE CAR OVER THE MOUNTAINS

Mountains provide the surroundings for some of my favorite activities: winter sports and hiking. No matter if you are a skier, snowboarder or you enjoy drawing snow more than playing in it, grab your pens and let's create a winter landscape together! This project will demonstrate how to start with the main object of the drawing and then work from the foreground backward. This is a good technique to create the correct overlap of elements, which gives depth to the drawing.

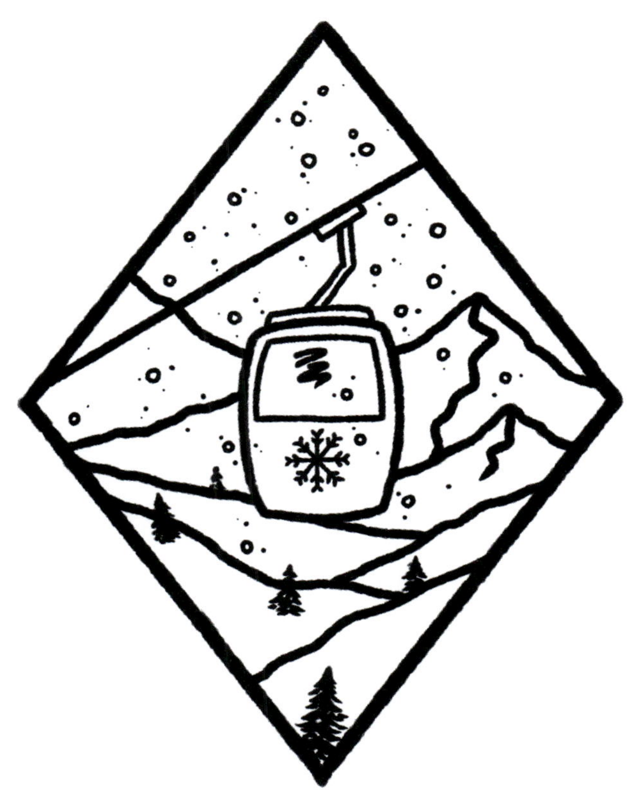

WHAT YOU NEED

Paper of your choice

Black pens in three sizes: 1.5, 05 and 01

Triangle ruler

Pencil and eraser

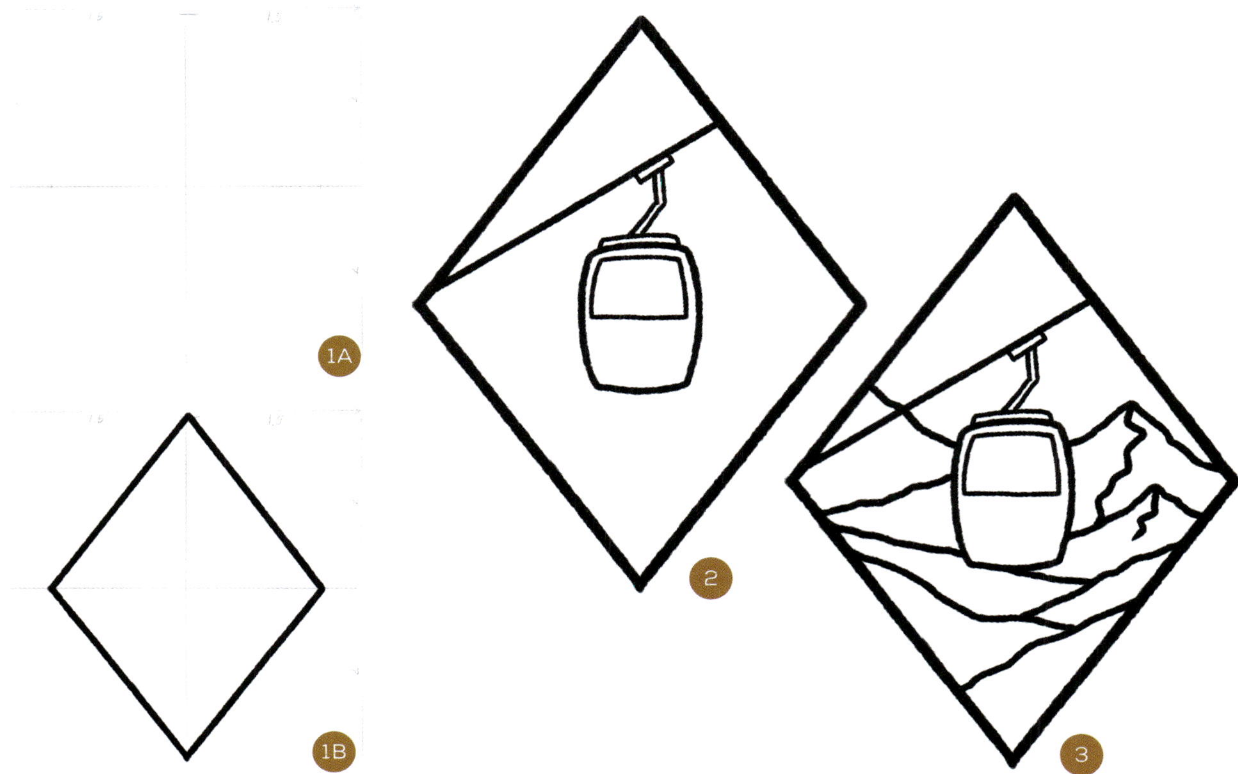

STEP 1

This drawing has a diamond frame. As a first step, we're constructing the frame. This will sound like a geometry class. Don't worry though—it's easy! Grab your pencil and ruler and draw two lines that intersect at a 90-degree angle. My diamond is going to be 3 x 4 inches (7.5 x 10 cm). From the intersection on the vertical line, measure 2 inches (5 cm) toward the top and toward the bottom, and mark those points. On the horizontal line, measure 1½ inches (3.75 cm) toward each side and make two more marks.

Use your thick (1.5) pen and the ruler to connect all four points that you just marked to get the outline of your diamond. Now, gently erase the construction lines.

STEP 2

The next step is to draw the gondola cable. Use the ruler and your medium (05) pen for this. Then, add the body of the gondola in the middle of the diamond. It has the shape of a rectangle but with curved sides. Use rectangle shapes to connect the gondola to the cable.

Switch to your thin (01) pen and draw the gondola window. The base is done, now on to the details!

STEP 3

In this step, we are adding the background. First are the mountain outlines. Use your medium (05) pen and start from the front with gently sloping hills. Continue to work toward the background, increasing the height and steepness of the mountains. On the mountains to the right of the gondola, add zigzag lines for the ridges.

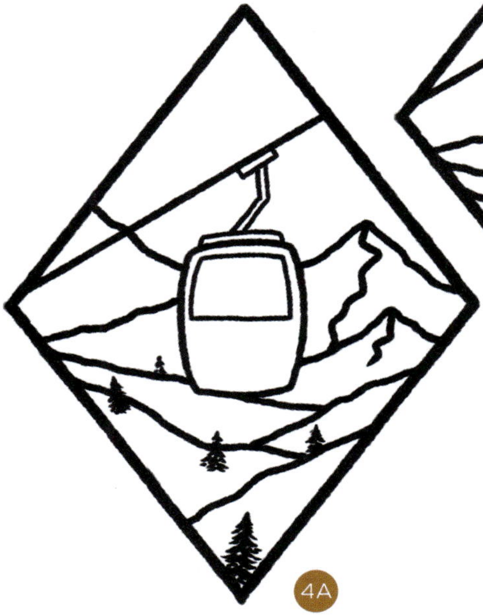

STEP 4

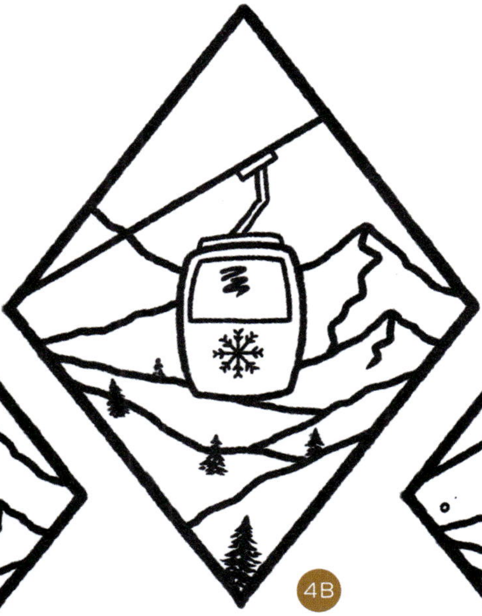

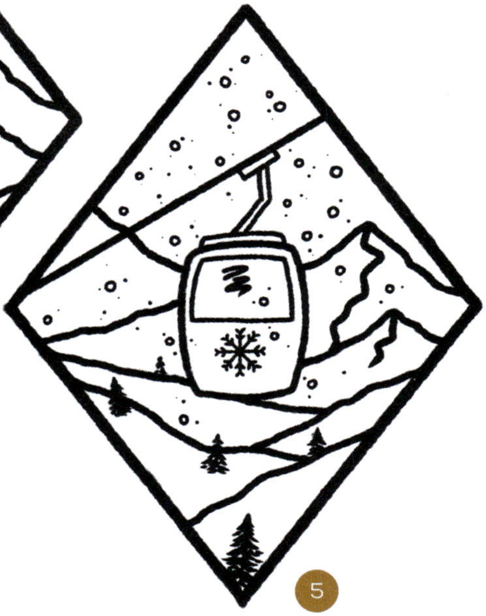

Now, to make the landscape below the gondola more interesting and natural, add some trees. I wanted a bulking style, as well as more black areas in general for some more contrast. To draw them, layer a bunch of outward-curving lines until you get a rough pine tree.

Use your medium (05) pen for the ones in the front and your thin (01) pen for the ones in the back. Make sure your trees get smaller and less detailed toward the back as they are farther away from the viewer.

Next, draw some details on the gondola with your thin (01) pen. I chose a snowflake, which I built like this:

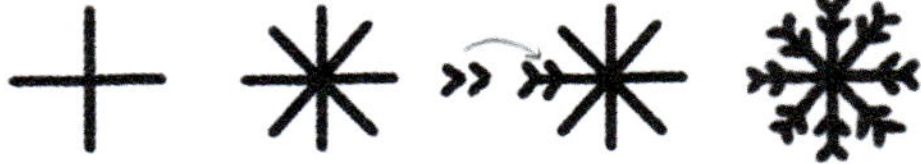

Or you could also use the logo of your favorite ski resort. Put a little zigzag line on the window to show the reflection of the light. Almost done!

STEP 5

Finally, add some details in the sky. Fitting the landscape and the gondola, I went for snowflakes. Use your thin (01) pen and draw very small circles and dots in two sizes (with your 05 and 01 pens) all over the sky. Make sure to put some in front of the gondola and the mountains too. And your winter wonderland drawing is ready!

VAN LIFE NIGHT SCENE

During COVID-19 lockdowns, every time I scrolled through my social media feeds, van life pictures would pop up. I even started researching van rentals for future travels . . . . Turns out my idea wasn't very unique, and because so many people were looking to book, prices were super high. So, I decided to draw myself a little van life scene instead. We'll be experimenting with different line depths, and I'm also teaching you my secret technique to drawing a perfect crescent moon in this project—it's worth millions!

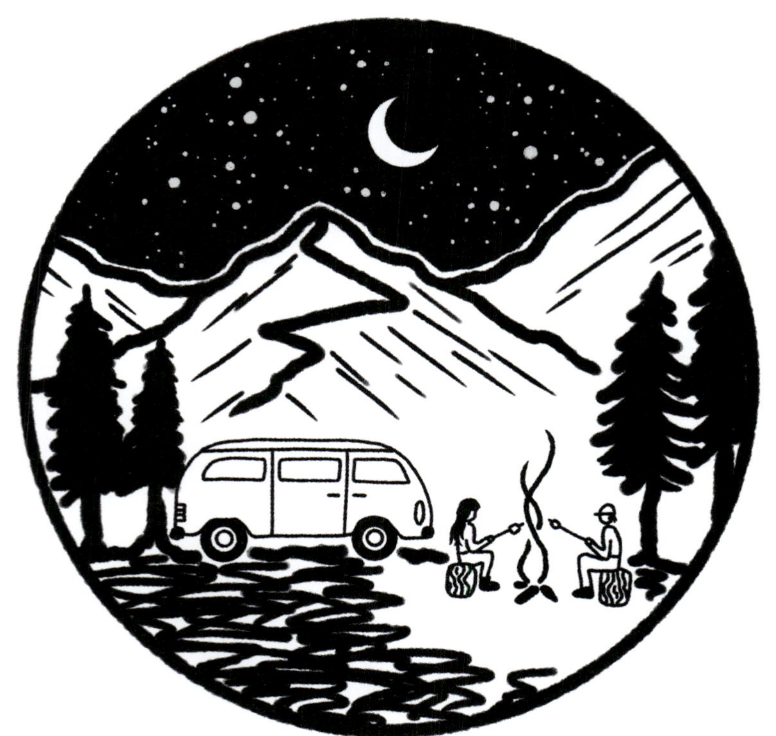

WHAT YOU NEED

Paper of your choice

Compass, circle tool or round object to trace

Black pens in four sizes: 1.5, 05, 01 and 005

Brush pen (for the trees and night sky)

Black liquid ink

White pens in different sizes, if you have them (10 and 08)

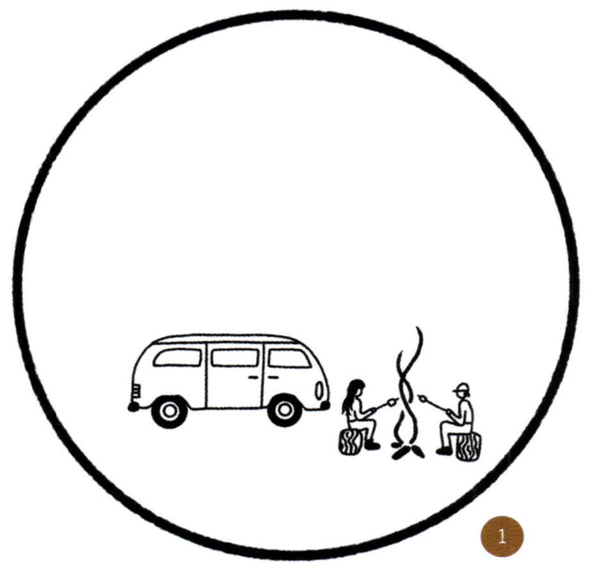

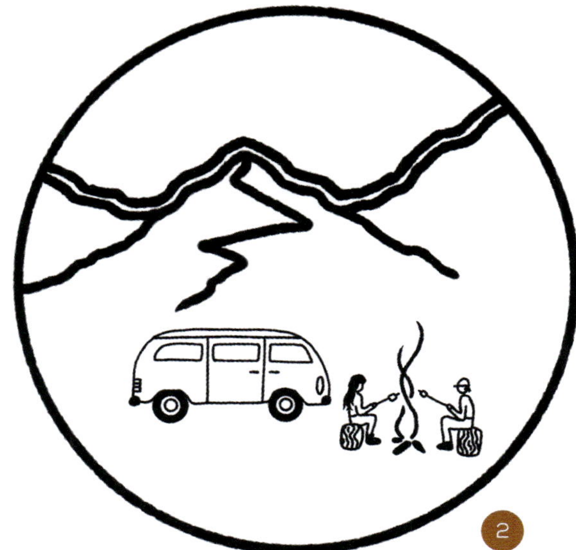

STEP 1

Start by drawing the circle frame of about 2 to 3 inches (5 to 7.5 cm). Use your thickest (1.5) pen for this. Next, draw the van. I searched online for a picture of a retro van that I used as a reference. To make it easier to draw, I kept it two-dimensional and left out most of the details. I used my two thinnest (01 and 005) nibs.

The couple making s'mores around the fire was composed in the same way:

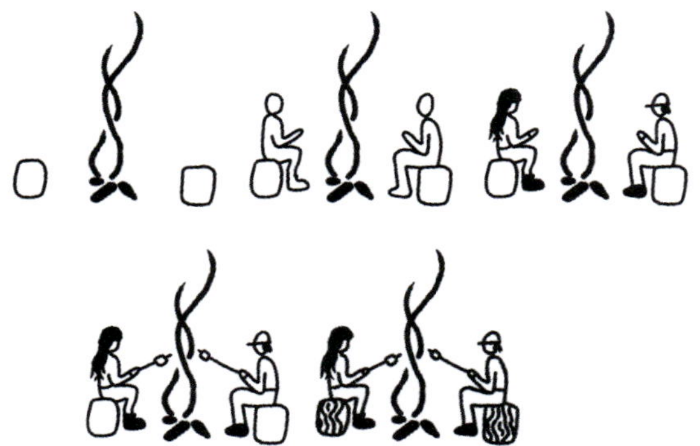

Ask yourself what features are absolutely necessary to recognize the subject of your drawing. Only put these on paper and ignore the rest. It keeps yourself from getting frustrated while still conveying the image.

STEP 2

Now, it's time to draw the mountains in the background with your thickest (1.5) pen. Add a zigzag line starting at the top of the mountain to show the mountain ridge. I wanted the mountains' outline to be clearly visible against the night sky later on; therefore, I added a second line with my thick (1.5) pen above the mountain outline. The thin white space between the two lines will accomplish my goal once the sky is painted black.

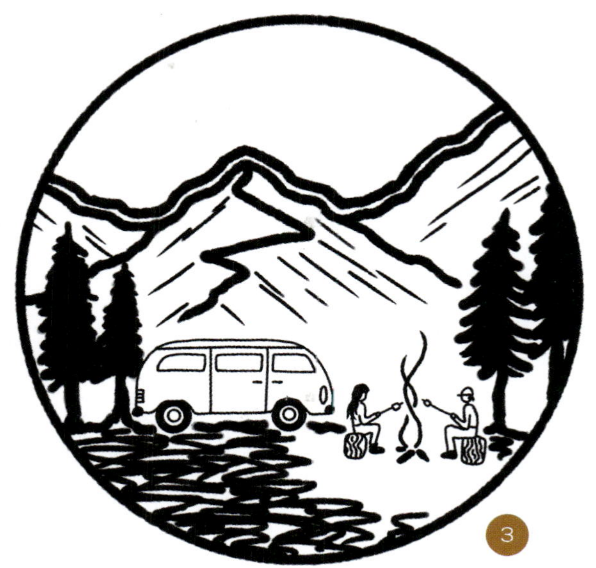

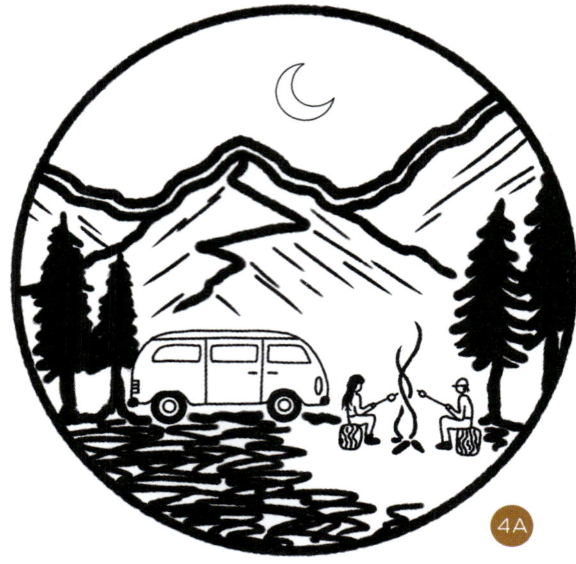

STEP 3

The main elements of the drawing are in place—good job! Let's move on to the foreground. Using the brush pen for the main body of the trees, and the thick (1.5) pen for the trunks and tips of the branches, add some tree silhouettes toward the left of the van and toward the right of the campfire.

Now, imagine yourself sitting next to the fire and looking around. You will see the space around the fire quite clearly. Beyond the reach of the firelight, it will be dark. Since the flames are moving, I always find that the shadows are moving too. Grab your thick (1.5) pen and fill most of the foreground with wiggly lines—these are the moving shadows. Keep an imaginary circle around the campfire free. This is the area where the fire sheds light. Use your thin (01) pen to add some lines to the mountains to give them some texture.

STEP 4

There is a crescent moon visible in the night sky and I'll show you a little trick to draw a perfect one: Draw a pencil circle in the size you want the crescent moon to be. Then, draw a pencil circle that is a little smaller, but place it slightly to the side and up. Draw the outline of the crescent moon created by both overlapping circles. Once the ink is dry, gently erase the pencil lines.

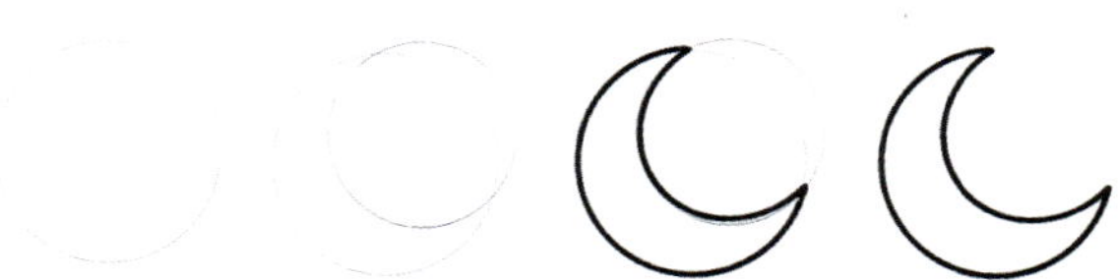

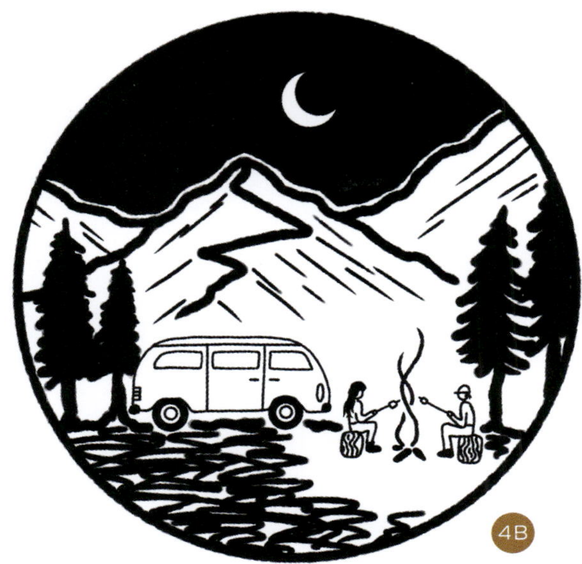

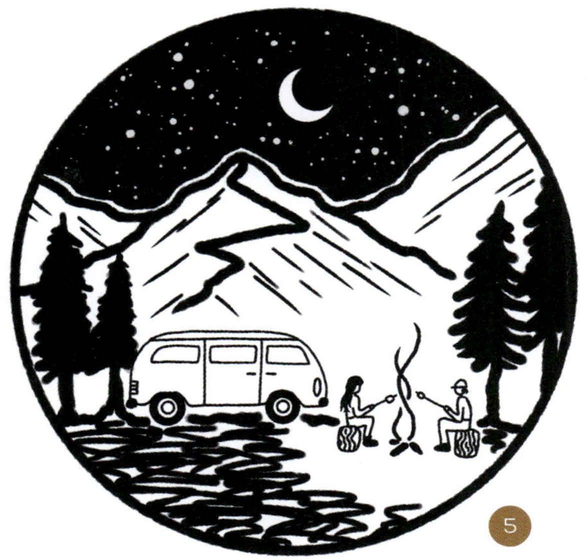

For larger black areas like the sky here, I fill them in with a brush and liquid ink to achieve an even, solid black. If you are using a felt-tip pen, the area might look a little uneven. You can do a second coat of black to get a better result and also go heavy on the stars in the next step. This will take the focus away from spotty areas.

STEP 5

To add the last touch, use your white pens to dot some stars in the night sky. I like to vary the sizes of the stars to imitate nature. The bigger dots represent brighter stars. Are you in the van life mood yet?

WINTER MOUNTAINS WITH SKI TRACKS

I don't know about you, but I am a big fan of skiing. On sunny days, the best part is taking a break on the terrace of a mountain restaurant, drinking hot chocolate and watching others ski down the slopes. This drawing differs from the other projects in its composition—there is no middle ground here. I wanted to highlight that the skiers are far away, so I dropped the transition that the middle ground provides between near and far elements. Don't you love how it looks?

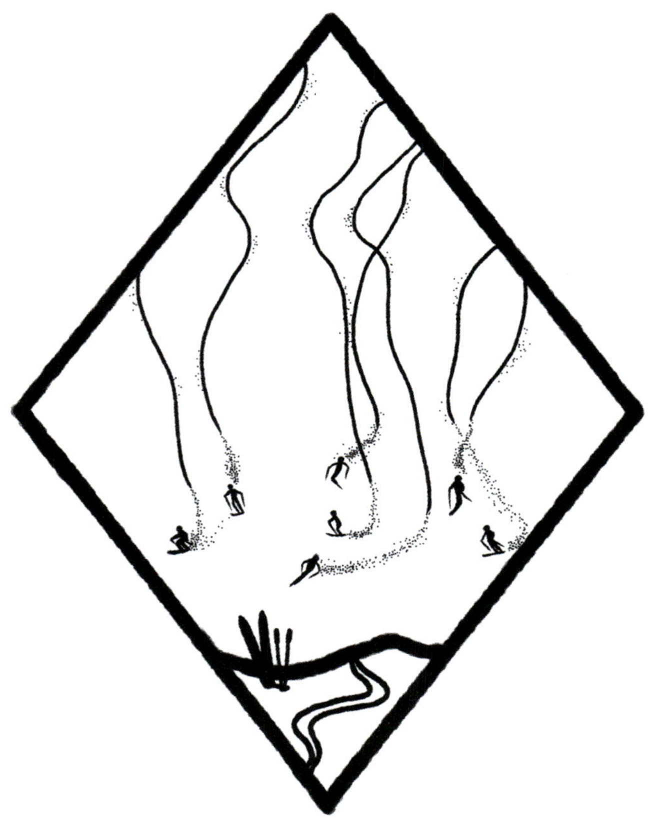

WHAT YOU NEED

Paper of your choice

Black pens in four sizes: 1.5, 05, 01 and 005

Triangle ruler

Pencil and eraser

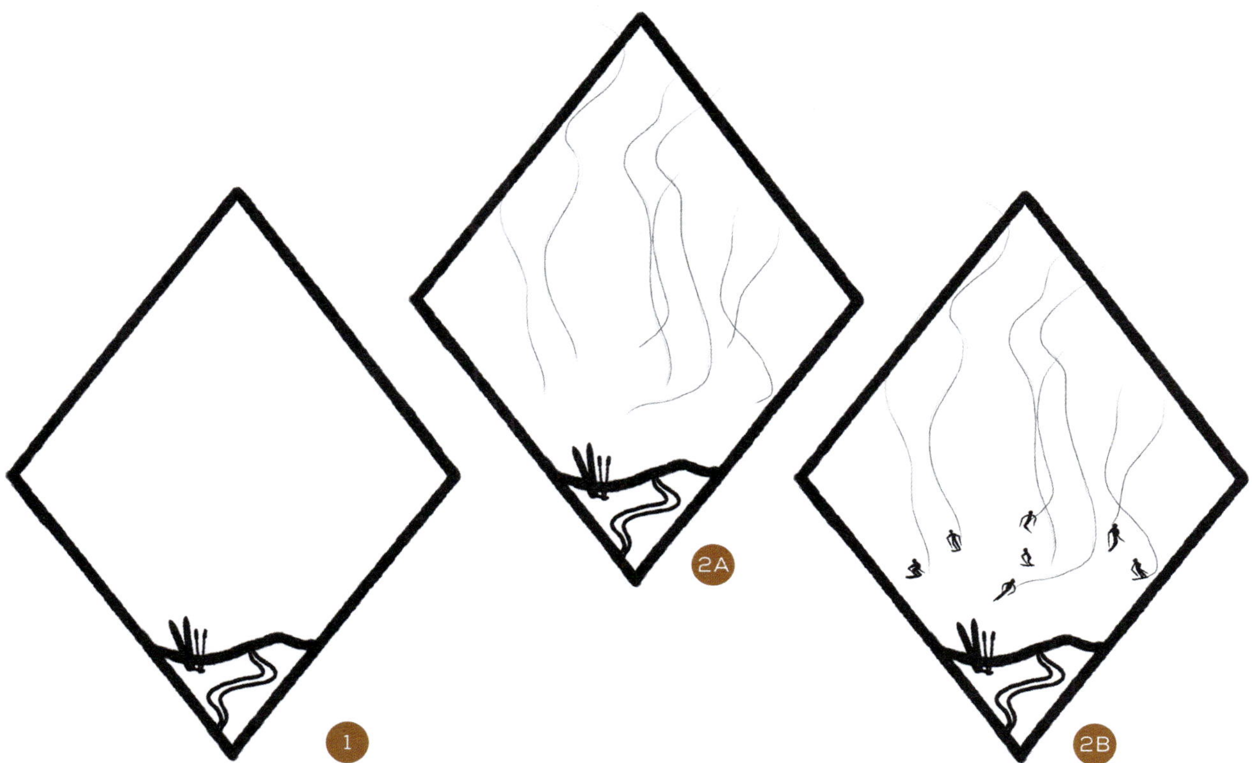

STEP 1

First, construct the diamond frame. See Cable Car over the Mountains on page 19 for the detailed explanation.

Add the slope line in the thicker (1.5) pen, then switch to a thinner (05) pen and draw the ski tracks in a gentle S-curve toward the bottom tip of the diamond. Add a pair of skis and ski poles toward the side in a combination of your 05 and 01 pens.

STEP 2

Next, mark the ski tracks for each skier in smooth pencil curves using your (05) pen.

In real life, the tracks will never be evenly spaced. I suggest playing around a little until you have them in a natural-looking pattern. At the end of each pencil line, place a tiny skier with a very thin (005) pen.

If you need an idea of how skiers move, find pictures of skiers on the Internet as a reference. The drawings of the skiers do not need to be very accurate as the skiers are very far away and you can only see them as a silhouette. I focused on getting the angle of the skis right in relation to the slope, as well as the size and proportion of the body and the arms.

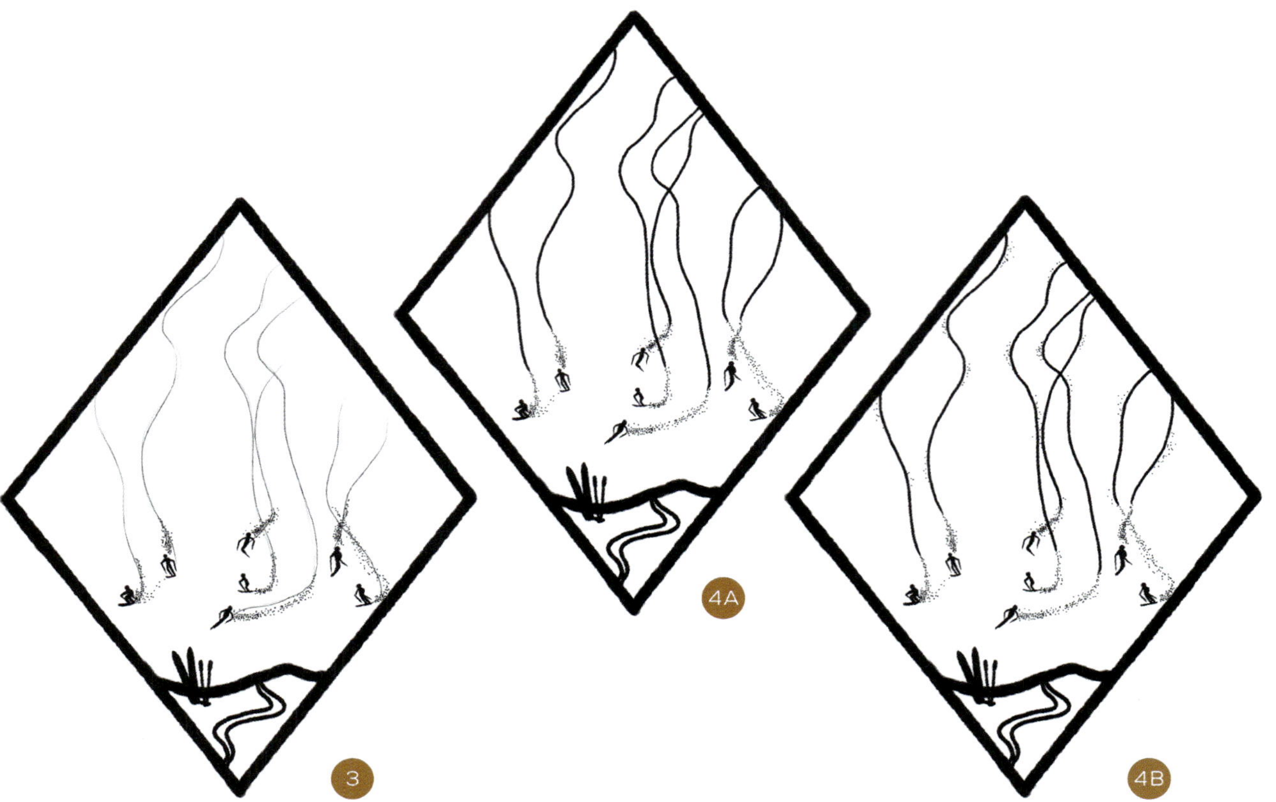

STEP 3

Behind each skier, place dots in thin (01) pen in the rough direction of your pencil line. This will be the snow dust that you normally see behind a moving skier.

STEP 4

Then, trace your pencil ski tracks for each skier with your thin (01) pen and gently erase the pencil lines. I also added some more dots with the same pen on the outside of each turn in the tracks. This is where the skiers normally kick up some more snow and the track is not as sharp. Happy skiing!

CIRCLE SCENE OF A FOREST CAMPGROUND

Some subjects are hard to draw. We can either practice a whole lot to achieve a realistic drawing or we can make it easier with the use of abstraction. This means we only draw the main characteristics of our subject and leave out any unnecessary details. That way, we can draw it without getting overly frustrated while the viewers will still recognize the object. This small circle scene uses abstraction for the pine trees, as well as the mountain slopes, to make them really easy to draw.

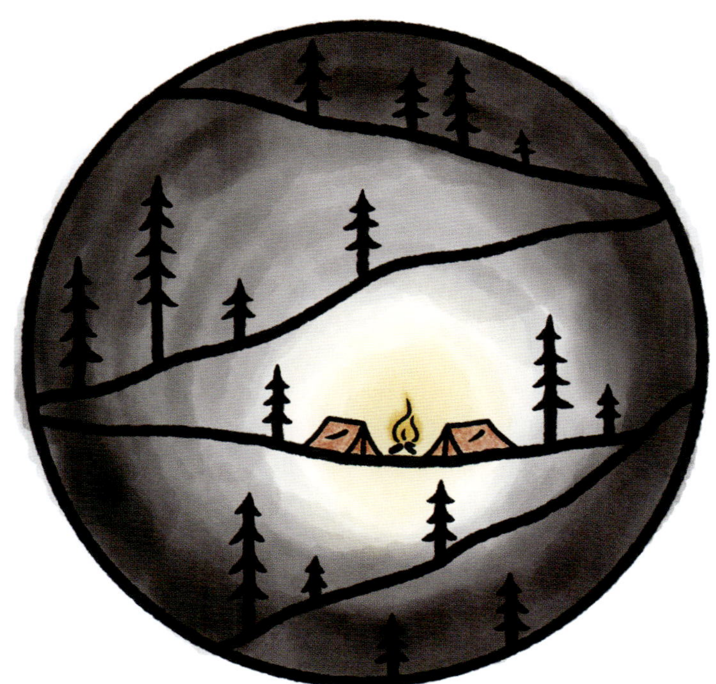

WHAT YOU NEED

Watercolor or mixed-media paper

Black pens in two sizes: 1.5 and 05

Compass, circle tool or round object to trace

Yellow and light red colored pencils

Watercolor or ink wash in tones of yellow and black

Small and medium round brushes

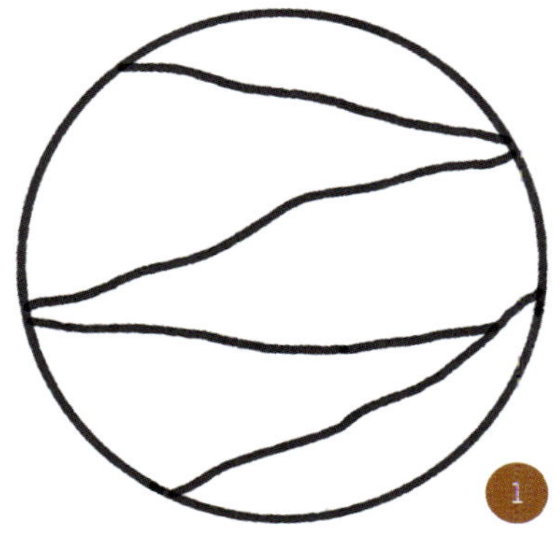

STEP 1

First, use your thicker (1.5) pen and draw the circle frame with a compass or a round object. I usually make circle drawings about 2 to 3 inches (5 to 7.5 cm) in diameter because they are quick to draw in this size. Feel free to use whatever size works for you.

Once you've completed the circle, lay down the mountain slopes. The lines should look a little like a zigzag line. I drew the second line from the bottom almost horizontally so I can place my campground on a flat surface.

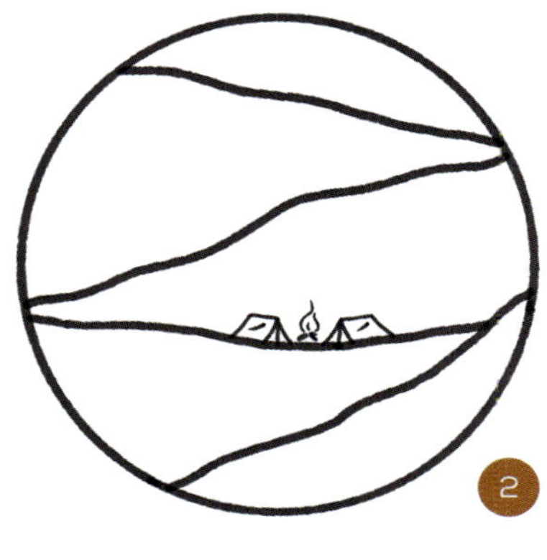

STEP 2

Time to add the campground. Use your thinner (05) pen for this. I like triangle tents and a campfire, so that is what I added.

If that's not your style, place a subject that makes you happy. You could just switch the tent type or draw a van or a cabin. Abstraction is also very helpful for the main subject; whatever you choose, go with a simple version without a lot of detail. That way, it will fit in nicely with the rest of the scene.

Animals also work really well in this setting. If you like things to be somewhat realistic, you could choose deer or mountain goats. For the fairy tale or fantasy fans, you could go with a unicorn or a dragon, for example. To find references for your favorite animal, you can do a Google image search, find drawing references on Pinterest or look at the covers of your favorite books.

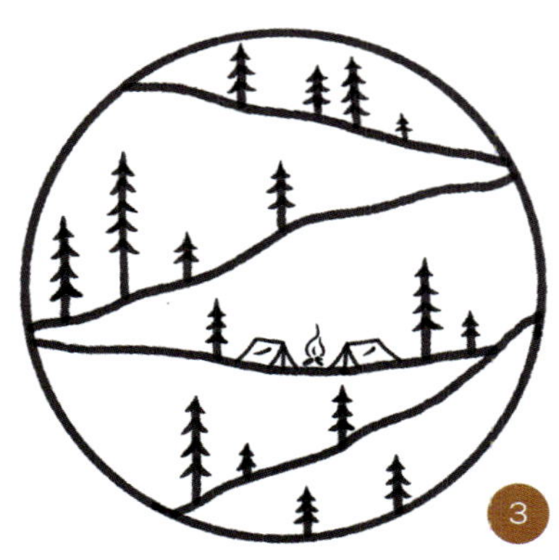

STEP 3

In this step, add in as many trees as you like. Use your thicker (1.5) pen, vary them in size and place them at uneven intervals to imitate nature. For the tutorial on trees, refer to the Linework Basics chapter on page 8.

You could stop drawing at this stage, with a minimalist black-and-white forest campground as a result. Well done!

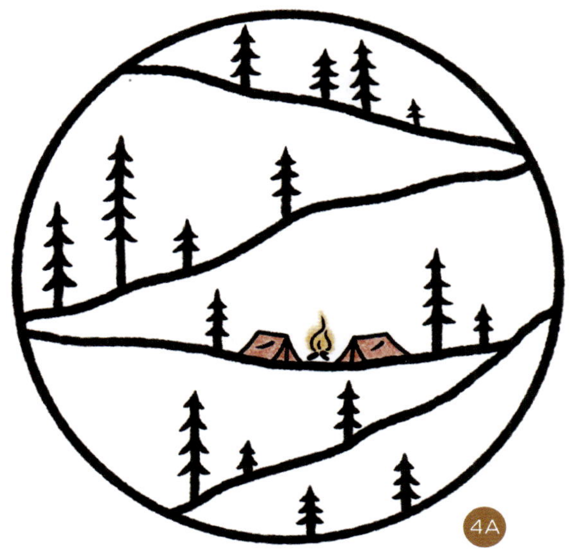

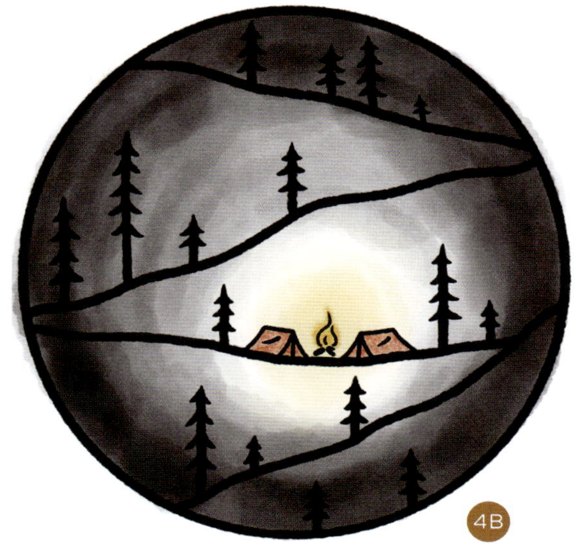

STEP 4

Keep going if you like experimenting with color . . . whatever color medium you choose is entirely up to you. My recommendation when filling your linework with color is to use a translucent color medium, so your ink lines stay visible. (Opaque media, like acrylic paint markers, for example, will cover up your ink lines. Of course, if that is your goal, go for it!)

I like to explore what black-and-white drawings look like when adding some color. My goal was to make the campfire glow and the campground pop so it would draw the eye at first glance.

So, to start, I used colored pencils in yellow and a light red to color the campfire and the tents. (Try not to cover your inkwork with the colored pencil; it dulls the black. If I have small "accidents," I will just draw over the black line again with my pen.)

The result did not make the campground stand out as I had expected. Erasing the colored pencil wasn't an option, as it would damage the paper. So, I decided to paint over it with diluted ink: a yellow splotch in the middle where the campfire is and gray around it to imitate the way the fire lights up only part of the grounds and the rest stays in the dark.

A QUICK NOTE ON INK WASH/ WATERCOLOR

Build the tone you want in layers—start with very little color in the water, and add more gradually. You will get a different effect when painting on dry versus wet paper. I painted on dry paper and also made sure that the yellow was completely dry before adding the black.

If you wet the paper first with clear water and then add the paint, the paint will spread over the wet surface and you have less control. If you use two colors, they will run and mix together where they meet. If you're not sure what you like better, I suggest experimenting with both effects on a separate piece of paper before coloring your drawing.

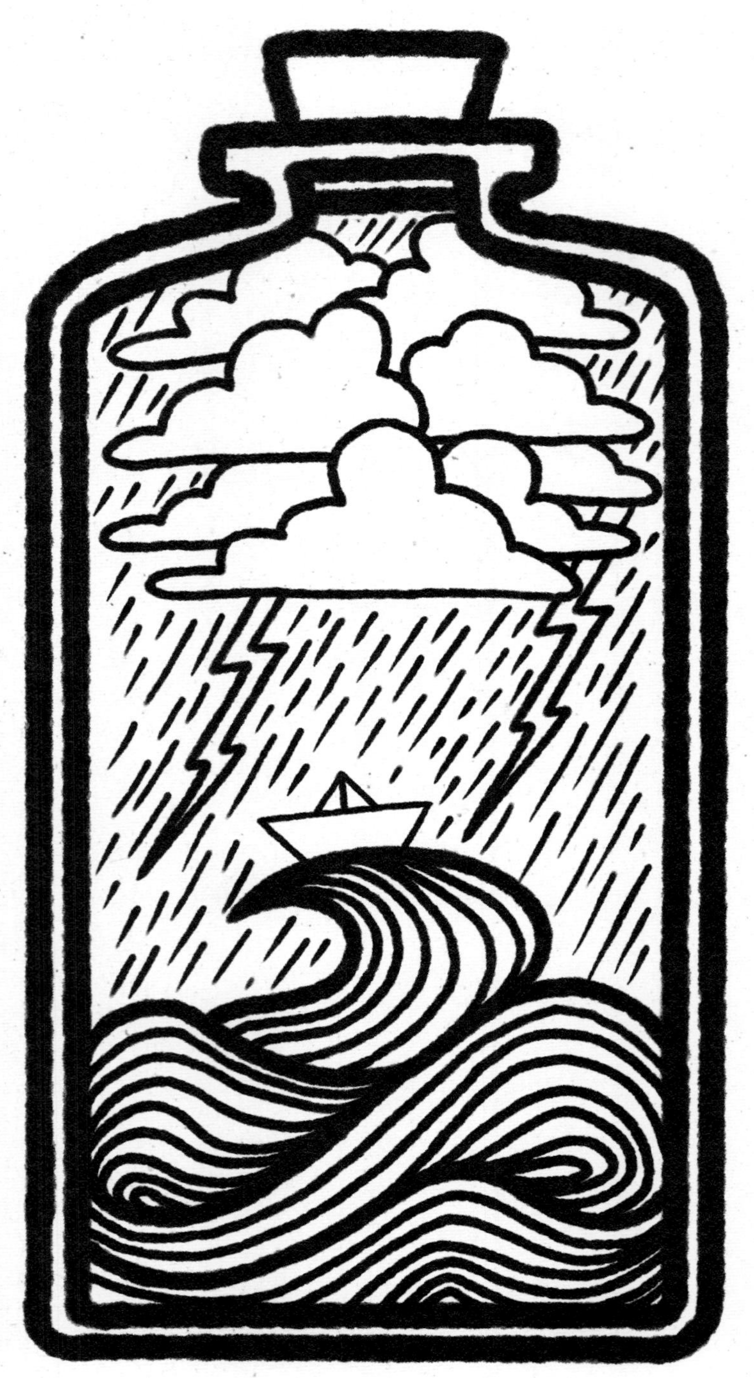

BEACH SCENES

How about some time off from the daily routine to go somewhere you've never been? Drawing landscapes—like books or movies—can take you to places near and far and you get to pick where you are going. I chose the beach today. Want to come?

In addition to showcasing serene landscapes that are fun to design and that will pop off the page, the following projects explore texture, perspective, silhouettes and, notably, how to draw palm trees. The former three topics are general lessons that will be useful in other projects in this book. The latter topic—palm trees—is there for a nice vacation vibe, and the leaf-drawing lesson will also help you with pine trees later on.

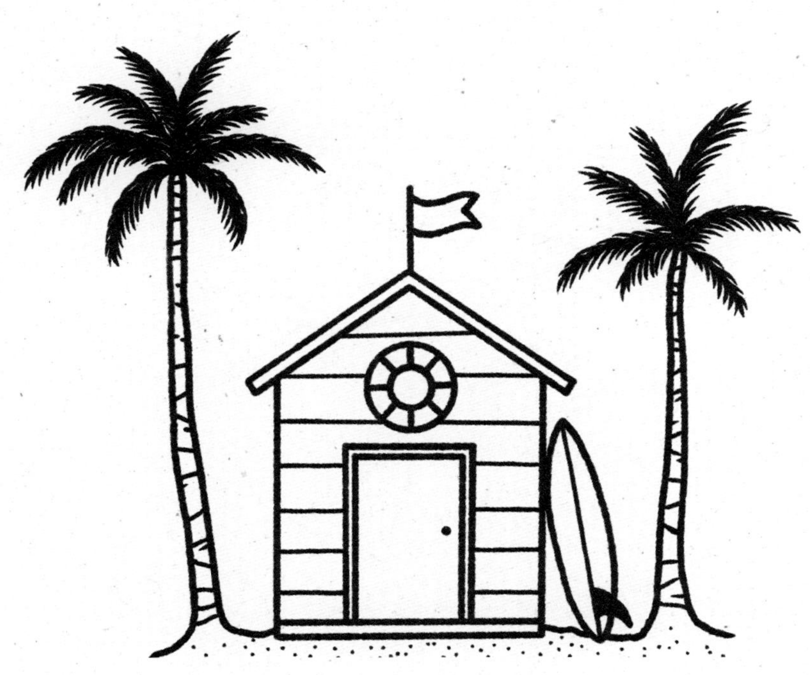

SURF SHACK

Are you bored or need a break? Bring some beach vibes to your house with this cute little surf shack! Although we're mostly looking at simple forms, we're going to be exploring more intricate things like sandy textures that will come in handy in following projects. As a side note: This makes a nice set with the Chill-Out Hammock Between Palm Trees (page 50) project.

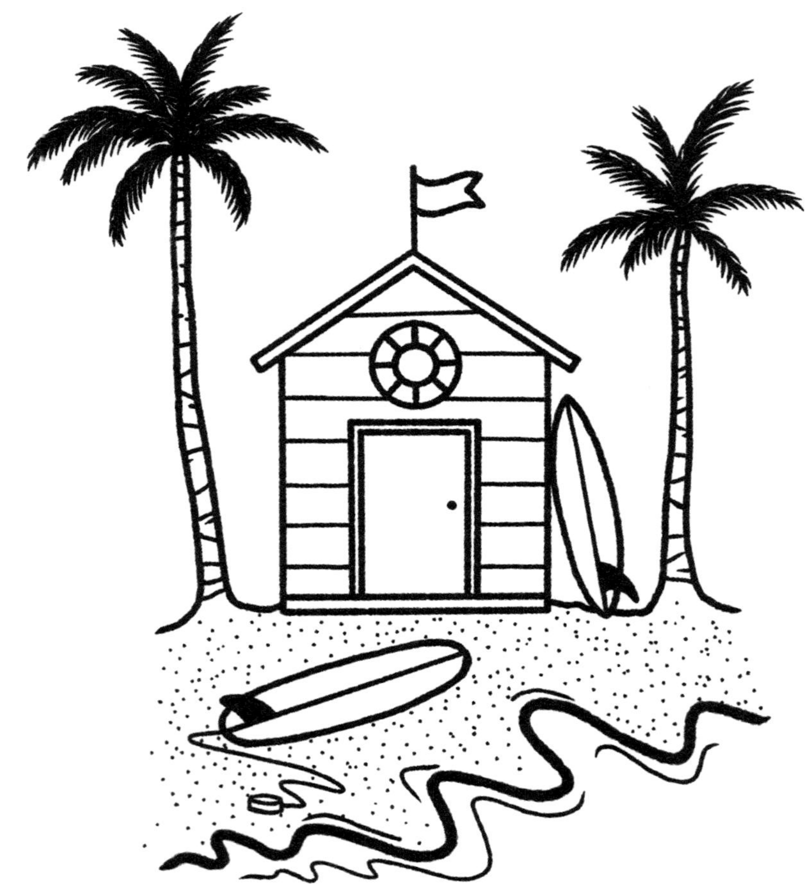

WHAT YOU NEED

Paper of your choice

Ruler

Black pens in three sizes: 1.5, 05 and 01

Brush pen

Compass, circle tool or round object to trace

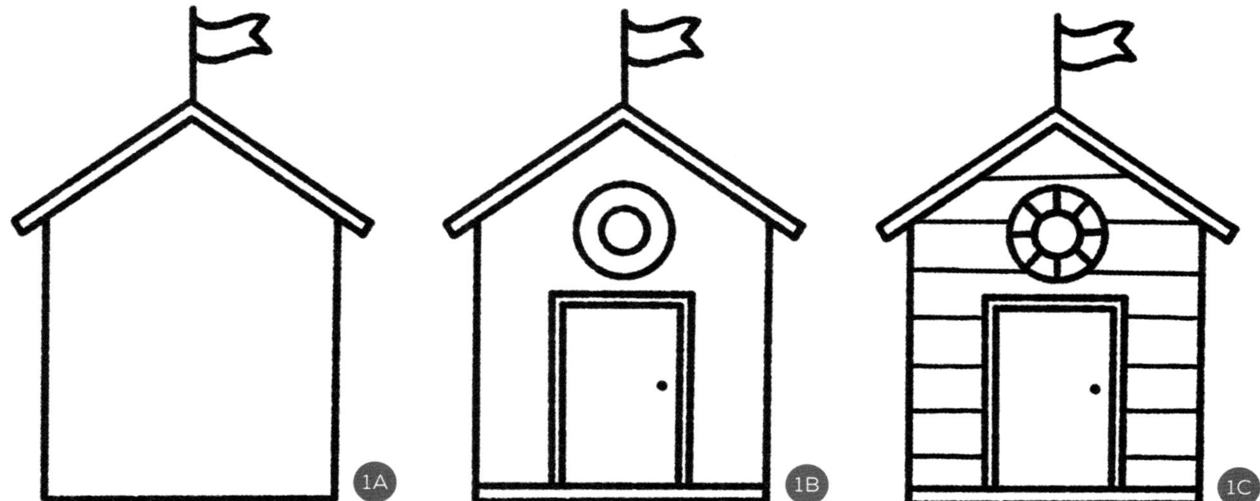

STEP 1

Start by constructing the shed with a ruler and a medium (05) pen. Draw three sides of a rectangle and close the top with a triangle for the roof. Make the triangle slightly wider than your rectangle base and add a second one above the first. Connect the end points and you have a nice-looking roof in three easy steps! Put a little flag on the roof top too.

One after the other, add more details: the door frame, then the door itself, including the doorknob.

The life belt above the door is made from two circles and a few lines to create the red and white segments. Finally, draw horizontal lines on the exterior wall but not on the door.

STEP 2

Draw the surfboards in front and beside the shack in medium (05) pen and use the thin (01) for the smaller details like the cord.

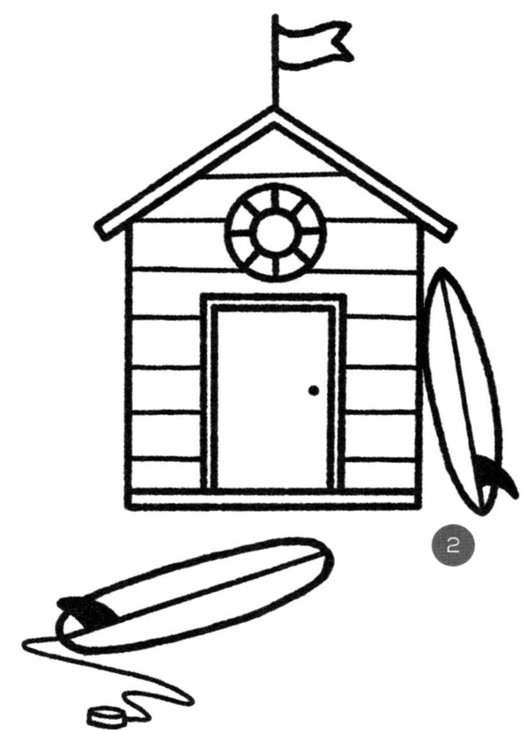

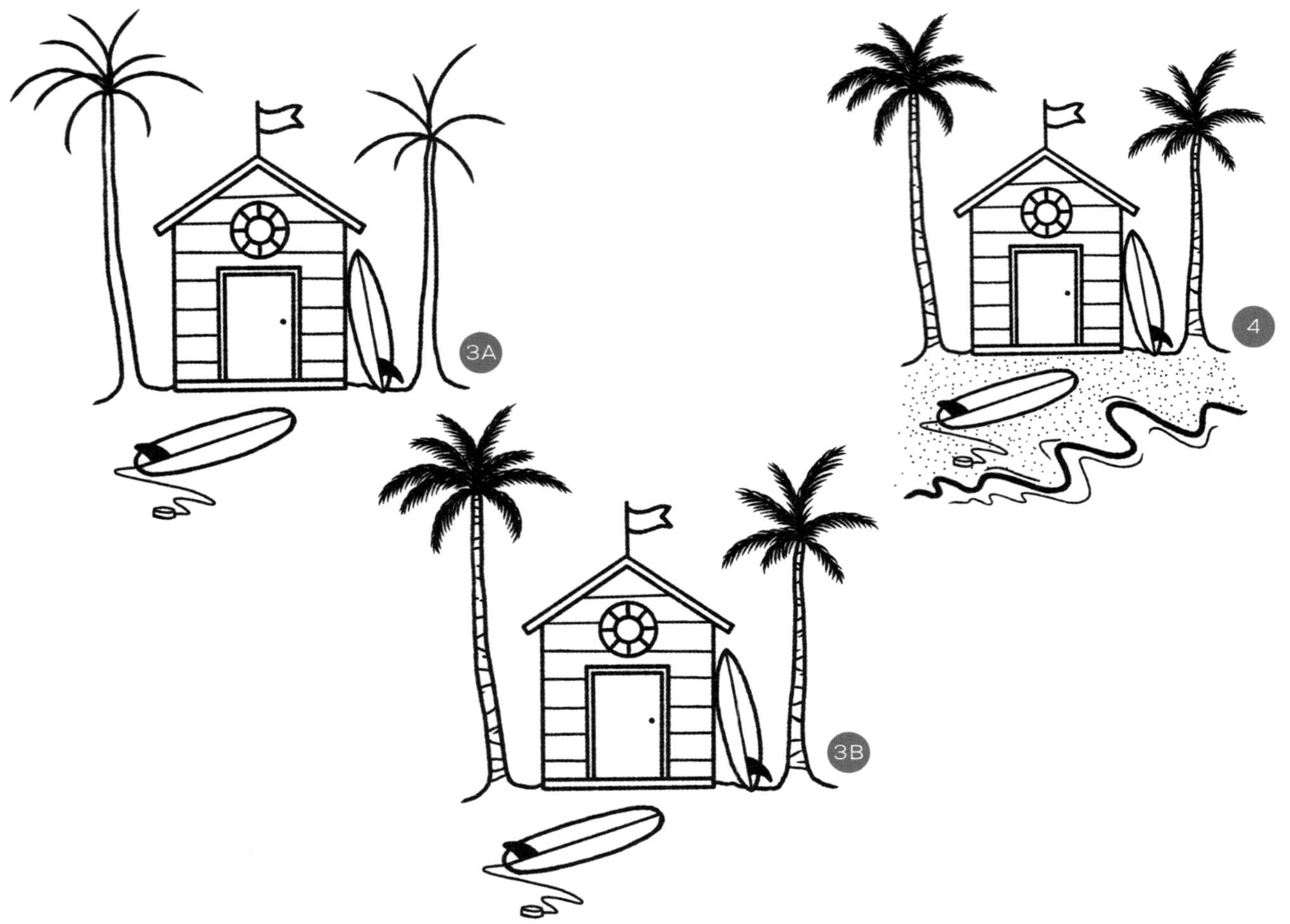

STEP 3

In the next step, draw the palm tree trunks and add some lines on the top as the leaf bases with your medium (05) pen.

Draw the full leaves onto the leaf stem with the brush pen. For a more detailed explanation, check out the Chill-Out Hammock Between Palm Trees project (page 50). For some texture on the palm tree trunks, draw some irregular and slanted lines in medium (05) pen.

STEP 4

As there is no surfing without water, the last step is to draw the water edge. Use your thick (1.5) pen and draw a curvy line in front of your cabin and surfboard. Accent some of the curves with a thin (01) pen line right beside them. I was trying to imitate the pattern that waves make when they roll onto the sand.

Create a sand texture by putting lots of small dots in medium (05) pen in the area between the shack and the waterline. Dotwork takes patience—well done for going slow!

SEAGULLS FLYING OVER THE DOCK

Wherever you look, you are experiencing some kind of perspective. Drawing one correctly is actually less difficult than you first think. In this project, we'll be using a one-point perspective to draw the dock.
Let me show you how to do it!

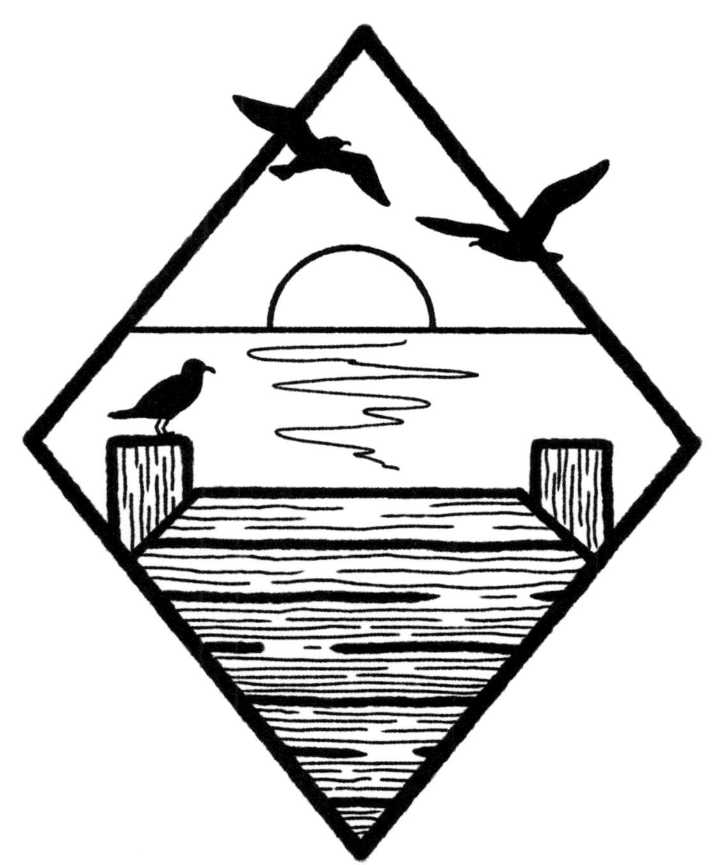

WHAT YOU NEED

Paper of your choice

Black pens in three sizes: 1.5, 05 and 01

Pencil

Triangle ruler

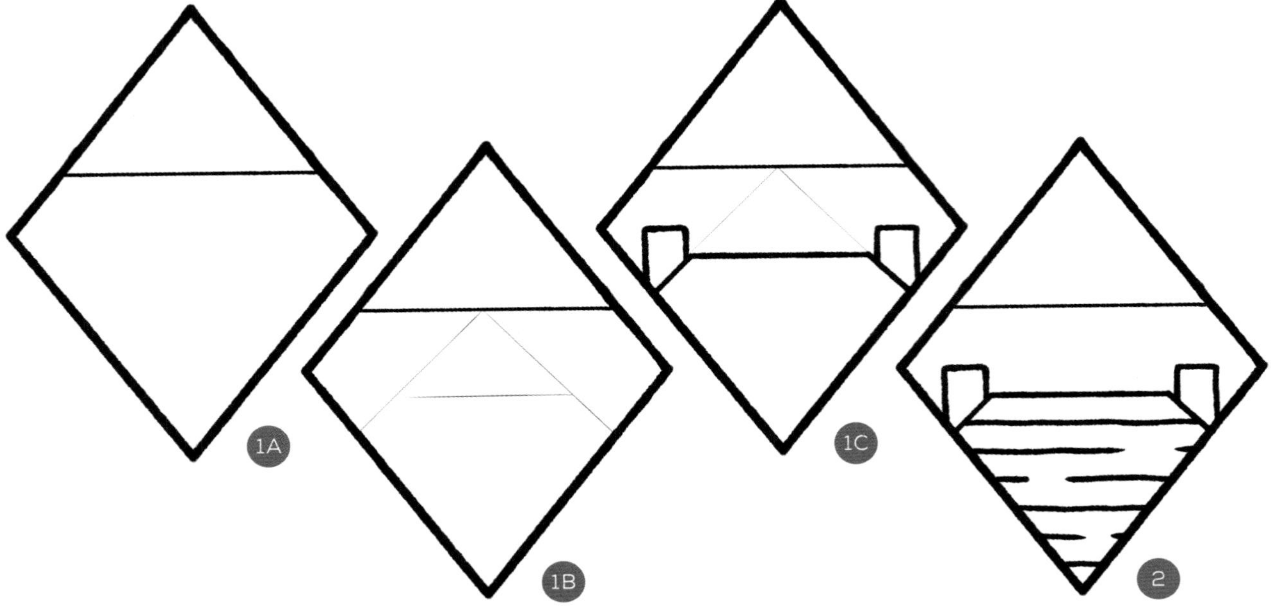

STEP 1

Draw the diamond frame with the thick (1.5) pen. Check out Cable Car over the Mountains (page 19) for detailed instructions. Draw the horizon line with a ruler and the thin (01) pen about one-third of the way down from the top of the diamond and find the middle of this line.

With the ruler, draw two pencil lines from the middle point toward the diamond outline. Parallel to the horizon line, draw the end of the dock. Ink the dock outline and draw the posts at the side of the dock in medium (05) pen. Make sure your ink is dry and gently erase your pencil lines.

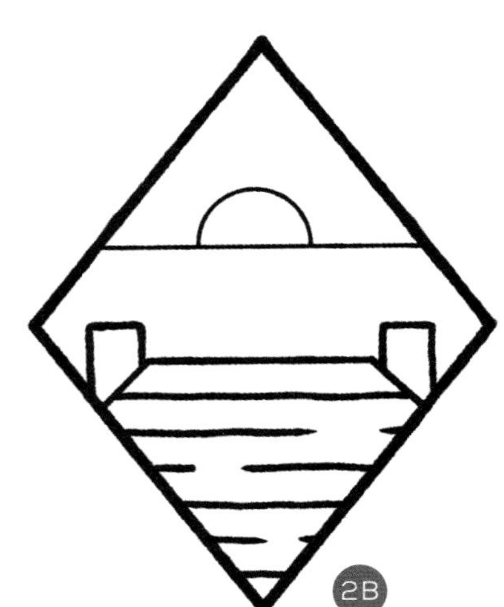

STEP 2

Add parallel lines to the dock to show individual wooden planks. I didn't use a ruler here and broke the lines in some places for a more organic look. Draw a half-circle for the setting sun in thin (01) pen. Sunsets make all landscape scenes more beautiful, don't you think?

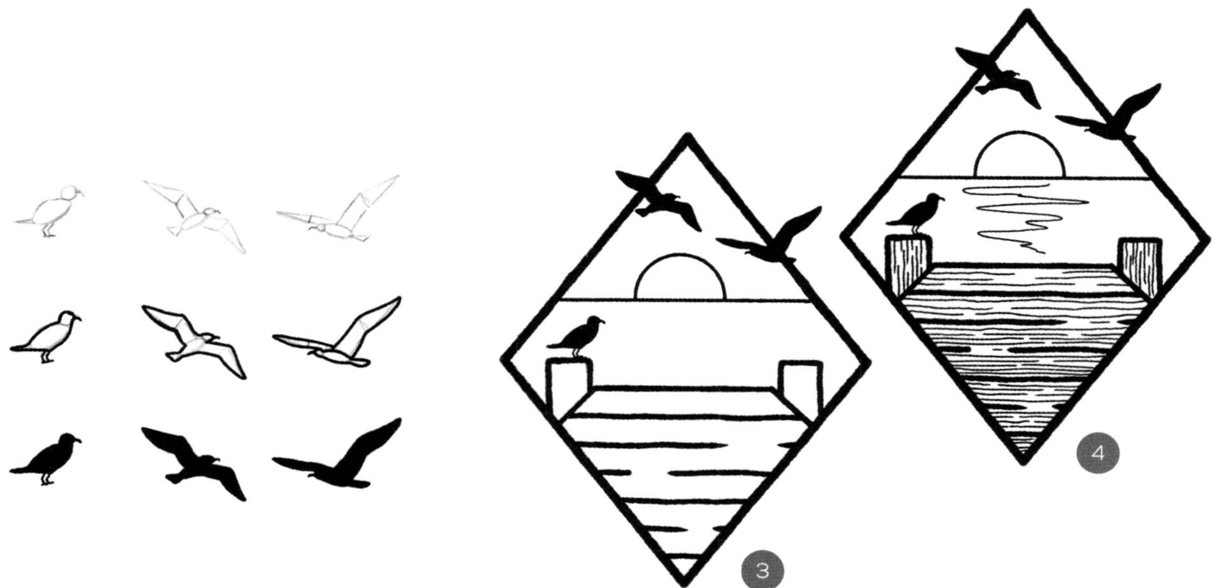

STEP 3

Draw the seagull silhouettes in thin (01) pen and fill them in. Again, I went online and looked for a picture—actually several pictures—for each seagull. Concentrate on their main features and forget the details to make them recognizable. For me, a seagull is different from other birds in its beak and the form of its wings when it's flying. For the one sitting on the dock, instead of the wings, I focused on the shape of the breast and back.

STEP 4

Add some lines in thin (01) pen to create a wood texture on the dock and draw a curvy line for the sun reflection on the sea surface as a final touch.

Congratulate yourself for drawing your first one-point perspective neatly—well done!

THE LIGHTHOUSE IN THE DUNES

Contrast is your friend when drawing in black and white. Often, the subject is in black or in gray tones and surrounded by white paper to achieve contrast and have your subject stand out. This drawing plays with the reverse by using a black background and leaving the main elements in white. The pros refer to this as "negative space." You will also learn how line weight can impact how close or far away a subject appears to the viewer.

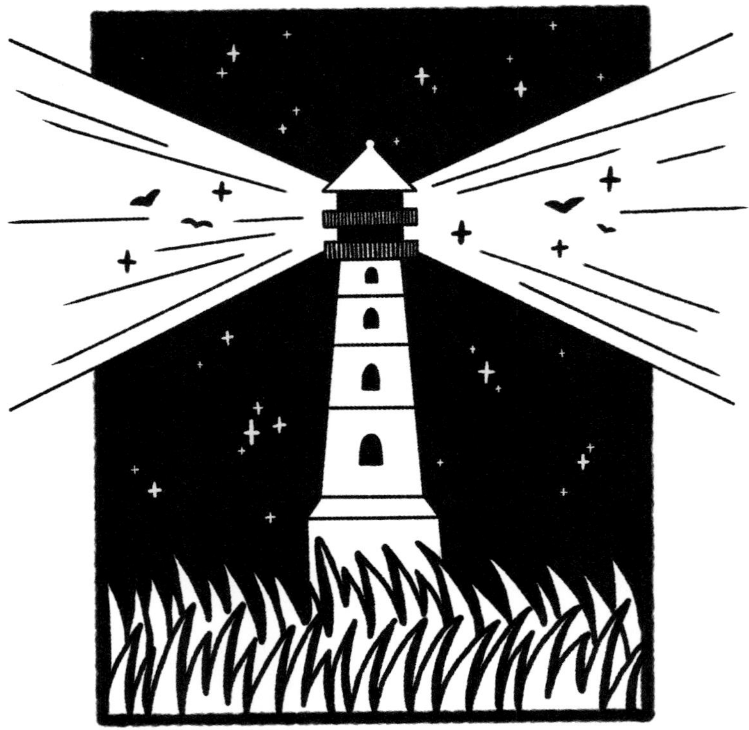

WHAT YOU NEED

Paper of your choice

Black pens in three sizes: 1.5, 05 and 01

Brush pen

Pencil and eraser

Triangle ruler

White pens in two sizes: 10 and 08

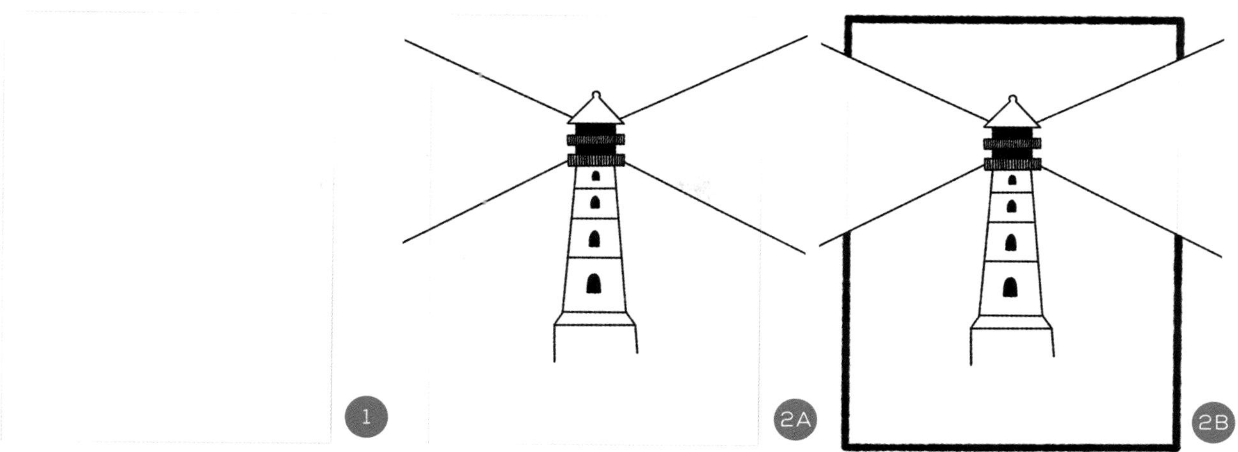

STEP 1

When working on pieces like this one with a partial frame, start with a pencil frame you can erase later. In this case, draw a rectangle in pencil of approximately 3 x 4 inches (7.5 x 10 cm).

STEP 2

Next, place the lighthouse in the center of the rectangle in thin (01) pen. I wanted the outline for the building to be sharp, so I used a ruler to draw all the lines. You don't have to use the same shaped lighthouse that I did. Draw one you like and switch up the details—they could look like this:

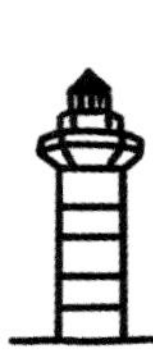
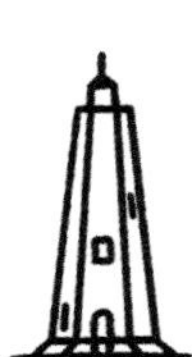
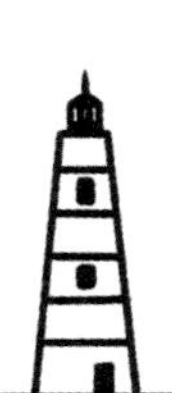
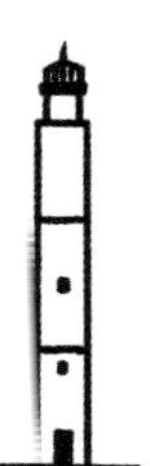
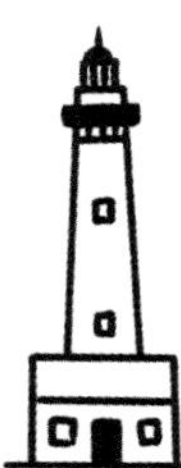

Add the edges of the light beams (see above for lighthouse options).

And, now, we are at the stage to draw the frame in ink. Use your thick (1.5) pen for that.

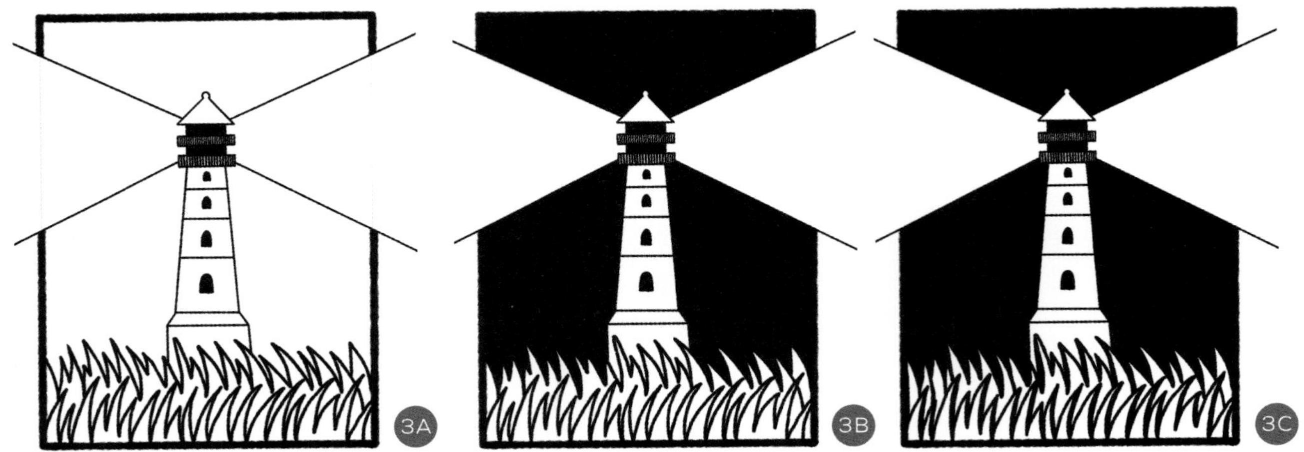

STEP 3

Between the lighthouse and the bottom line of the rectangle, add some dune grass with the medium (05) pen. I guess you could also interpret those jagged lines as very strong waves . . . or you could go ahead and make them more wavelike if you imagine your lighthouse sitting on a rock and the sea is dramatically wind-whipped below it.

Fill the background with a black brush pen to create the night sky.

After doing that, I realized that I needed to make the grass pop a little more so it appears in front of the lighthouse rather than the same distance away. So, I thickened the lines on the grass on one side of the blades. The thicker line weight brings it to the front more, don't you think?

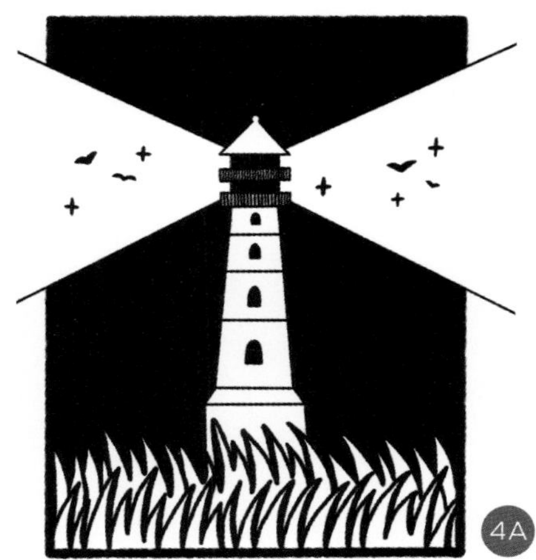

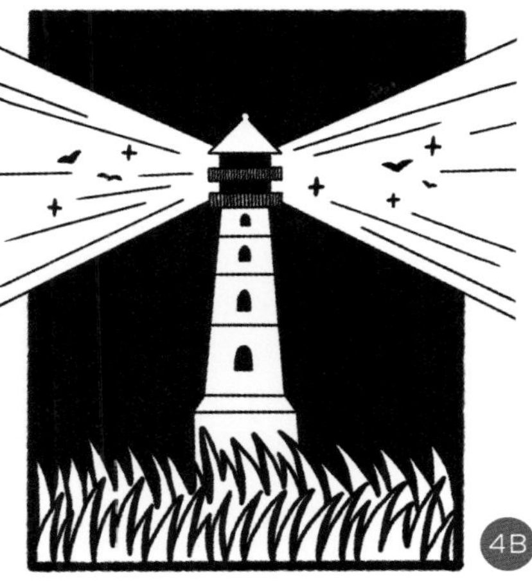

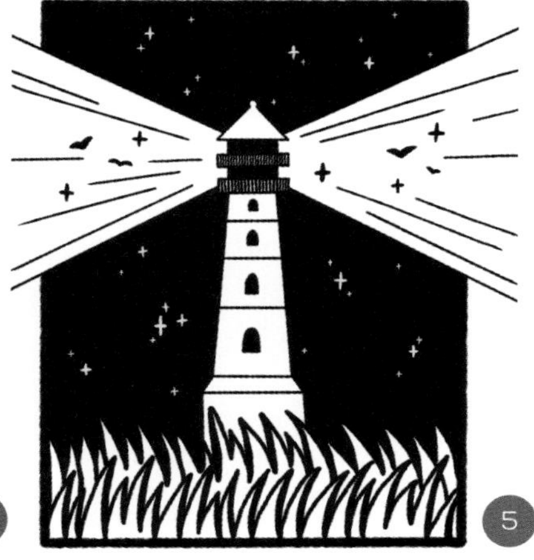

STEP 4

We're on the final stretch here—let's add some details! First, add a few birds and stars within the light beams using a combination of pens. Afterward, use your ruler and your thin (01) pen to draw some fine lines radiating outward from the lighthouse. Be careful to spare the birds and stars you just drew.

STEP 5

As the last step, add some stars in different sizes with your white pens. If your black sky is not as smooth as you'd like it to be, add lots of dots in different sizes for an instant fix.

If you want to add some color, I suggest red for every other lighthouse segment and a light and bright yellow for the light beam. Maybe also a grayish green for the grass or blue if you want it to be waves.

THUNDERSTORM OVER THE SEA

I love a good thunderstorm—not on a ship or anywhere outside really—but when watching from a dry place with a cup of tea in hand. To me, it's a spectacular display of the power of nature. To translate this power into the next drawing, you will work on stacking many curved lines to show the strong movement of the sea, as well as straight lines to express the heavy rain and to depict lightning.

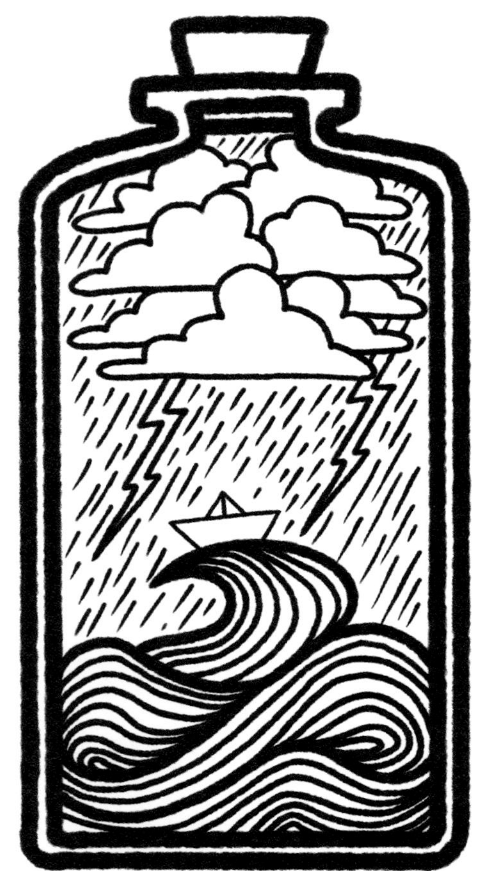

WHAT YOU NEED

Paper of your choice

Black pens in three sizes: 1.5, 05 and 01

Ruler

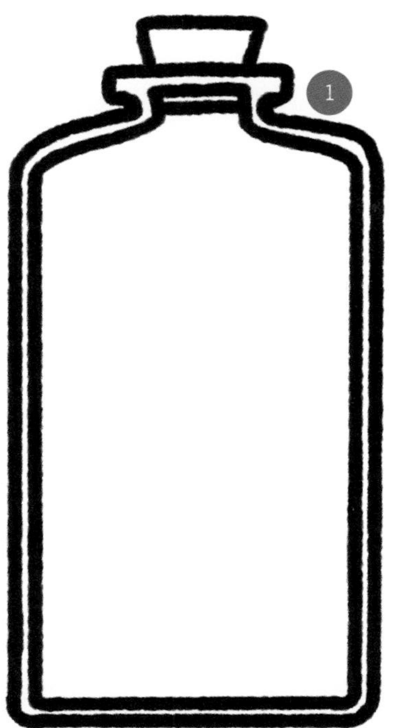

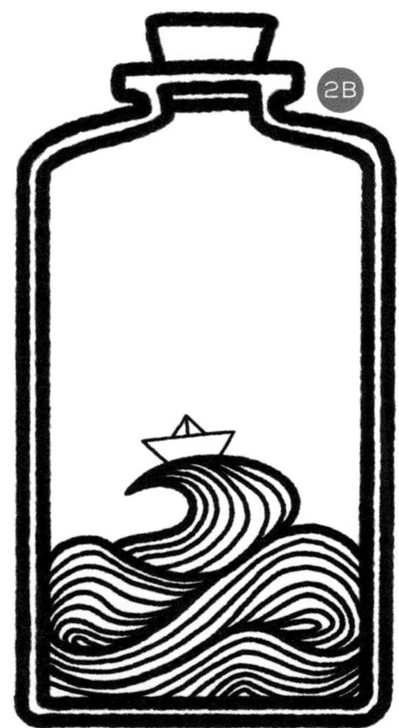

STEP 1

Draw the outline for the bottle with your thick (1.5) pen. The bottom part is basically a rectangle with slightly rounded corners. I drew the lines with the ruler without connecting the corners, then ditched the ruler and drew the corners freehand. The top is a little trickier. Try to get even and symmetrical curves toward the mouth of the bottle. The cork comes last, and if you want, use the ruler again to create its cylindrical shape.

STEP 2

Move on to the sea now. Start from the bottom with your medium (05) pen and do the thicker outlines first, then switch to a thin (01) nib and place thinner lines inside to create movement.

OPTIONAL, BUT CUTE: Place a small paper boat on top of the waves.

STEP 3

Near the top of the bottle, pile up some clouds with your thin (01) pen. It's easiest to start from the front and work backward, so the only cloud with a complete outline is the one in the front. Continue placing clouds toward the top and sides until you get to the outline of the bottle.

STEP 4

Now, it's time to add the lightning, continuing with your (01) pen. Draw as many as you want and make them somewhat parallel. Just try to avoid hitting the boat
too closely.

STEP 5

The final detail in this project is the pouring rain. Draw lots of short lines with your thin (01) pen, parallel to the lightning strikes. When drawing the rain, I sped up my movement toward the end of the line and used less pressure to get a smaller, pointier line.

SAILING AROUND TROPICAL ISLANDS

Living close to the mountains but far away from the sea, it took until my gap year to set foot on a sailing boat for the first time. I was a bit worried I might get seasick. Luckily, the sun was shining and the sea was mostly nice and flat, so it was quite the relaxing experience. In this drawing, the relaxing part is drawing the waves. There are lots of repetitive strokes to practice consistency. Imagine the sun on your face and chill for a bit!

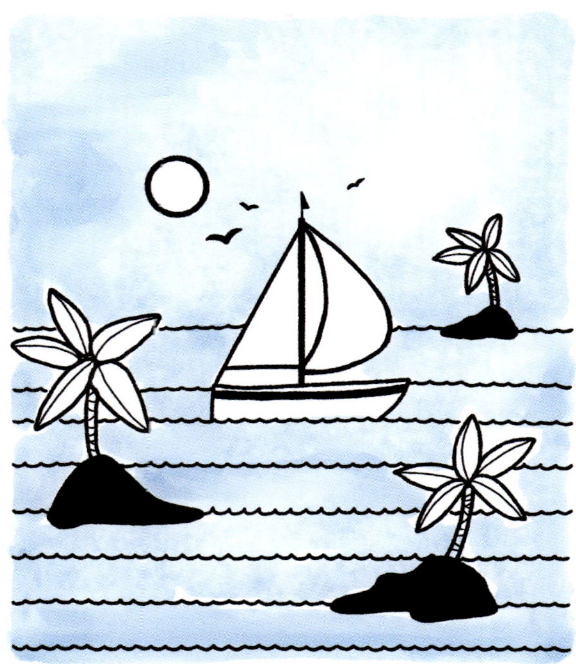

WHAT YOU NEED

Watercolor or mixed-media paper

Pencil and eraser

Ruler

Black pens in three sizes: 1.5, 05 and 01

Compass, circle tool or round object to trace

Watercolor or ink in tones of blue (optional)

Medium round brush (size 3) (optional)

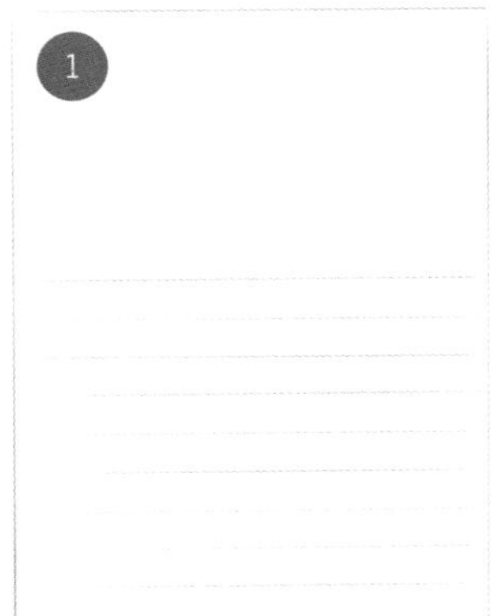

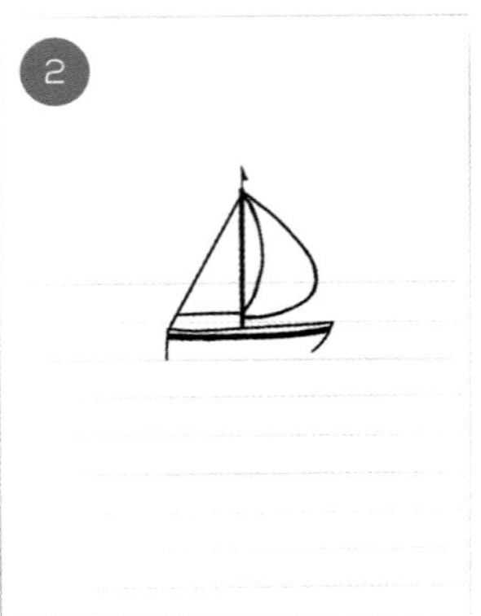

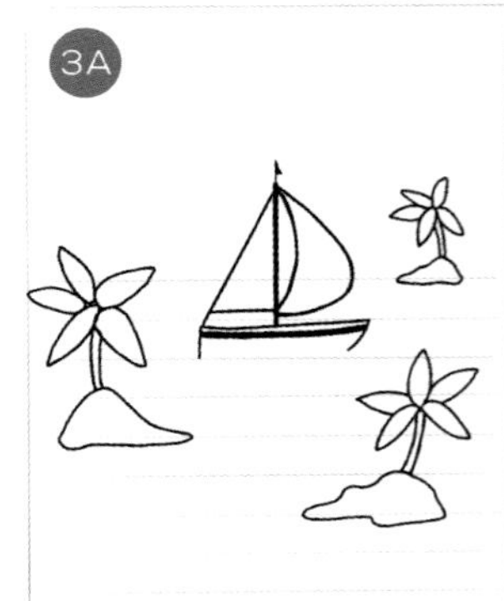

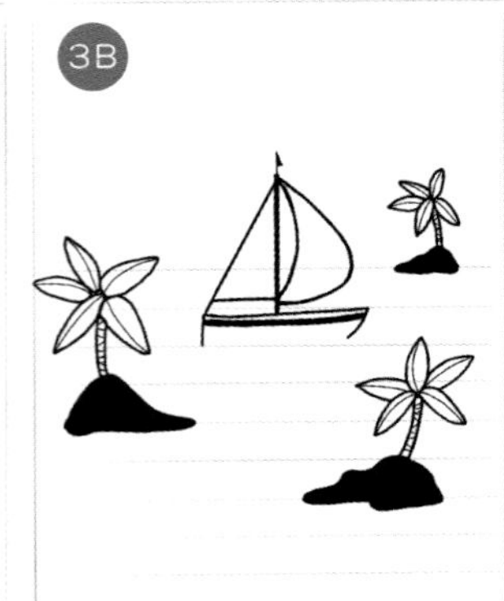

STEP 1

To keep this drawing tidy, you need some guidelines. Set up a rectangle in pencil. It doesn't have to be very accurate as we'll erase it later. Using a ruler, add parallel lines every ¼ inch (.5 cm), from the bottom to about two-thirds of the way up.

STEP 2

Draw a sailboat in the middle with your medium (05) pen like this: Start out by drawing the hull—the top is a straight line and the back is also quite straight. The front part is slightly curved. Place it on one of the pencil lines and don't draw the bottom of it completely. This is where the boat would be underwater. Draw the mast next. It's a straight line again; I doubled up here to make it a little thicker. Then, move on to the sails. You can use triangle shapes here on both sides of the mast or you could use curved lines for a spinnaker sail, like I did.

STEP 3

Now, we are moving on to the islands and palm trees, still with our medium (05) pen. I put two islands in front of the boat on either side and one in the far background, so three altogether. For the palm trees, draw two parallel lines for the stem and put five leaves on top of each stem. There actually is a drawing rule—or maybe it's a mathematical one—that says most objects in nature appear in uneven numbers. Observe your surroundings the next time you're outside or look at paintings by master artists and you will see why I often apply this rule in my drawings.

We don't have much contrast in this piece for now, so color the islands in black with your thick (1.5) pen or brush pen. I also added a thin (01) pen line to each palm leaf for some added detail.

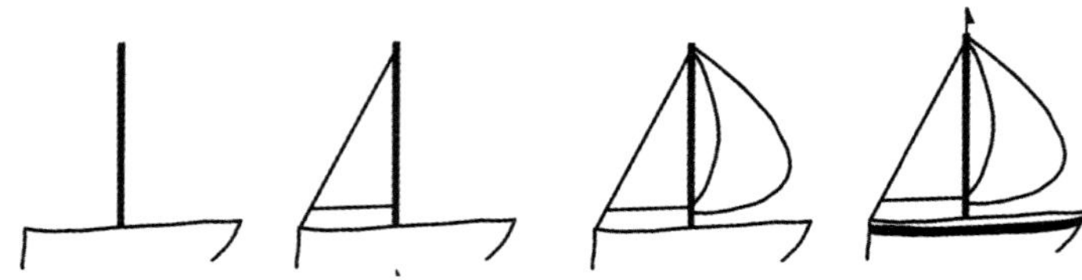

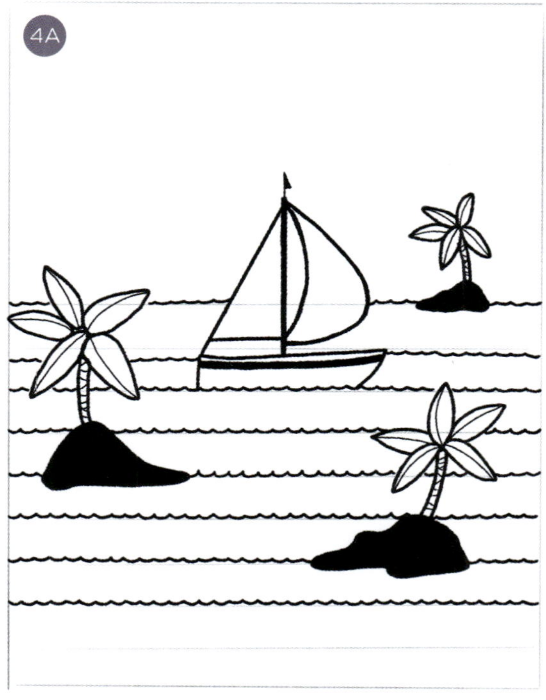

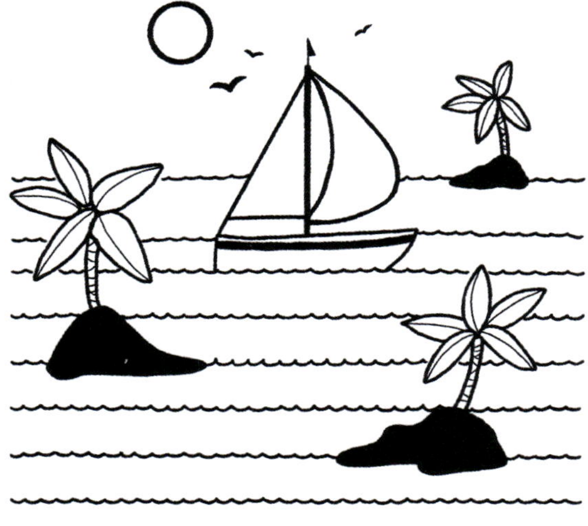

STEP 4

And here comes my favorite part of this drawing: the wavy water surface. On each pencil line, lay down a scalloped line with your medium (05) nib. I see this as a bunch of UUUUs connected to each other. Go slow and concentrate on making all the Us the same width. Meditative moment right here. Who needs yoga class when you can draw waves instead?

As finishing touches, I added a circle for the sun and some flying birds. Make sure your ink is dry and then gently erase the pencil lines.

OPTIONAL: Paint the rectangle in the nice bright blue of a summer day but leave the sun, the sailboat and the palm trees white.

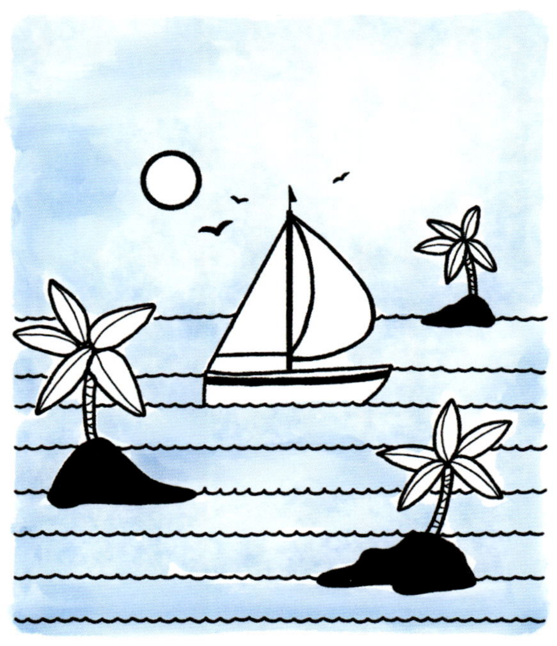

CHILL-OUT HAMMOCK BETWEEN PALM TREES

Who doesn't dream of a hammock on a deserted beach from time to time? Take yourself on a beach vacation with this drawing! Here, in addition to adding color to convey a beautiful sunset—as well as adding a sandy texture at the end—we'll be playing with lines to evoke the sunlight shining on the water surface.

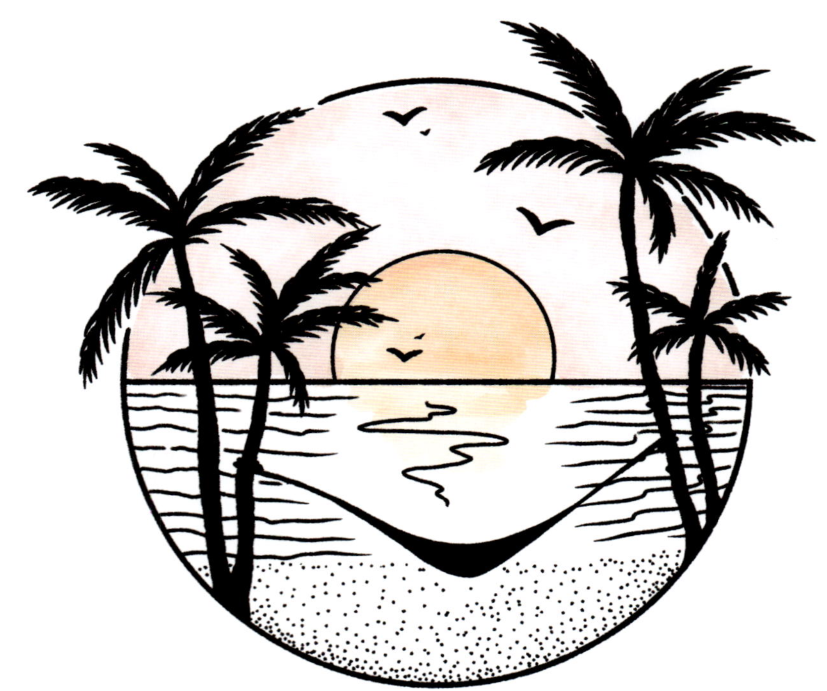

WHAT YOU NEED

Watercolor or mixed-media paper

Black pens in three sizes: 1.5, 05 and 01

Compass, circle tool or round object to trace

Ruler

Brush pen

Watercolors in tones of pink and orange

Medium round brush (size 3)

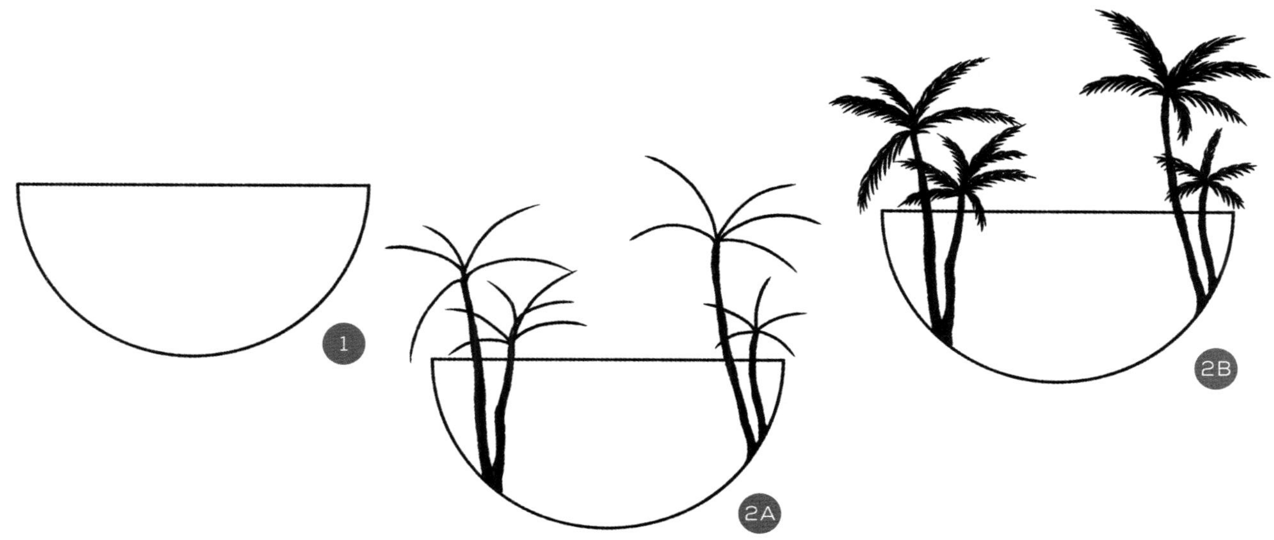

STEP 1

Draw the bottom half of a circle with your medium (05) pen. I find it easiest to draw a straight line and mark the middle. Then, use a compass to draw the half-circle.

STEP 2

On the left and right side of the circle, draw the trunks of the palm trees in medium (05) pen and fill them in. At the top, add five curved lines for the leaves.

Next, fill in the leaves with the brush pen. Begin with more pressure so the line is thicker at the start and ease up toward the tip of the leaf while also speeding up your stroke so the line tapers into a pointy end. Check out this detailed sketch:

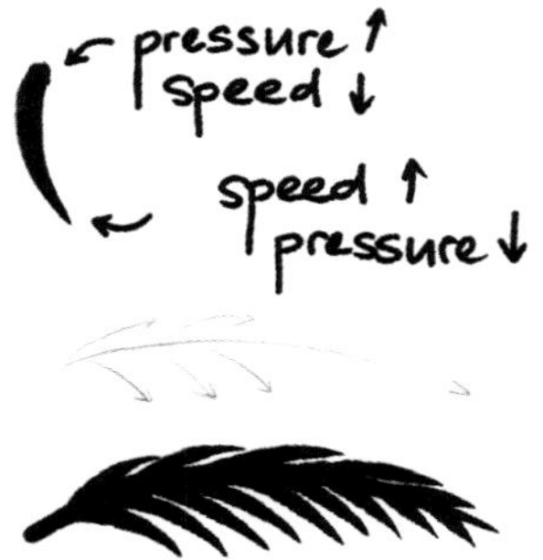

Also, note how the individual leaves curve the same way as the stem. By the way, if you don't have a brush pen, you can achieve the same shape with a regular pen with a thin nib. It's just slightly more work because you'll have to draw two separate curved lines that connect at their tip and fill in the space between them with black.

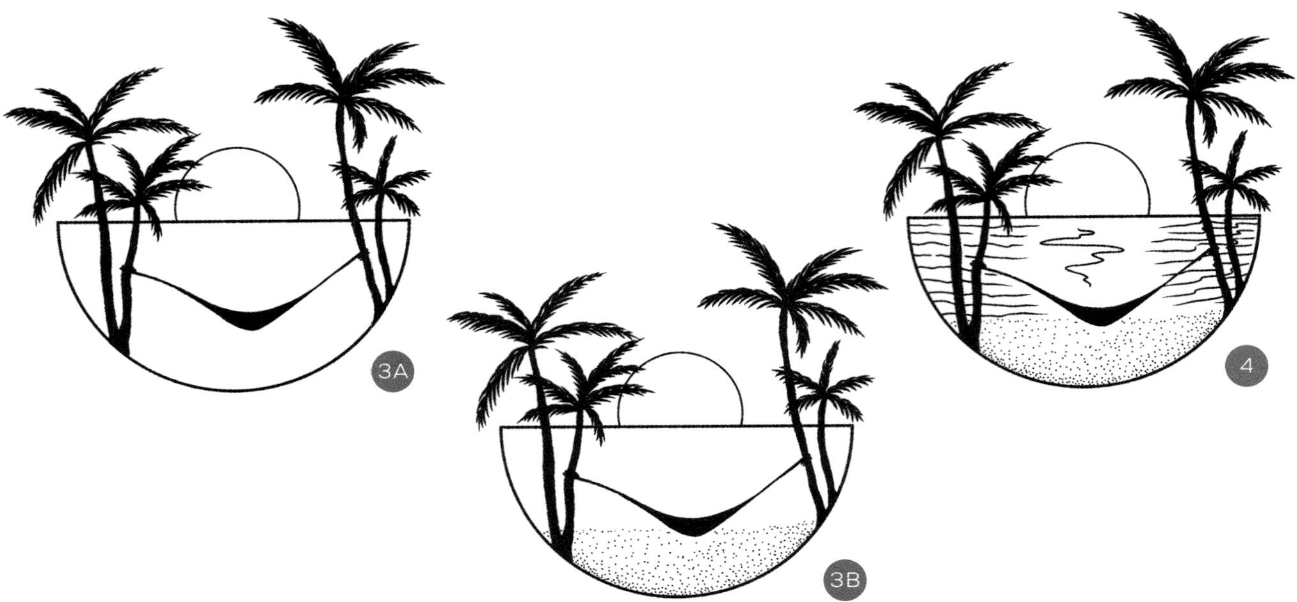

STEP 3

In this step, you'll draw the setting sun in thin (01) pen and add the hammock silhouette. For the sun, use your compass or your round object and trace it with the thin (01) pen. For the hammock, you can draw a curved line and just fill in the curve with more black. (If you want to experiment, you could also add a person sitting in the hammock, possibly having a cocktail.)

Put lots of thin (01) pen dots at the bottom of the circle underneath the hammock. This is the sand on your deserted beach. When laying down the dots, go slowly so the dots don't accidentally become dashes. Also, place them in an irregular pattern for a natural look.

STEP 4

What makes lying in a hammock even more relaxing? The sound of the ocean! So, next up are the waves. Use your thin (01) pen. From the edges of the circle, draw uneven lines toward the middle. Don't draw them in front of the sun, though; this is where it reflects on the water surface and it usually looks silverish-white. Because the surface is so bright there, you will not be able to see many details.

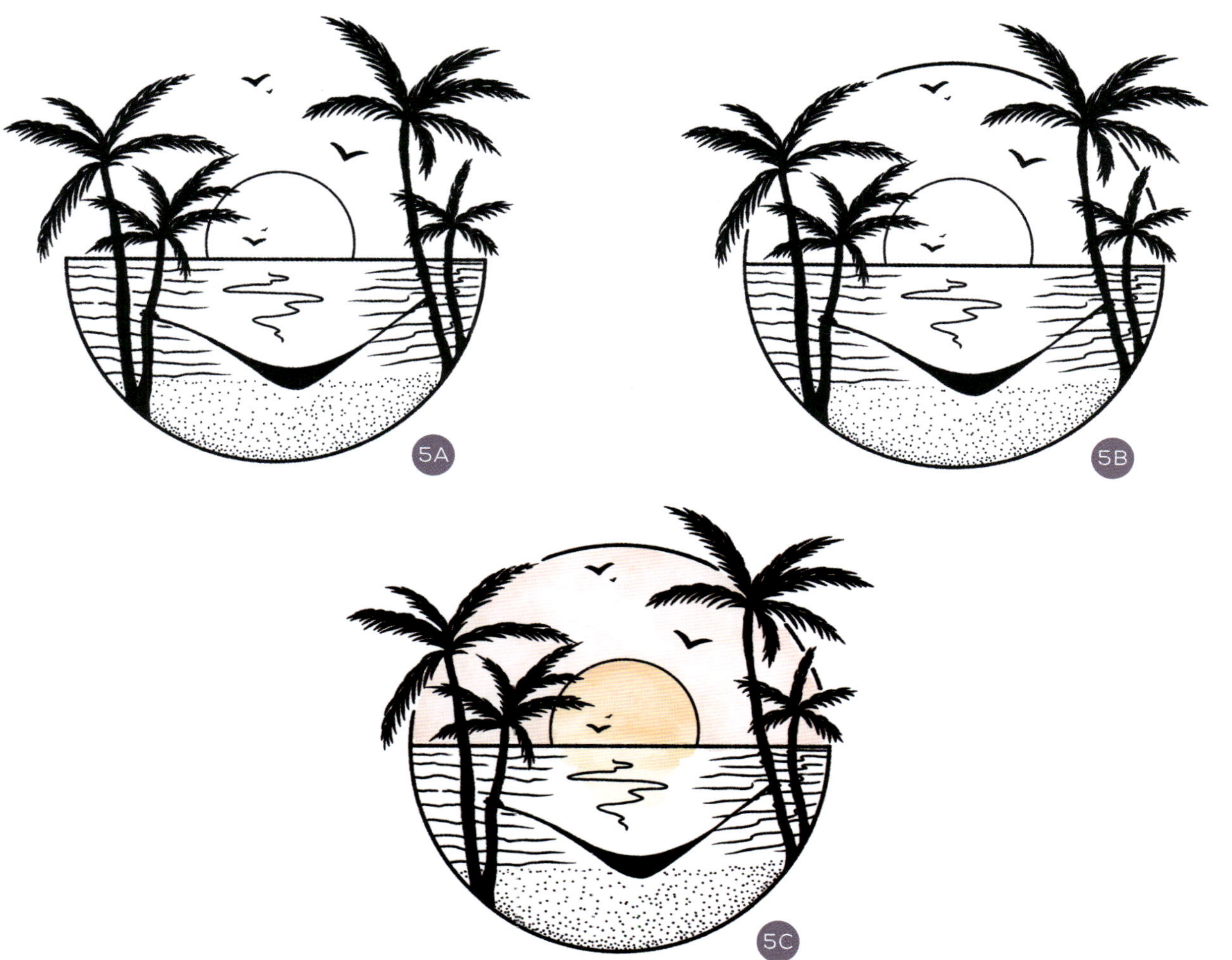

STEP 5

Finishing touches! Draw the birds in the sky (refer to the warm-up exercises in the Linework Basics chapter on page 8 for a detailed how-to) and, optionally, the rest of the circle outline, all in medium (05) pen. I break the outline before it meets the palm leaves so they are clearly visible.

If you want to add some color, this is the perfect piece for watercolor. I added a smooth light pink wash to the sky and painted the sun orange to give a sunset vibe to the whole project.

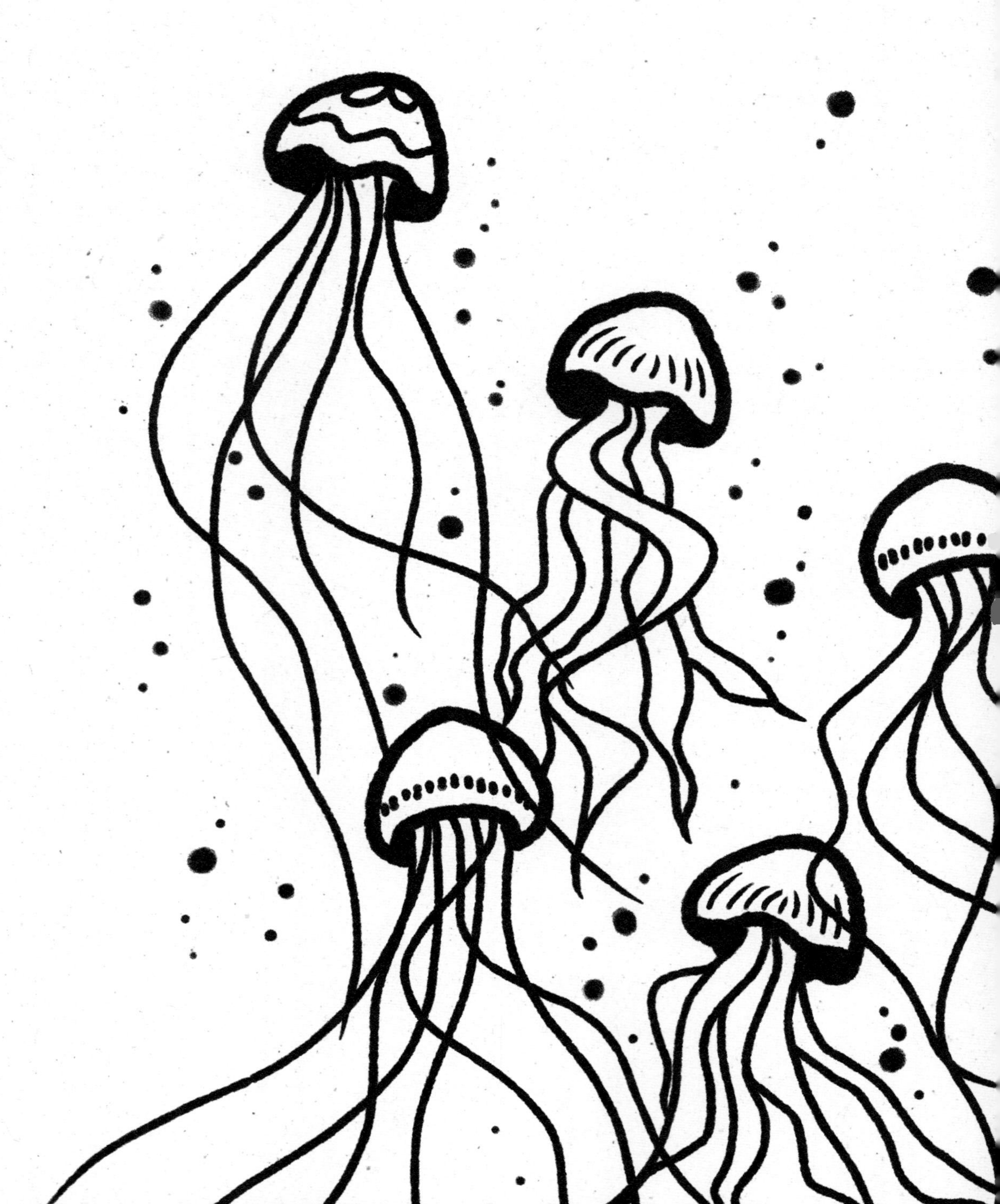

UNDERWATER SEASCAPES

The deep sea must be a fascinating place. I admit that my knowledge of this world comes from documentaries and movies. Also, from some of the novels I've read, sometimes there are divers among the set of characters (not sure if that counts . . .).

None of the projects in this chapter are an accurate depiction of marine life—just nice drawings with a lot of artistic freedom, which will push you as an artist. The more you look at things in a creative way, the more this will show in your work.

Additionally, many animals will show up in the next projects that we will have fun drawing: baby seals, whales, turtles and lots of small fish. Last but not least, you will learn a skill many budding artists dream of—namely, how you can "draw" water using different elements like waves or bubbles.

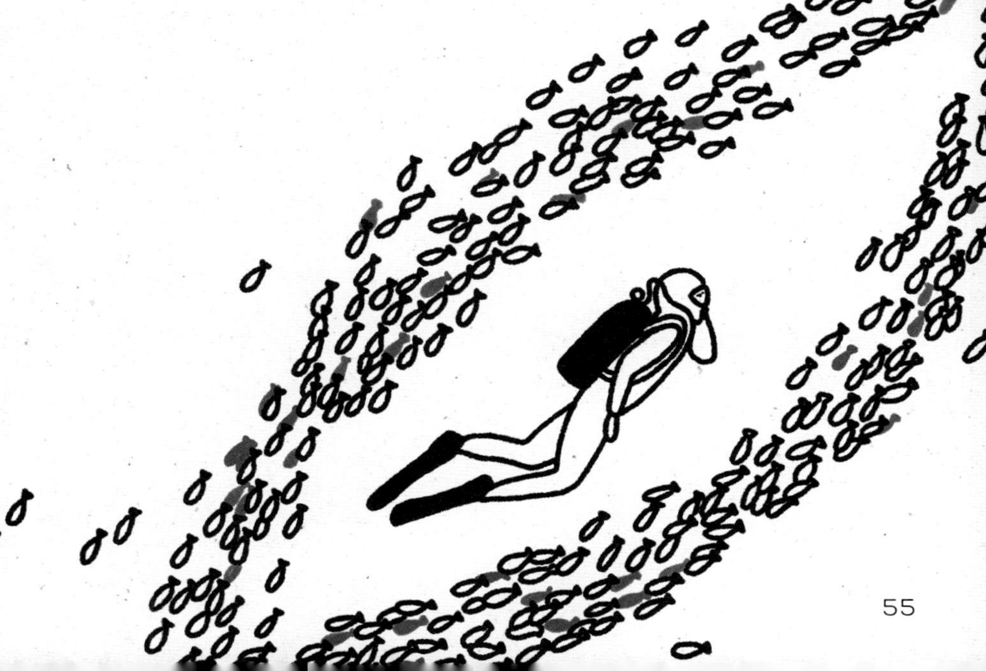

BABY SEALS PLAYING IN THE WAVES

There is no better motivation than a baby animal to try and make a delightful and charming piece that will make you smile (and make a great gift for a new baby!). In addition to working with a borderless composition, in this project you will also practice expressing water through drawing elements like small waves, bubbles and small fish.

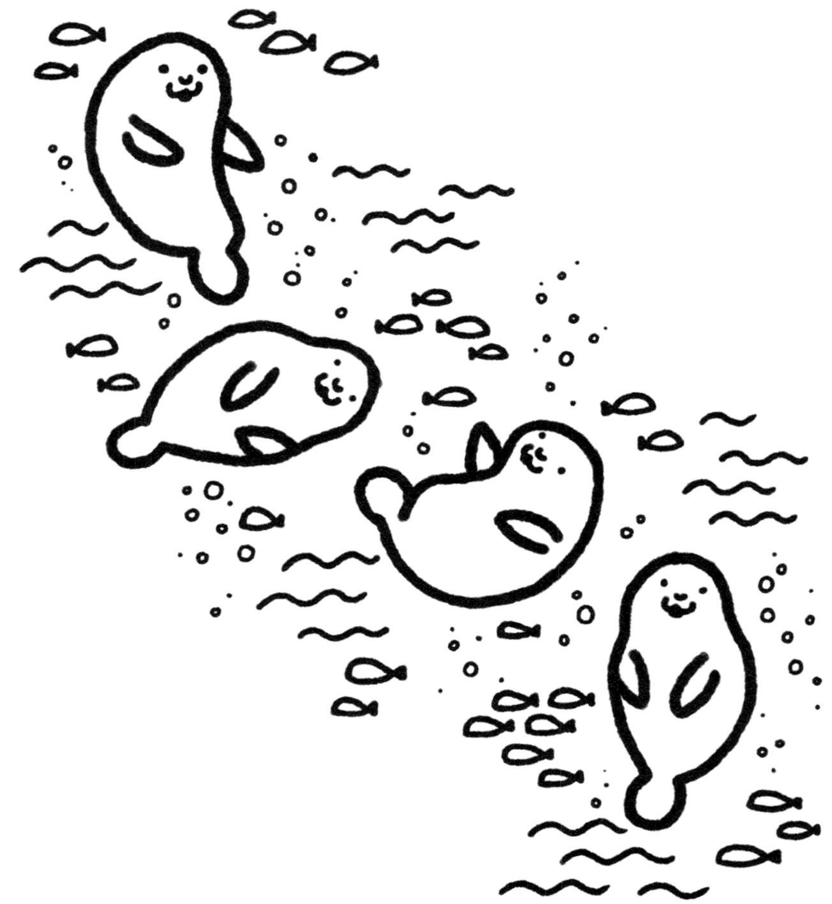

WHAT YOU NEED

Paper of your choice

Black pens in two sizes: 05 and 01

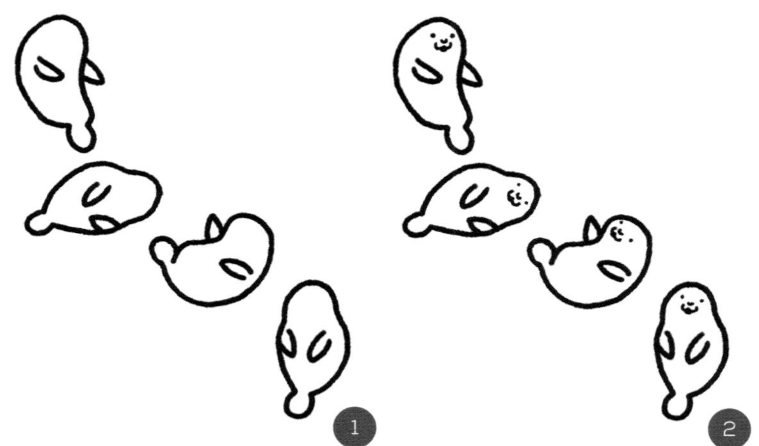

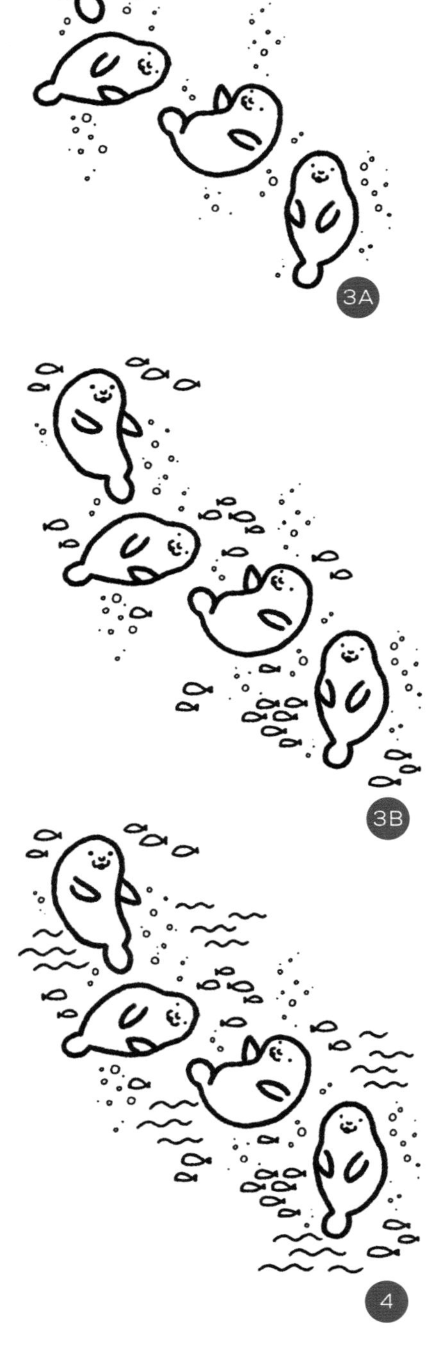

STEP 1

There is no frame on this project, so dive right in by drawing the baby seal outlines with your larger (05) pen. I think they resemble kidney beans, with a small round shape added on for the tail and two pointy shapes for the fins. Place four seal outlines on an imagined diagonal line. If you examine my drawing closely, you can see that I only use two outlines really. The first and the third, as well as the second and the fourth, are very similar, just positioned differently.

STEP 2

What makes the baby seals cute? Their friendly faces! Add a smiling snout, whiskers and eyes in thin (01) pen. And that's the main subject of this drawing completed—nice work!

STEP 3

In this next step, give the baby seals a background, all in thin (01) pen. Whenever I see non-fish animals swimming underwater in documentaries, there are bubbles around them. Draw circles and dots in different sizes to create some.

Then, add some small fish. Note that I kept each group swimming in the same direction and alternated directions between the groups. A more detailed tutorial on how to draw small fish can be found in the Whale with Small Fish Friends project on page 64.

STEP 4

As the final touch in this drawing, complete some wavy lines in the rest of the space around the baby seals. Aww, still cute!

JELLYFISH SWARM

Has anyone else sat in front of the jellyfish tank at SeaWorld® for a long time and found it super relaxing to watch them float in the water? This drawing might not transfer that same level of zen, but it's still a fun project with lots of curved lines, so let's get started! (*Psst:* There is an opportunity to practice overlap here when you draw the tentacles. This will show the viewer which of the jellyfish are closer to the aquarium glass and which ones are farther away.)

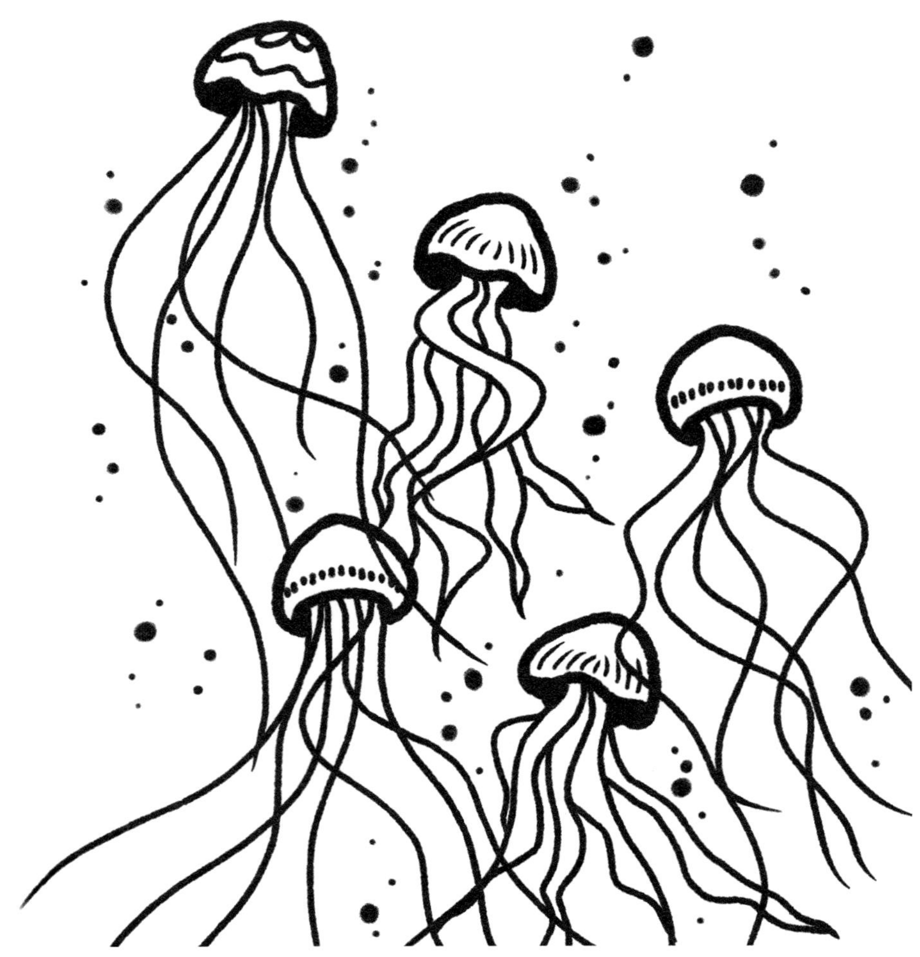

WHAT YOU NEED

Paper of your choice

Black pens in three sizes: 1.5, 05 and 01

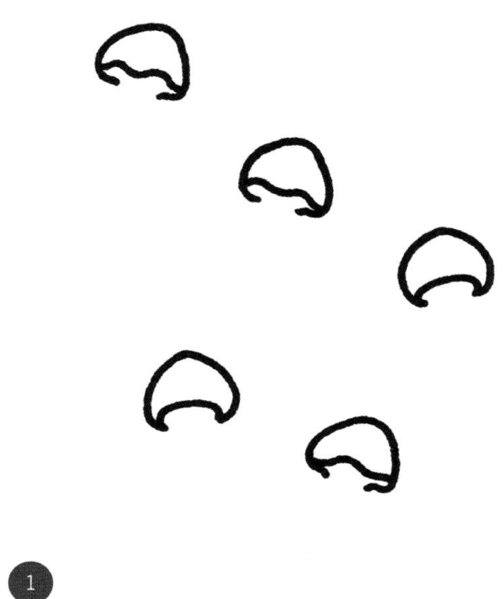

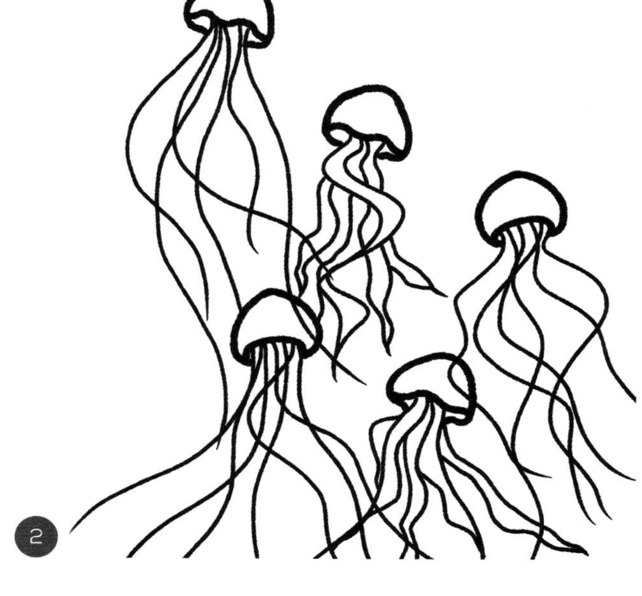

STEP 1

Draw the jellyfish bodies with your thickest (1.5) pen. To me, they are a pointy half-circle that curves inward at the bottom. I drew five of them because we are on a 15-minute time limit. You can draw as many as you want though. On a big piece of paper, this could become quite a large swarm and keep you drawing for days . . . .

STEP 2

Once the bodies are finished, move on to the tentacles. Use the medium (05) nib here. Have them overlap for a more natural look. Note the different types: on three jellyfish I did just lines. On the other two, I drew a thicker shape. Of course, there are even more variations if you feel like mixing it up some more.

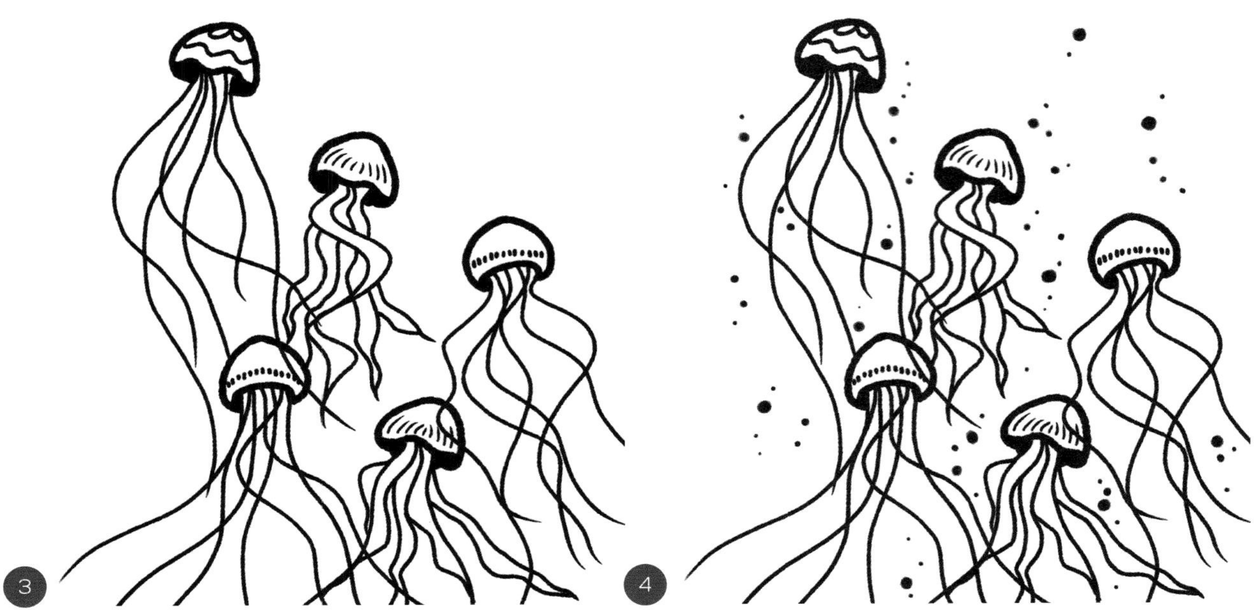

STEP 3

Decorate the jellyfish bodies with medium (05) and thin (01) pen lines. These are the edges that glow in the black light of the SeaWorld® tank. Fill in the bottom of the bodies in black on both sides of the tentacles.

STEP 4

The drawing is almost finished; it's only missing a background. If this were colored work, it would be easy! With ink drawings, it's a little more complicated when it comes to things that are very lightly colored in real life, like water or air. You need to find shapes that express what you want to draw as you don't have the option of color.

And what did I choose here? Drumroll . . . my water favorite: bubbles!

Draw lots of black dots in a variety of sizes—you can use all your pen sizes for that.

OPTIONAL: Color the jellyfish and/or the water with watercolor washes of your choice. Recently, I've read about pink jellyfish; that would be a striking combination with a blue water background.

DIVER SWIMMING THROUGH A SCHOOL OF FISH

When you see large swarms of fish on TV, the movement and the sheer number of individual fish is always an amazing sight. The diver in this drawing gets to see them up close. I wanted to show you, with this design, that you can create larger shapes by putting many small items close together. I arranged the fish swarm in an almond shape, as I assume that this is how it would look in nature. You could also go for something funkier, like a spiral for example.

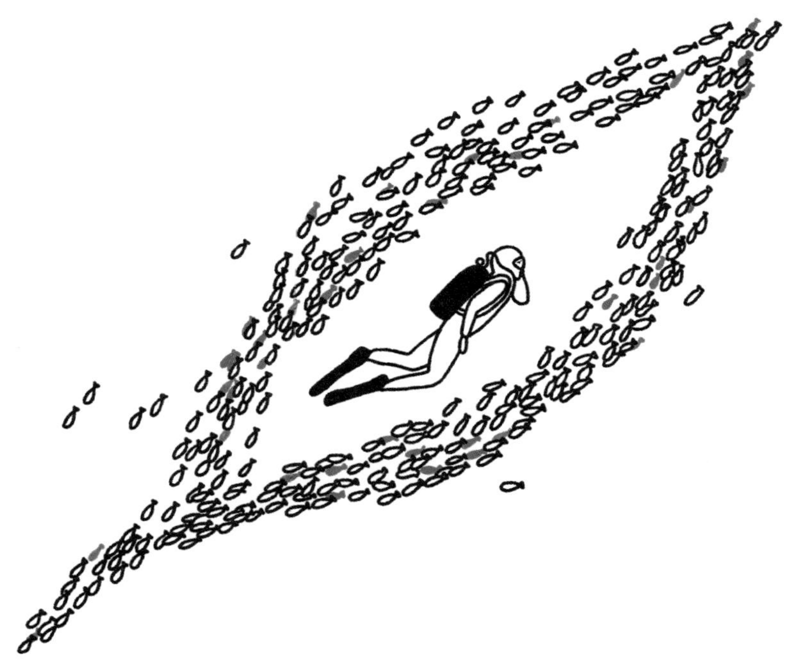

WHAT YOU NEED

Paper of your choice

Black pen in one size: 05

Pencil and eraser

Gray felt-tip pen or ink wash

Small round brush (size 3)

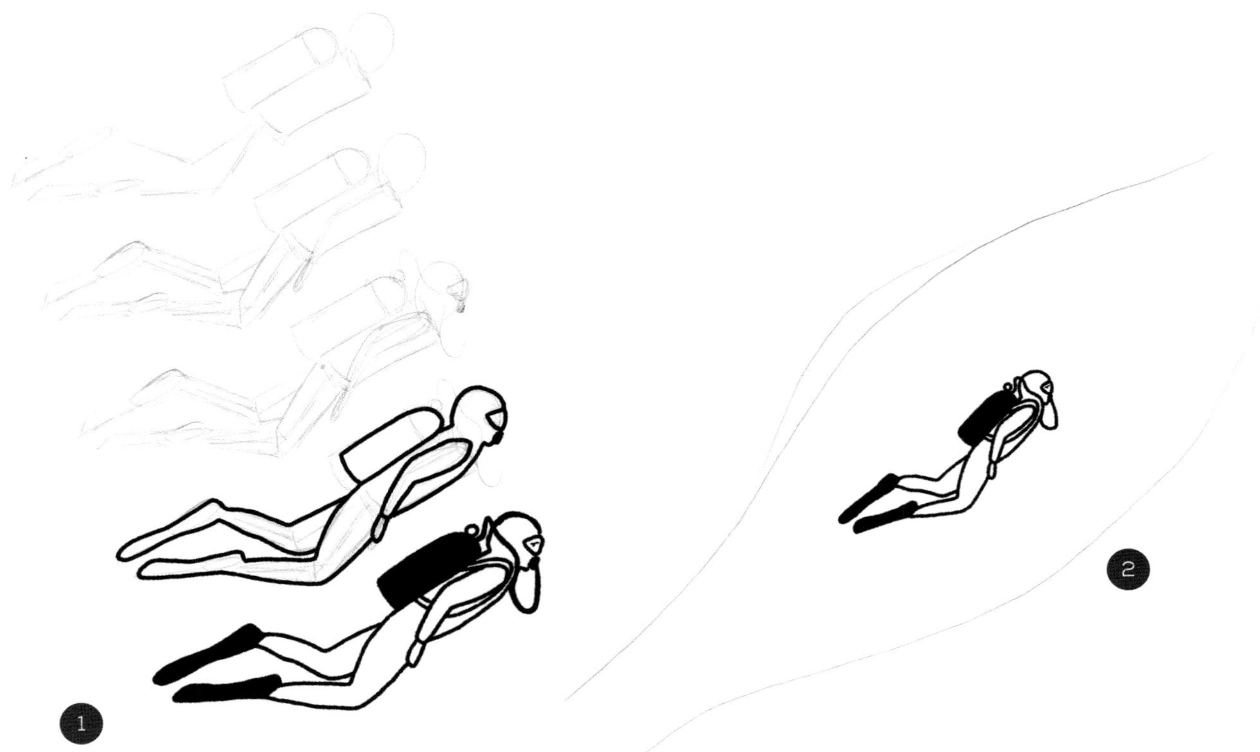

STEP 1

Let's start out with the diver in medium (05) pen. With people as subjects, pay attention to the proportions, otherwise they don't look quite right. Again, I kept the details to a minimum and used abstraction to make my life easier. Look at the hand of the diver, for example, no fingers. Here is the step-by-step process to get from rectangles, sticks and circles to the finished diver:

Fill in the tank and the fins in black for some contrast. You could also draw the whole diver in black and turn it into a silhouette with even less detail.

STEP 2

Draw a guideline for the fish in pencil.

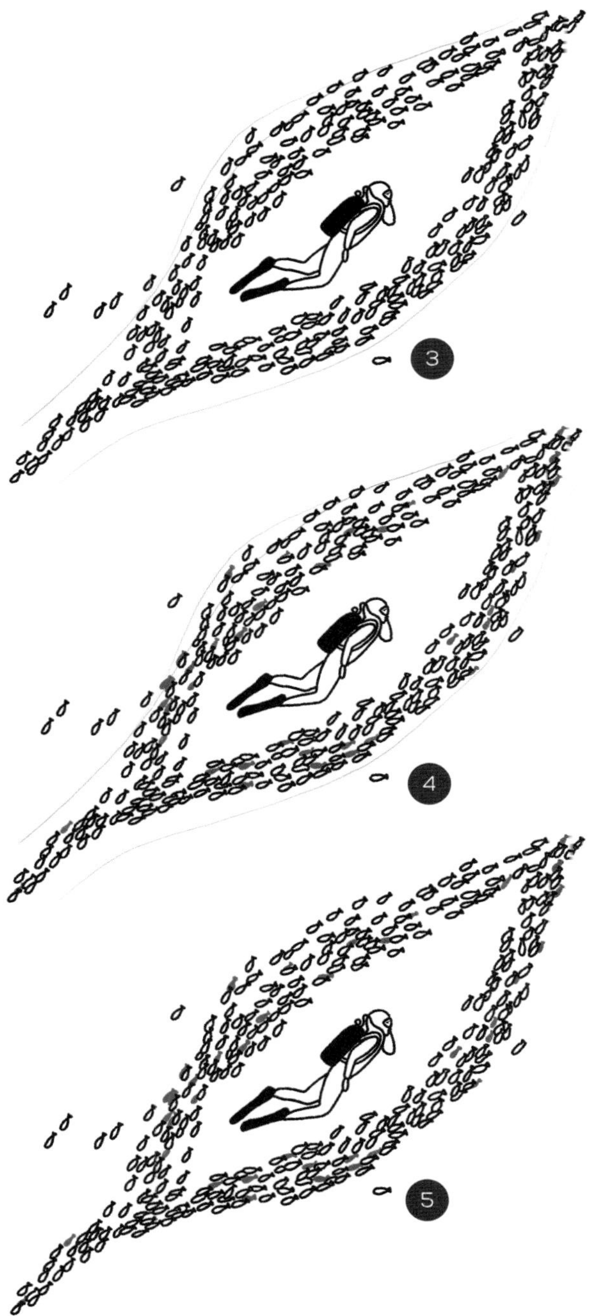

STEP 3

In this step, it gets a little meditative again. Add lots of small fish swimming in the same direction around the diver. A more detailed explanation on small fish can be found in the Whale with Small Fish Friends project on page 64. Try to overlap your fish on occasion to show that they are in front of each other and that there are many of them.

STEP 4

For an extra background layer, use your gray pen, ink wash or pencil and scatter small gray fish behind the others and at the edges of the swarm.

STEP 5

Last but not least: Erase the guidelines. You finished another project. High-five your pens and be happy about it!

WHALE WITH SMALL FISH FRIENDS

Every time I scroll through social media, whale puns and jokes show up in my feed. Here is one that describes the next project: What do whales need to stay healty? Vitamin Sea!

In this project, we'll practice showcasing the water's movement expressed here through long and gently curved lines. It will also give examples for drawing corals and algae on the sea bottom.

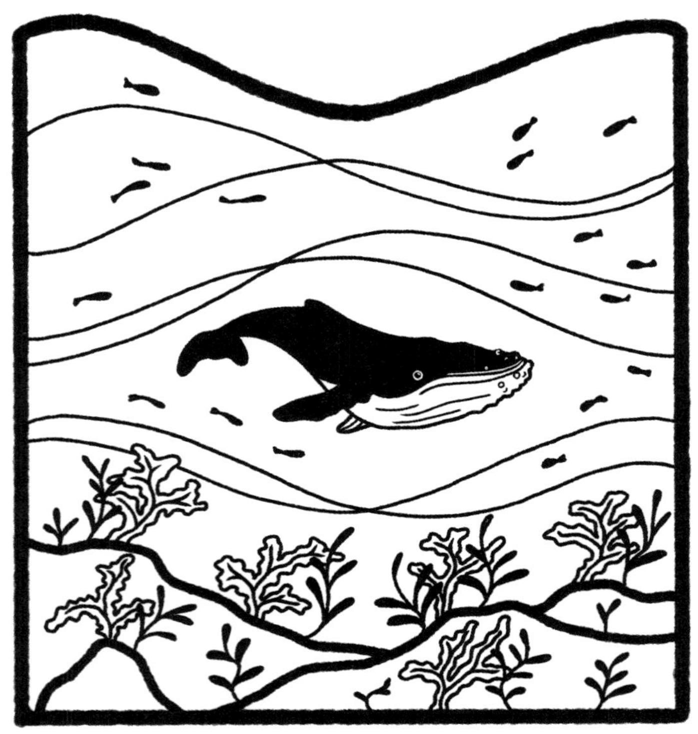

WHAT YOU NEED

Paper of your choice

Black pens in three sizes: 1.5, 05 and 01

White pen in one size: 08

Ruler

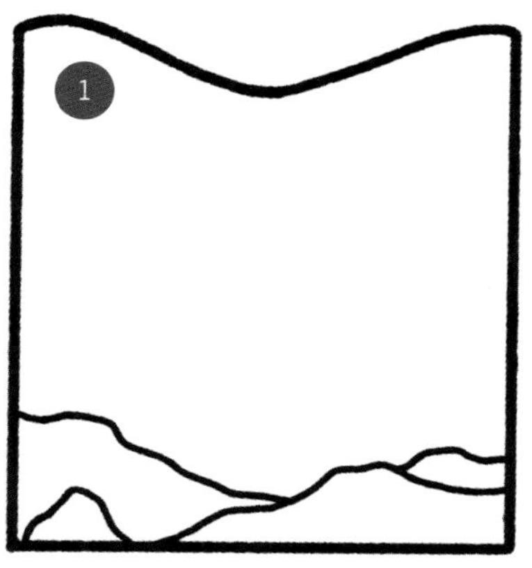

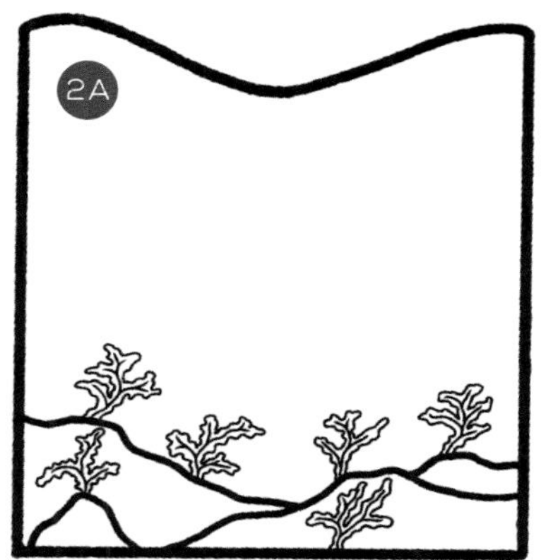

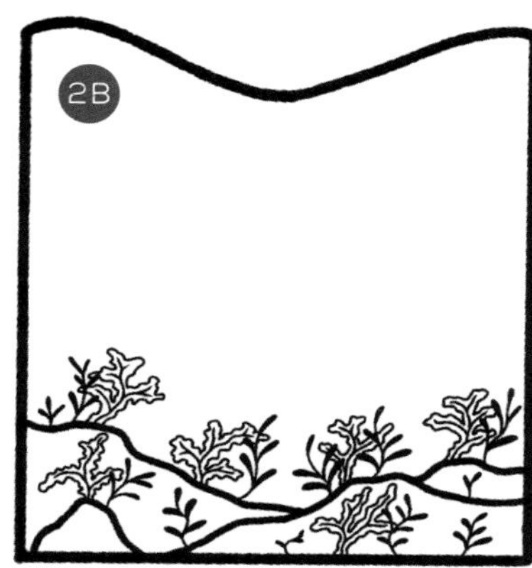

STEP 1

As with most of our drawings, start with the frame in thick (1.5) pen. Draw a rectangle bottom and leave the top side open. Connect both sides of the rectangle with a curved line that resembles a wave.

In the bottom of the rectangle, add a few irregular lines in medium (05) pen. This will be the bottom of the sea.

STEP 2

Of course, we also need some corals and algae. For the corals, first draw the stem in thin (01) pen. It kind of looks like a little tree. Then, add a curvy outline all around. For the algae, start with an S curve and add leaves to it. Fill in the leaves with black like me or leave them blank.

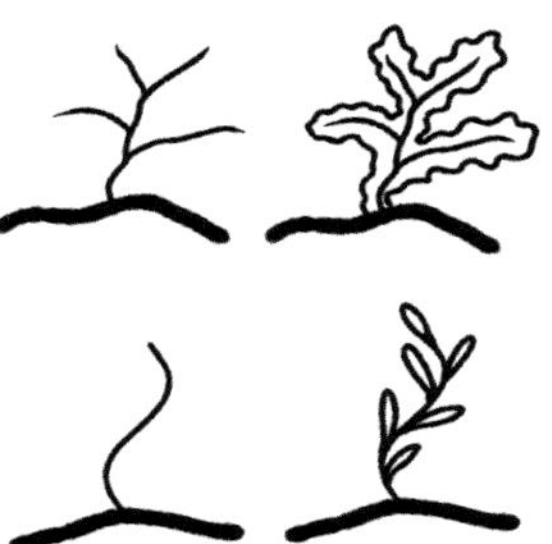

Distribute as many corals and algae over the bottom as you wish. (I think I went a little overboard because it was fun to draw them.) It's good to put some of the algae in front of the corals (for example, just drawing over them). This creates a little depth in the drawing.

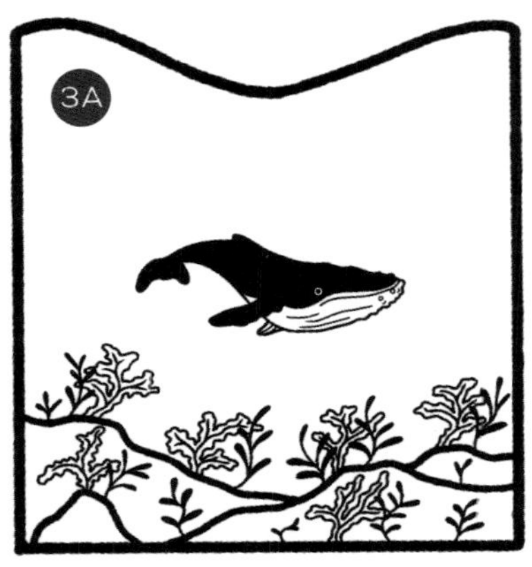

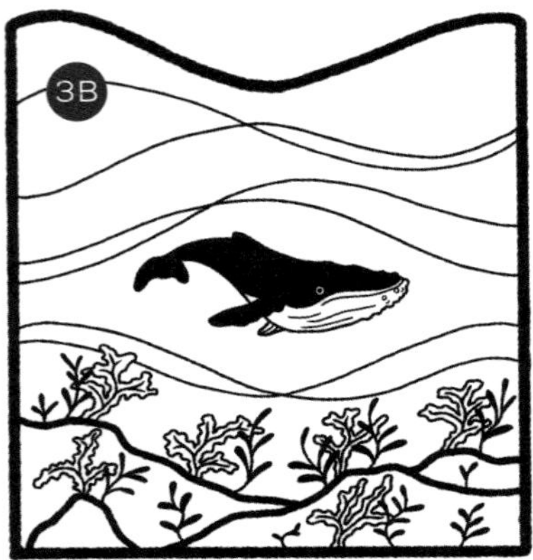

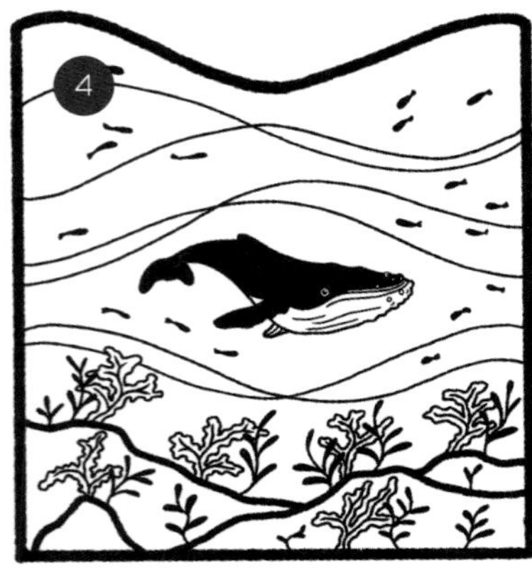

STEP 3

Now, it's time for our focal point: the whale! Look online for a reference picture to help you (I found this grumpy whale that I really liked). This is how you break down the drawing process:

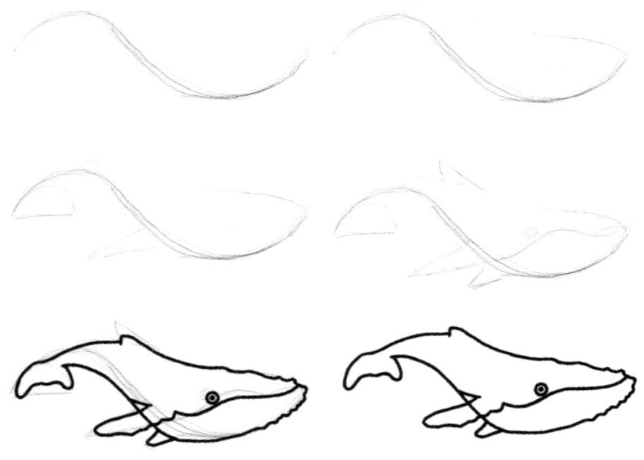

Draw the whale in thin (01) pen within your rectangle and fill in the black areas with your brush pen.

It doesn't matter what kind of whale you draw, just make sure that you color some larger areas in black. This will make the whale stand out in the drawing as it's the darkest element.

Here is an example for a less detailed orca as an alternative:

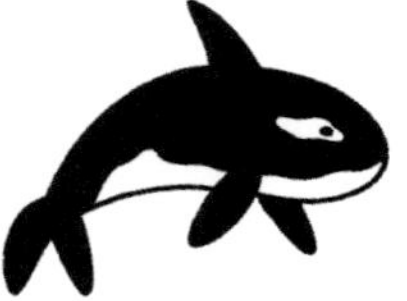

Above and below the whale, add some curved lines in thin (01) pen as more waves. You've completed 90 percent of the drawing—almost there!

STEP 4

The last step is for completing the small details: little fishes with a small (01) pen. They are all made of the same basic shapes that are stretched in different directions and filled with black:

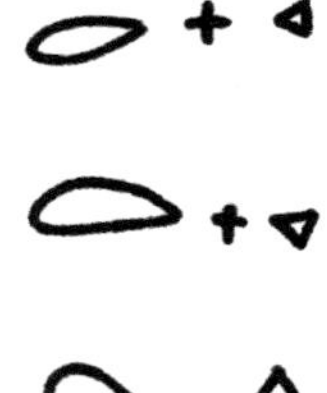

Lastly, grab a thin white pen and add some white accents on the whale. I chose to put a highlight in the eye, the upper lip and added a few sea pox as well. Whale done!

TURTLE SWIMMING OVER SEAWEED

This project will teach you a fun (and somewhat meditative and soothing) way to doodle seaweed. And the great part about it? Your lines don't need to be super accurate and it will still look good.

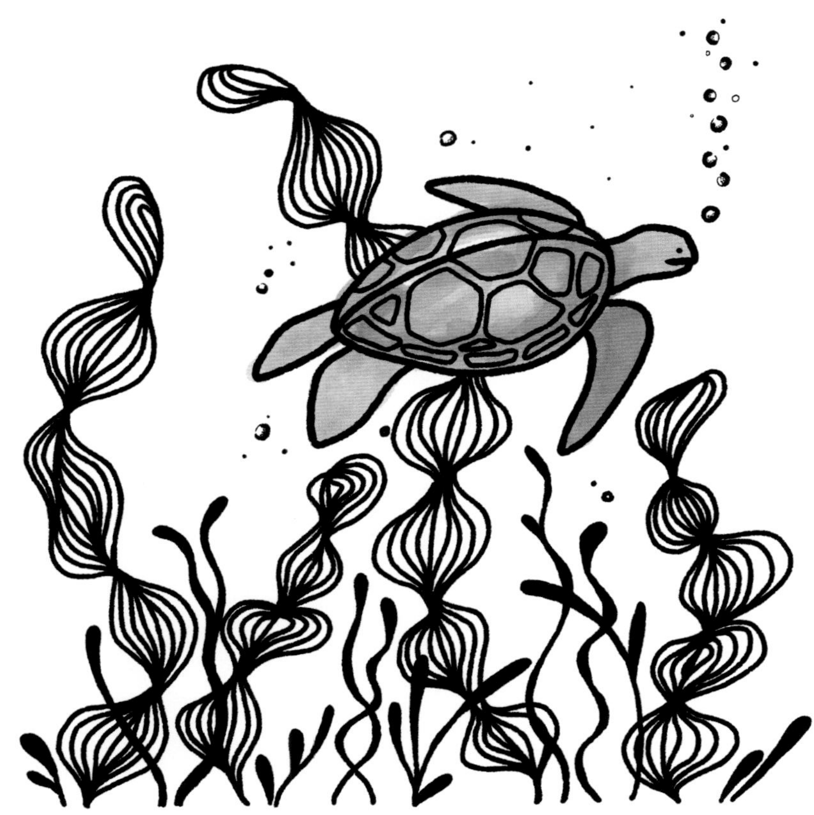

WHAT YOU NEED

Watercolor or mixed-media paper

Black pens in three sizes: 1.5, 05 and 01

Pencil and eraser

Ruler

Watercolor or ink in tones of green (optional)

Medium round brush (size 3) (optional)

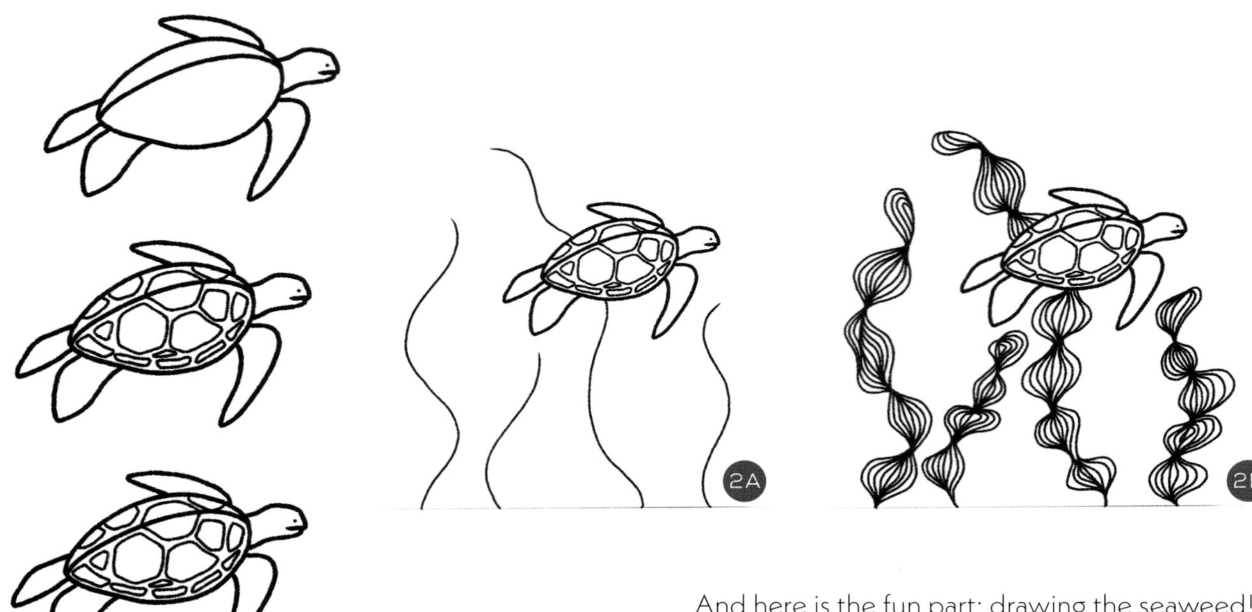

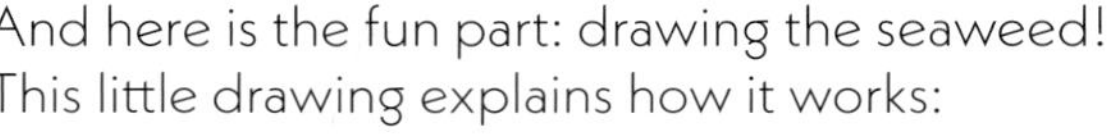
And here is the fun part: drawing the seaweed! This little drawing explains how it works:

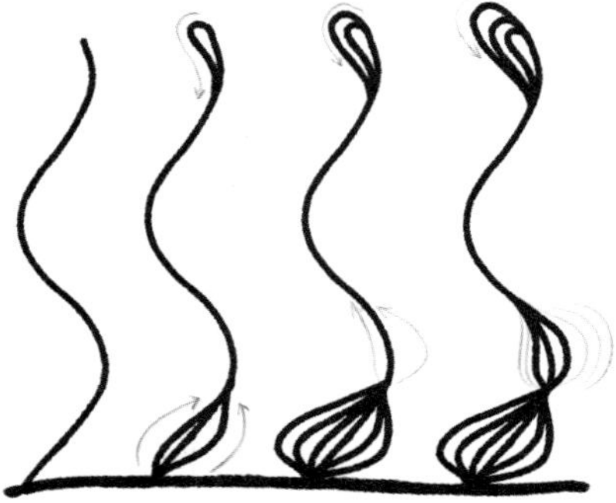

STEP 1

We're putting the turtle in the middle of our paper. Use your medium (05) pen for the outlines of the body, the fins, and the head and a small (01) pen to add some details. Again, simplify the turtle as much as you can to make it easier to draw. I think the pattern on the turtle's back is unique to turtles; therefore, this is the only detail I kept besides the outlines and the face.

STEP 2

Draw a pencil line below the turtle for the bottom of the sea. From there, draw some curved stems in thin (01) pen for the seaweed. I decided to have one long stem that passes behind the turtle. It will look like the turtle swims in front of it in the final drawing.

Start at the bottom and draw a curve on each side of your stem. They start at the bottom, and after curving outward, they meet a bit higher up on the stem. The curves don't have to be symmetrical, in fact it's better if they aren't. Add more curves like these somewhat parallel (but not too tidy) to the first pair, again making sure that all curves meet at the same point on the stem. Once you like the volume, start with a new set of curves at the endpoint of the first group and repeat the steps. The end of the stem works in a similar way, just draw the curves toward one side only.

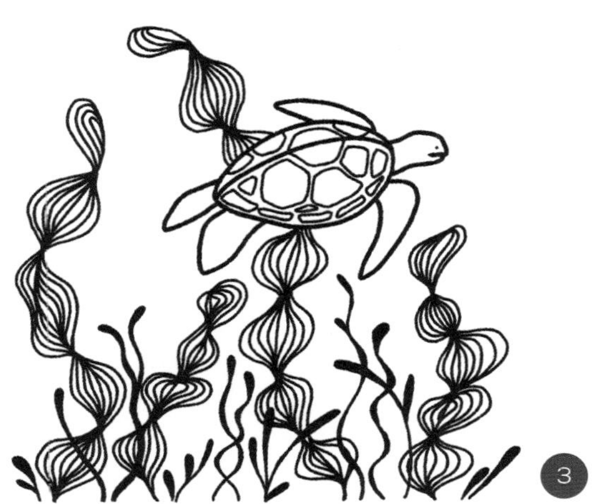

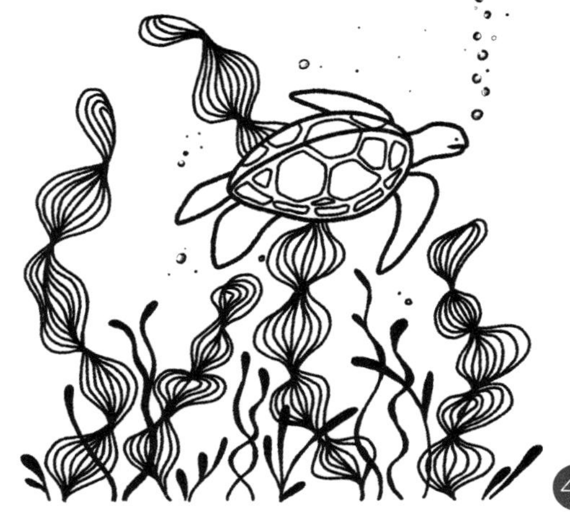

STEP 3

Draw the smaller algae by starting with curved lines and rounding them at the end. I also made the stems a little wider in some parts. Make sure your ink is dry and gently erase the pencil lines once you've finished with the algae.

STEP 4

For details, add some bubbles in different sizes around the turtle and, especially, rising above the head.

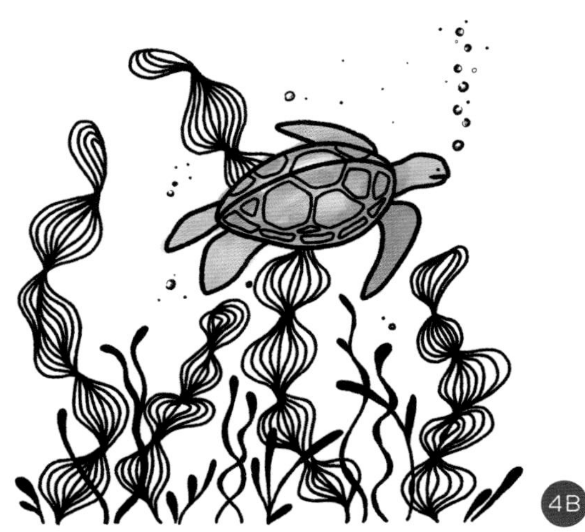

OPTIONAL:

I chose to add some color as I felt the turtle got a little lost in the drawing. (You might say I didn't pay enough attention to the composition!) By painting the turtle green, it becomes the point of focus in an otherwise black-and-white drawing. You can also outline it in green watercolor, ink or pencil, if you prefer.

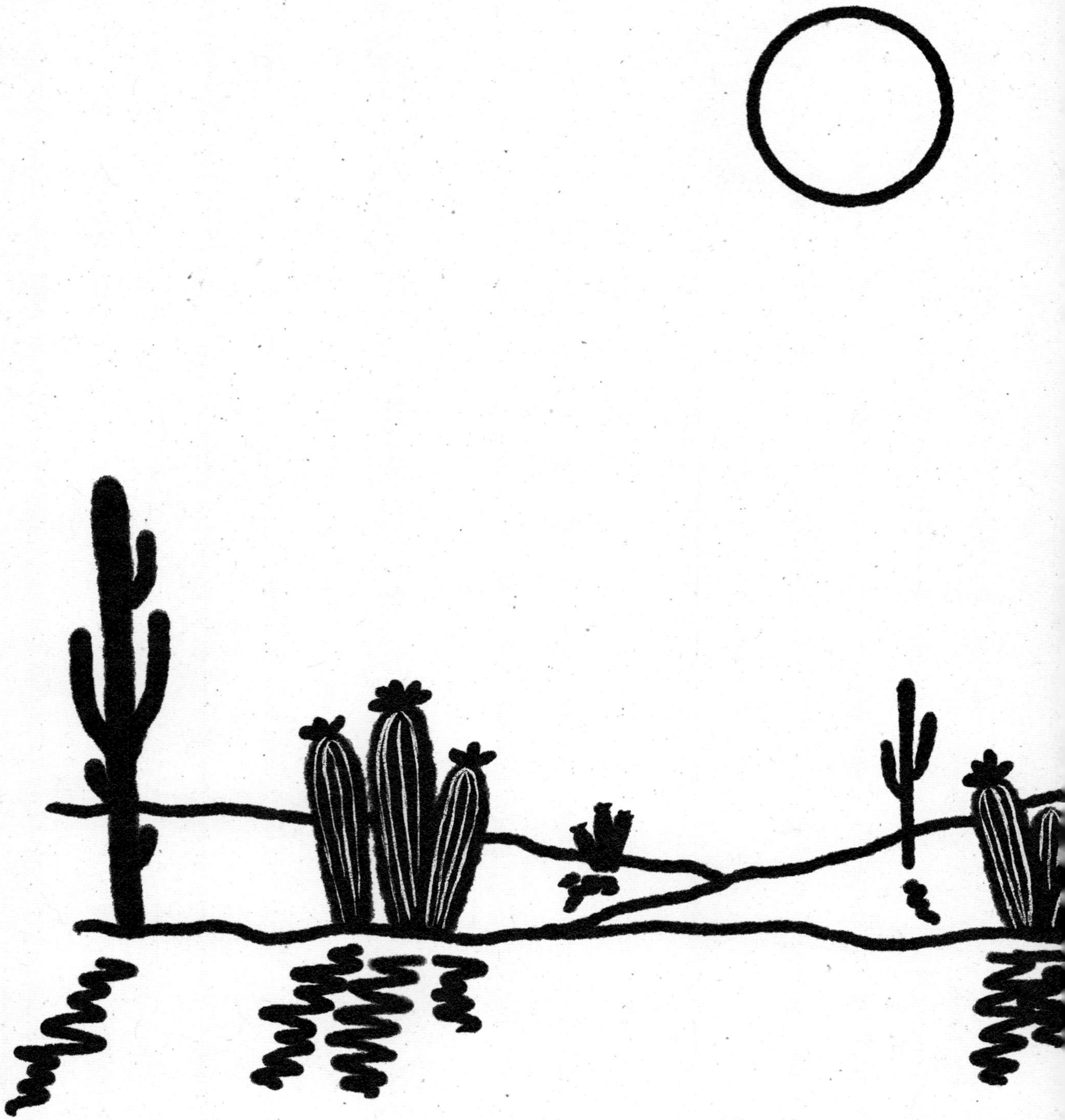

DESERT LANDSCAPES

For the next section of drawings, I went through my photo albums of a road trip to the Southwest of the United States. Needless to say that we stopped at all the (many) national parks in the area. It was amazing! I hope to show you, through describing my process, how you can translate personal experiences into drawings. I hope it will encourage you to draw your own later. (*Psst!* The Wrap-Up chapter on page 170 contains more tips.)

More specifically, through these atmospheric desert-inspired compositions, we'll be exploring topics like simplifying shapes (page 72) and playing with the contrast of white details on black backgrounds (page 81), as well as designing intricate-looking borders (page 78).

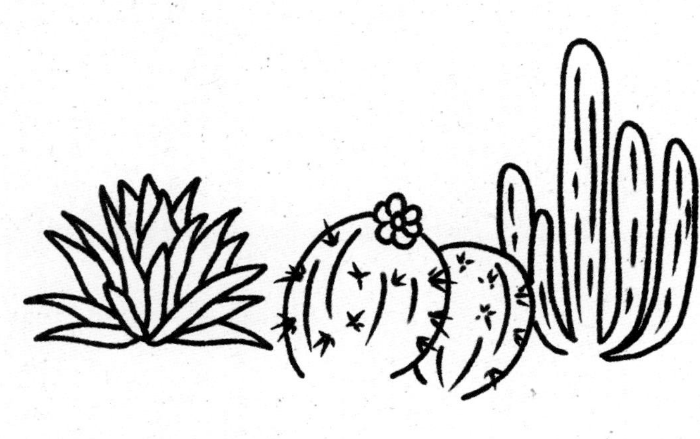

ROCK FORMATION LANDSCAPE

You make the rules for what you draw. If you want to, you can combine elements in a drawing that do not really go together or arrange them in a way that is different from reality—let's just call it artistic freedom. For this one, I wanted to combine two things that stood out to me on the road trip I mentioned earlier. The first were the huge sandstone buttes in Monument Valley and the second were the Joshua trees.

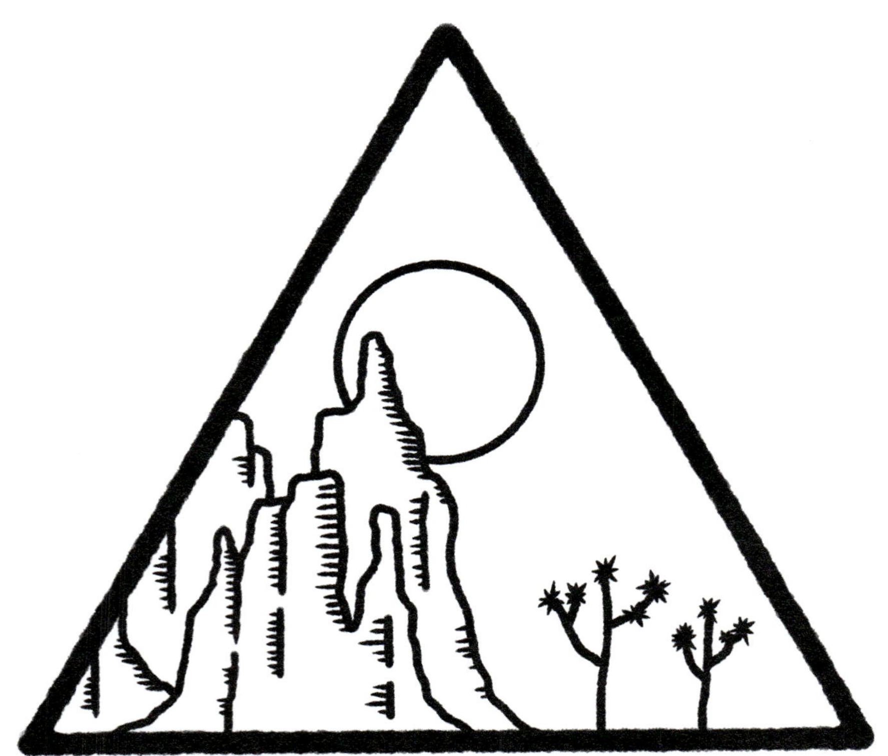

WHAT YOU NEED

Paper of your choice

Black pens in three sizes: 1.5, 05 and 01

Compass, piece of string or triangle ruler

Ruler

Pencil and eraser

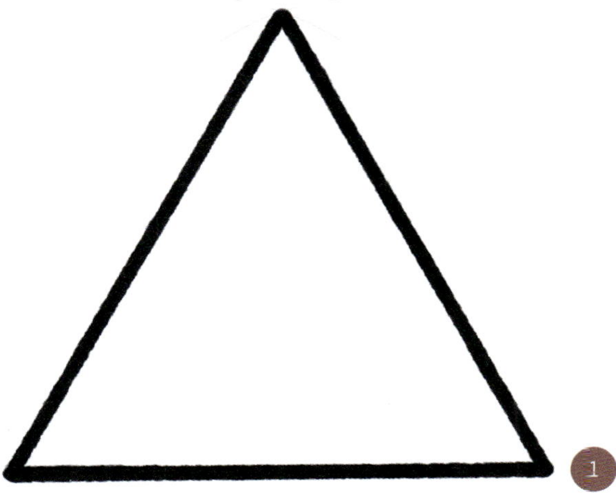

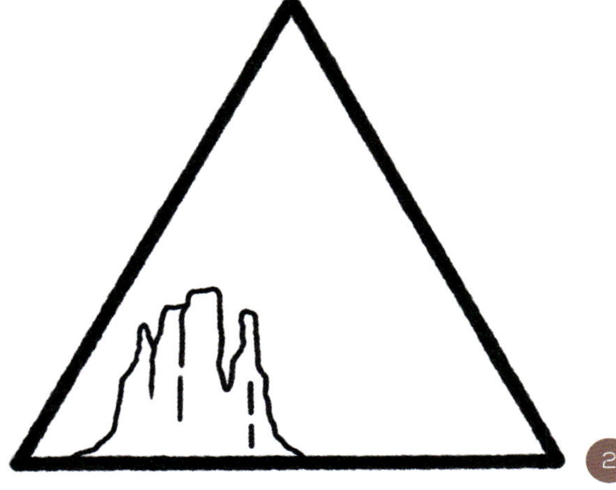

STEP 1

This is a drawing with a triangle frame and all the sides are the same length. Beware: geometry lesson coming up. I'll make it easy though, I promise. The easiest way to create such a triangle is with a compass. Draw your base line in thick (1.5) pen. Stick the needle end of your compass in one end of the line and open your compass to exactly that length. Swing the pencil tip over the middle of the line and make a small mark. Do the same thing from the other end of the line.

Where both pencil lines cross marks the tip of your triangle. Connect this point to your base line on both sides to get your triangle and erase the pencil. End of geometry class!

OPTIONS IF YOU DON'T HAVE A COMPASS:

Tie your pencil to a piece of string. Measure the line with your piece of string and hold down the string on the end of your line. From there, pull your pencil over the middle of the line and make a mark. Then, do the same thing from the other end of the line.

Use your triangle ruler to measure a 60-degree angle on each end of your baseline and draw the sidelines. I suggest doing that in pencil first until you know where both pencil lines meet.

STEP 2

After all that geometry work, let's move on to the actual subject. Draw the outlines for your rock formation with the medium (05) pen. I placed all my rocks toward the left because I need some space on the right for the Joshua trees. Start with the formation closest to the viewer and work backwards.

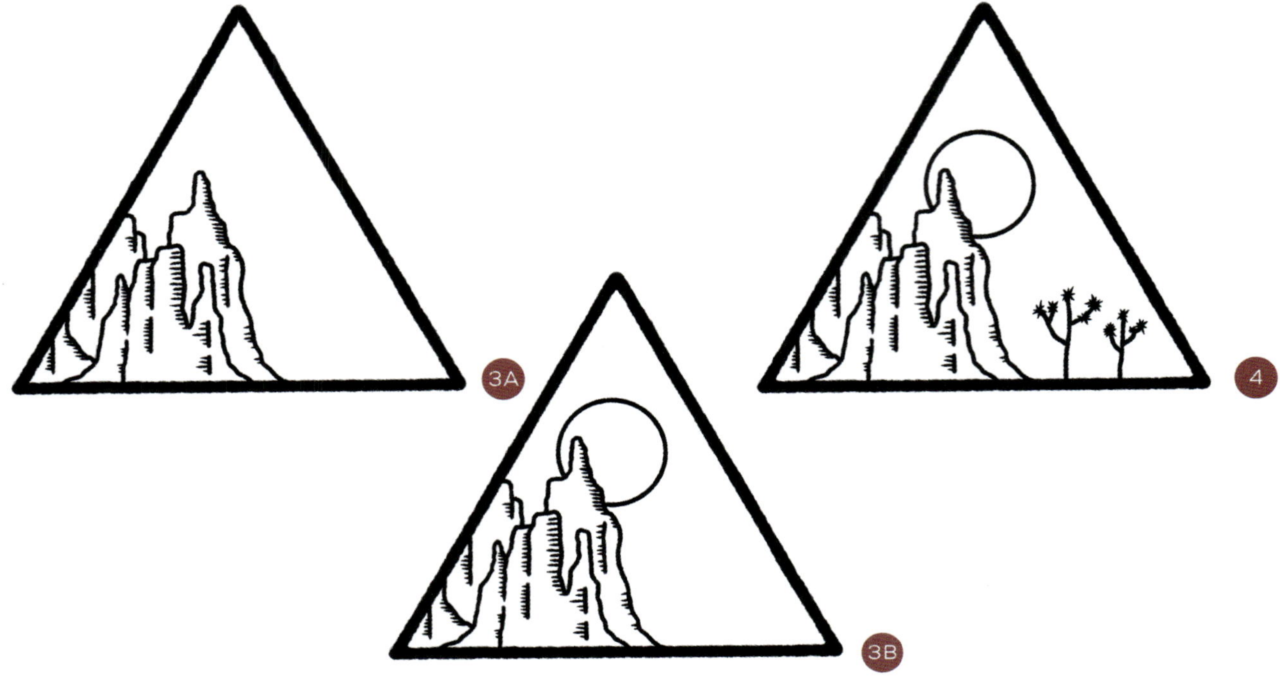

STEP 3

Make the different rocks overlap, so it looks like they are behind each other, and draw some smaller textures onto them with the thin (01) pen. I thought the sandstone looked like it had vertical lines on it, so that's what I tried to show here.

Behind the rock formation, draw a circle for the sun in medium (05) pen.

STEP 4

Final details! I simplified the Joshua trees to just a couple of lines in medium (05) pen with a starlike shape at each end in thin (01) pen.

Even though this combination is not something I observed in reality, I do think it looks nice. Thanks for sticking with me, and hopefully it has inspired you to have more fun with artistic freedom in future drawings of your own!

CACTI IN THE DESERT

While clicking through my digital photo albums, it occurred to me that I had taken hundreds of photos of different kinds of cacti. Two-thirds of those pictures are really bad for the same reason. Why? I did not pay attention to the sun and the resulting shadows and, therefore, most of the pics show a shaky silhouette of a cactus with a really bright sky. So, it's worth it to dedicate a drawing to my random cacti pictures (I'm way more skilled with a camera these days, I hope!) and practice laying down shadows in different directions.

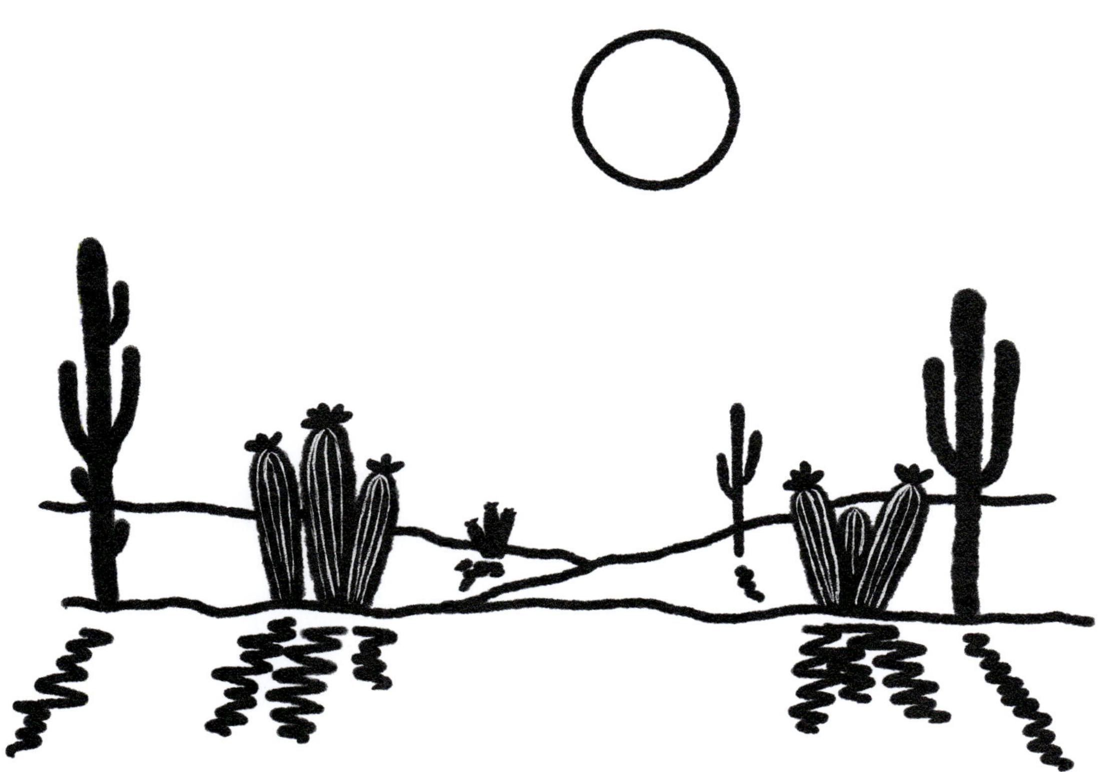

WHAT YOU NEED

Paper of your choice

Black pens in three sizes: 1.5, 05 and 01

Brush pen

White pen in one size: 08

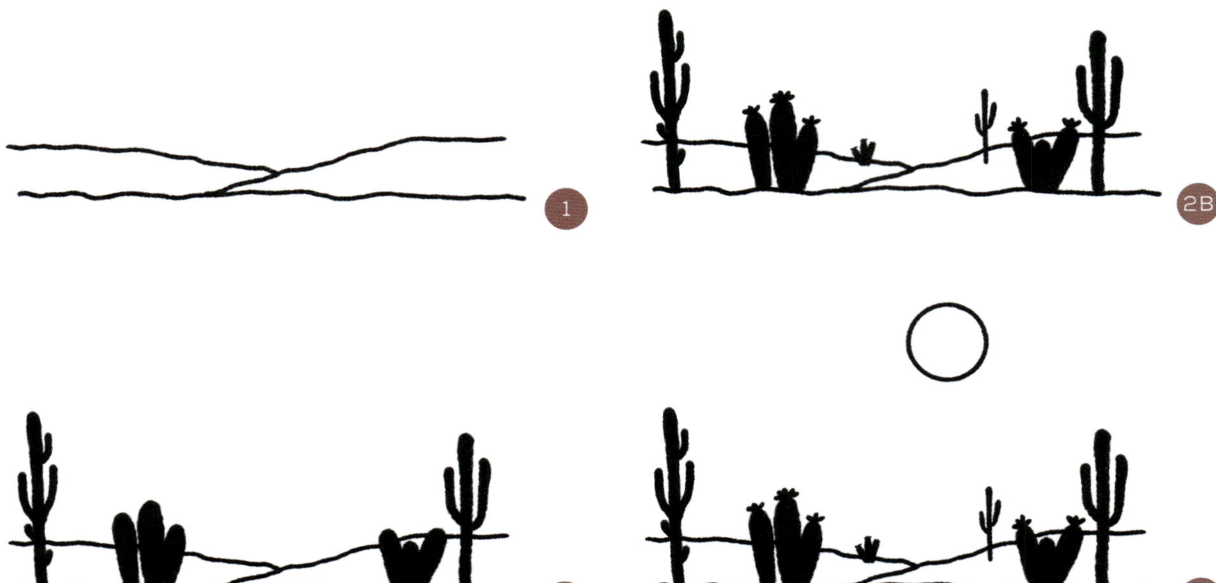

STEP 1

Start out with irregular lines for the ground in medium (05) pen. As all of our cacti will be silhouettes in black, you do not need to break the lines. Just draw over them.

STEP 2

Place the cacti silhouettes on the foreground line. I arranged mine almost symmetrically with slight variations to the plants on each side.

As the shapes of the cacti in front are so similar to each other, the drawing can look boring. I employed some creative freedom and added flowers to the bulkier type of cacti.

Next, switch to your thin (01) pen and add some very small cacti in the background. As they are far away, work with little detail. Just the distinct shape is enough to make them recognizable.

STEP 3

Next up is the circle for the sun—easy!

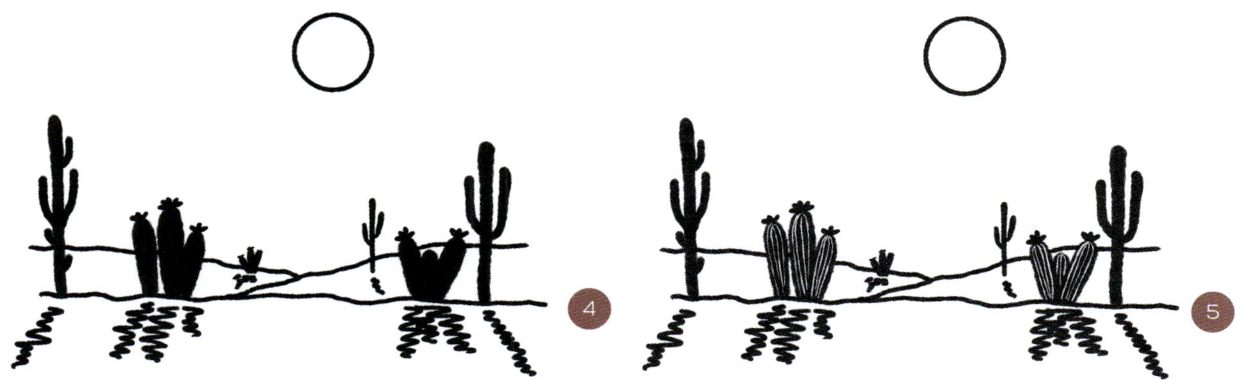

STEP 4

To add another important detail I found in my photo fails, draw some wiggly lines for the shadows cast by the cacti in medium (05) pen.

For this step, it's important where you placed the sun, as this will dictate in which direction you need to lay down the shadow. Check out this drawing for a hint:

STEP 5

To finalize the project, draw some texture on the cacti in white pen. I swear the completed piece is so much cooler than any of my pictures!

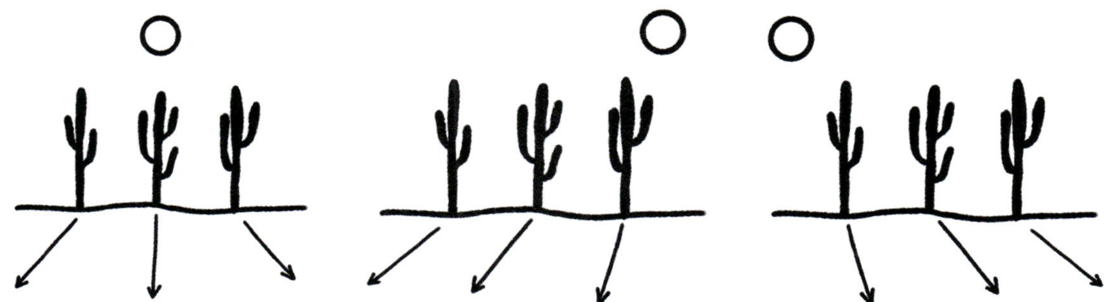

ADOBE HOUSES AND A SNAKE

Where I live, people don't build adobe houses. Naturally, I was quite curious and examined a few of them closely. They are super easy to draw, as their basic shape is very simple already. To make this project more interesting, let's add a special frame! If you've tied friendship bracelets in the past or someone has ever gifted you one, you might recognize the pattern. That's where I got it from. By the way, the snake is just there for fun. Feel free to leave it out or add something else.

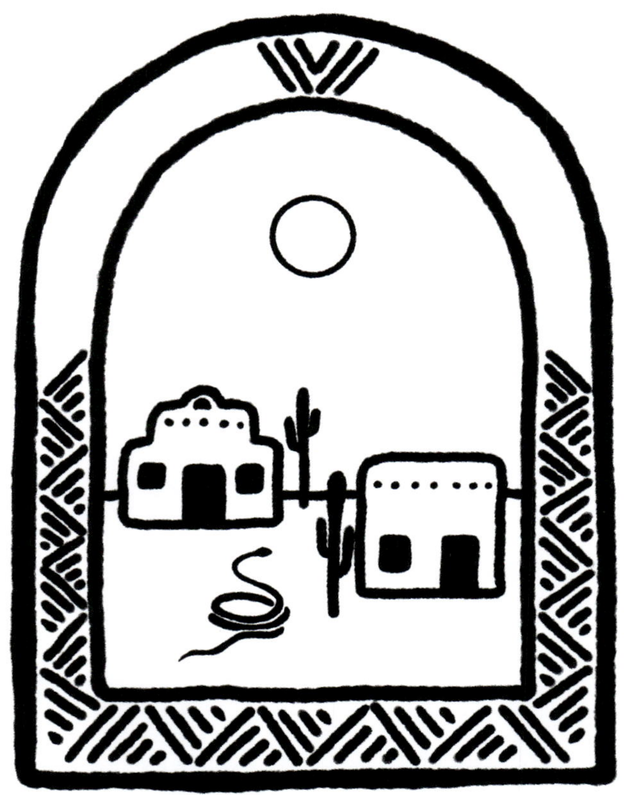

WHAT YOU NEED

Paper of your choice

Black pens in three sizes: 1.5, 05 and 01

Ruler

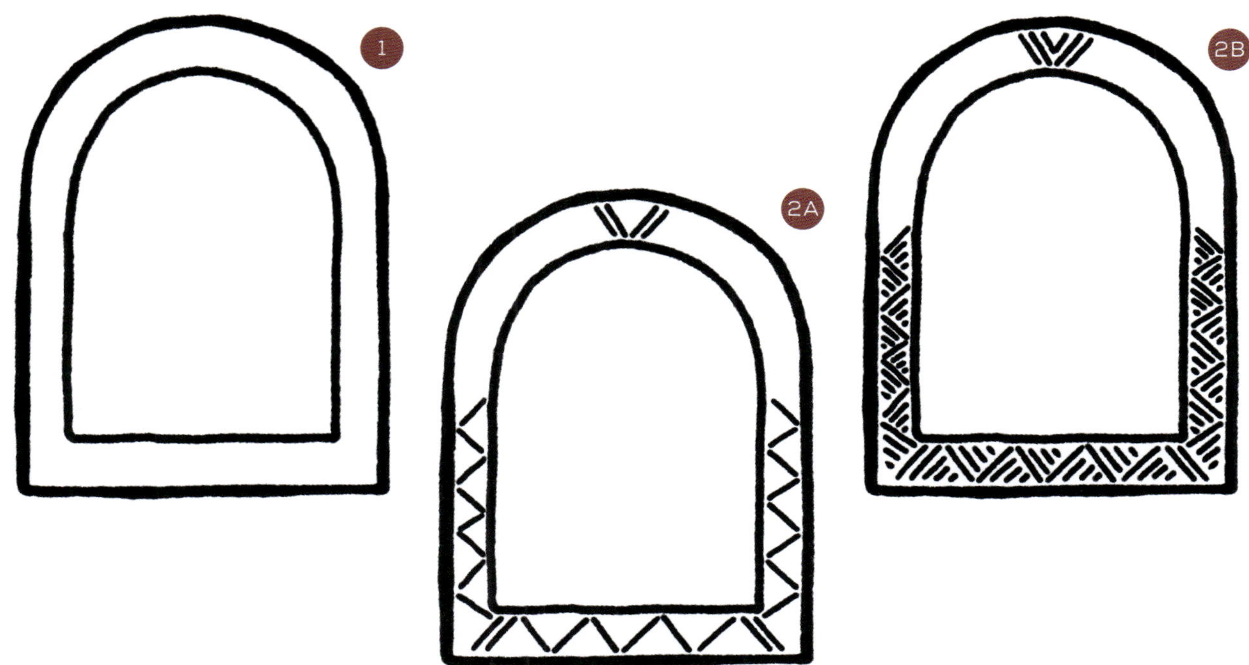

STEP 1

Draw a double window frame. For the outer line, use your thick (1.5) pen. For the inner line, use your medium (05) pen. I drew the shapes without a ruler for a more organic look.

STEP 2

Now, we are completing the pattern with the medium (05) nib. I started with the longest lines in a zigzag pattern and then filled in the remaining spaces with shorter lines. Refer to the drawings for a better understanding of the process.

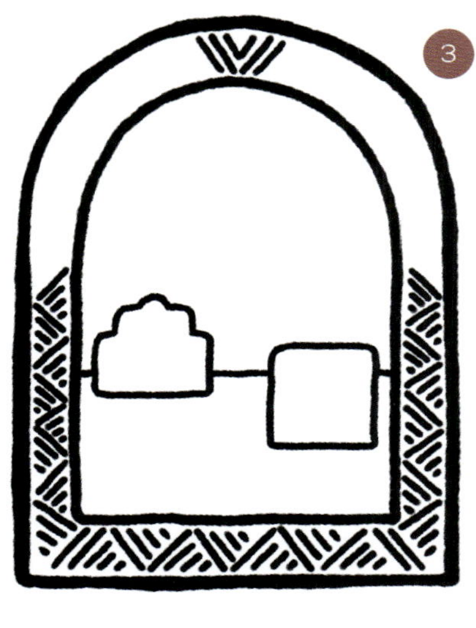

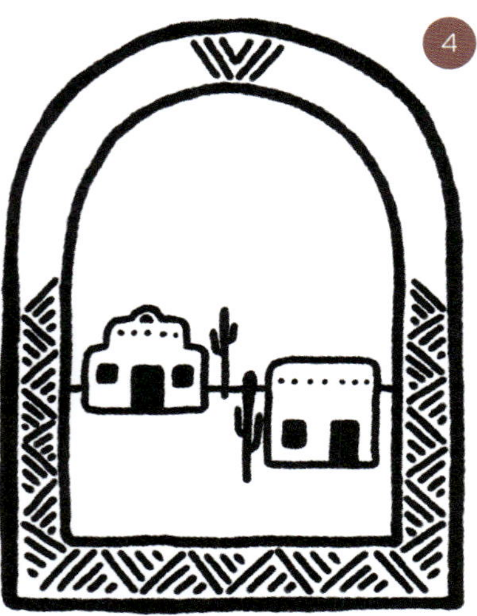

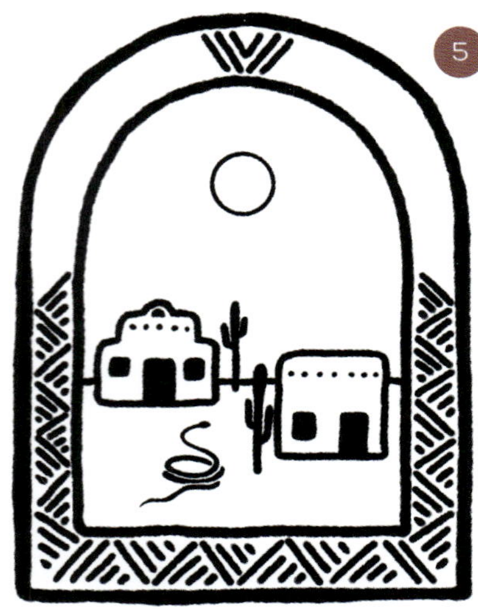

STEP 3

Draw outlines for the adobe houses and add the horizon line in medium (05) pen. Make sure that you are on the exact same level on each side of the houses, so that the lines are matching. It's a common mistake to disregard this and then wonder why the drawing somehow looks wrong. (I'm guilty of this too; I have enough old drawings to prove it.)

STEP 4

Your houses still need some detail and so do their surroundings. Draw some windows and doors and add some dots to indicate wooden beams. I also planted two cacti in the yard. Go with what you like here.

STEP 5

Last up, are the final details. Draw a circle for the sun and add the snake in the foreground.

DESERT NIGHT SKY

One thing that really amazed me on that long-ago trip was the night sky in the middle of nowhere, specifically the startling amount of stars. So, I designed one drawing to remind me of that. For a focal point in the sky, I picked the constellation of Orion, surrounded by lots and lots of stars. By placing the cacti in front of the night sky, they help to express the distance of the stars from the viewer and will help you better grasp perspective.

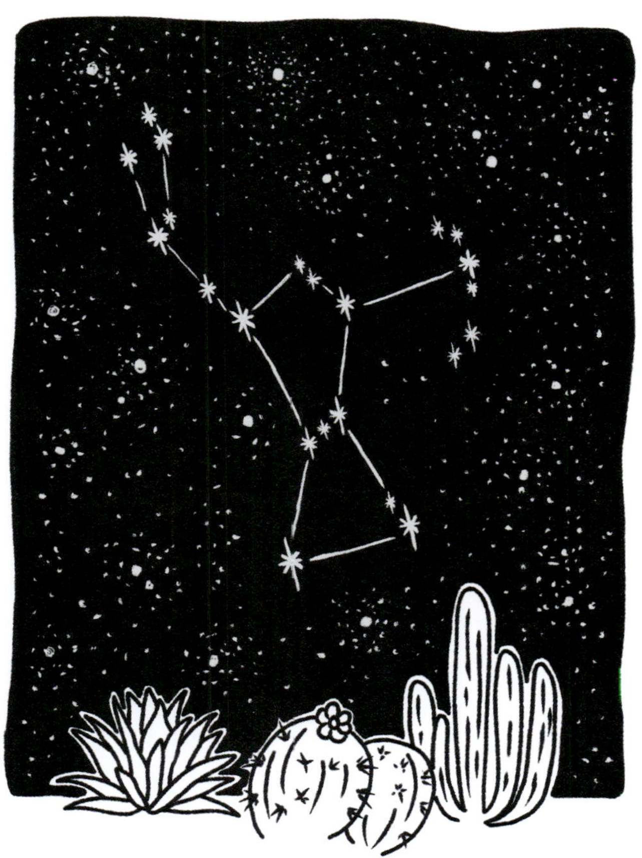

WHAT YOU NEED

Paper of your choice

Black pen in one size: 05

Brush pen

White pens in two sizes: 10 and 08

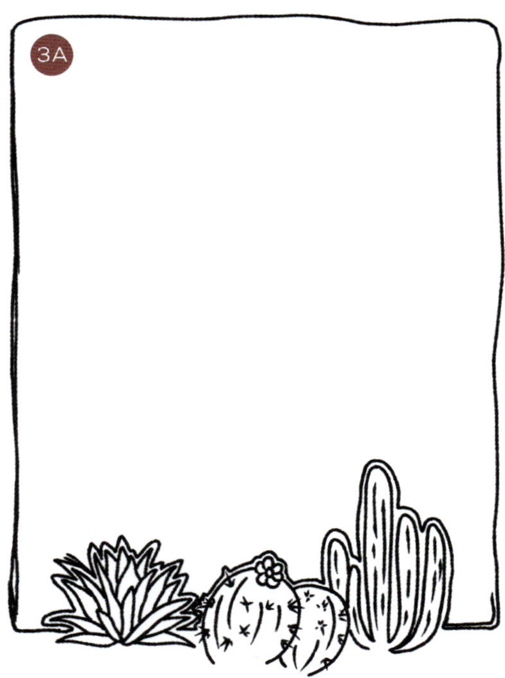

STEP 1

Begin your drawing with the leaves for the agave on the left in medium (05) pen. I often tell you to start with the parts that are in front, closer to the viewer, then work backward. Look at the images above to see what I mean.

STEP 2

Once you have completed the agave plant, draw some more cacti on the right-hand side of it.

CACTI PROCESS

Note how I did not put all the plants on the same level and how there is some overlap as well. Both of these things create some depth in the drawing and make it seem less "flat."

STEP 3

Now, you're ready to fill in the sky with black. Around the cacti, I wanted some white space so they are clearly separated from the sky. (I use this technique a lot and you will find it in other projects too.) So, draw a line around the top of the cacti and then complete it into a rough rectangle shape.

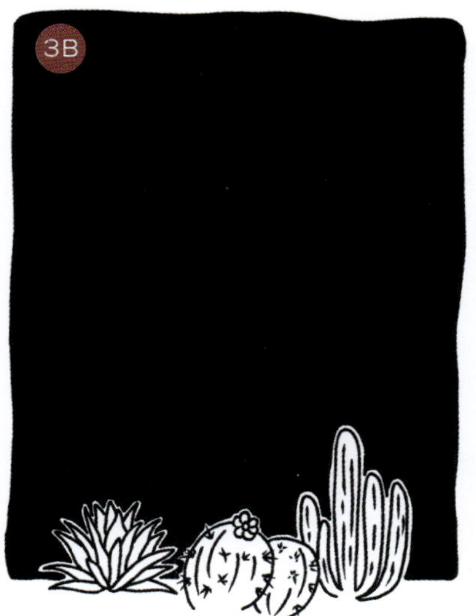

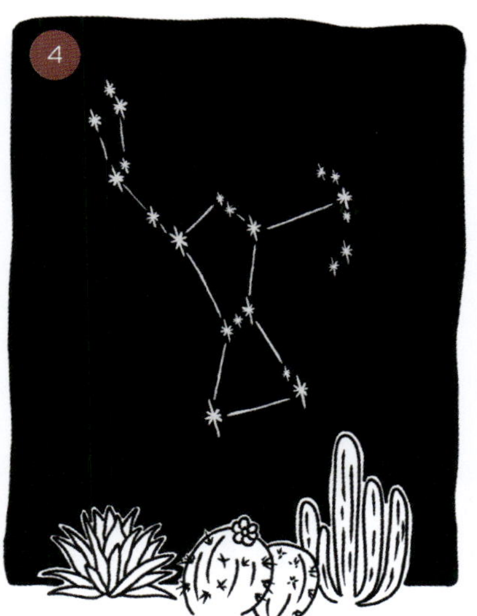

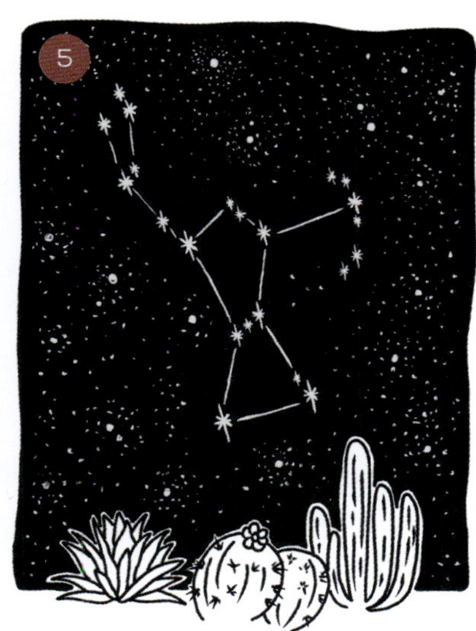

I eyeballed it and used some irregular lines to create a more organic frame than the 100 percent straight lines drawn with a ruler. Naturally, if you prefer a sharper edge, do that! Whenever we create an outline for a space we later fill with black, it's only important to work tidily on the outside. Any lines that are drawn on the inside will disappear later on, so feel free to relax and be a little sloppy here! Once you have a frame you are happy with, fill it in with black.

STEP 4

Draw Orion (or any constellation of your choosing) with white (10) pen. I usually refer to Wikipedia for constellations. They have some great imagery that makes it easy to draw them correctly.

STEP 5

At last, fill the sky with millions of white (size 08) pen stars—or at least as many as you have the patience for!

OPTIONAL VARIATION: If you happen to own gel pens in metallic colors (and unlimited patience), they would be awesome to create a Milky Way drawing.

LINEWORK CANYONS

One of the highlights of that much-mentioned trip was, of course, the Grand Canyon. I will use it to show you a super-easy and fun way to do mountain shapes or canyons. It's so easy that you can do two motifs in one session. Basically, you draw a bunch of mountain outlines, then fill that in with cross-contour lines. I'll even add some color. The way the canyon landscape changed color with a different light was stunning and made it totally worth getting up at 4 a.m. to see the sunrise.

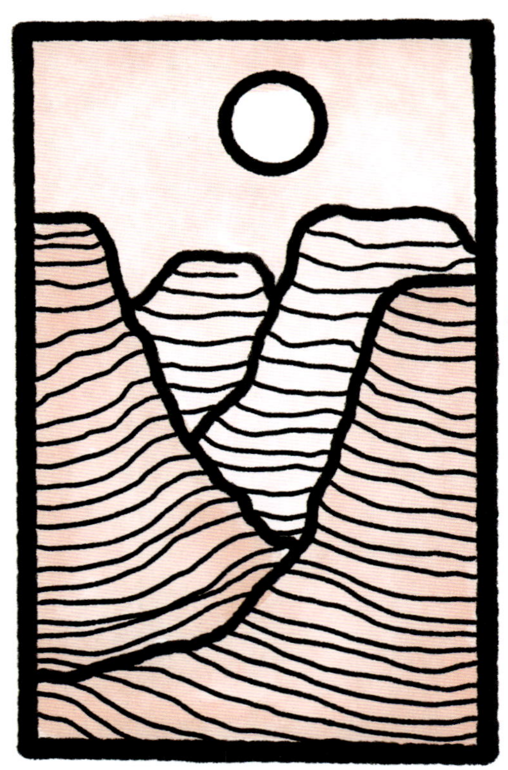

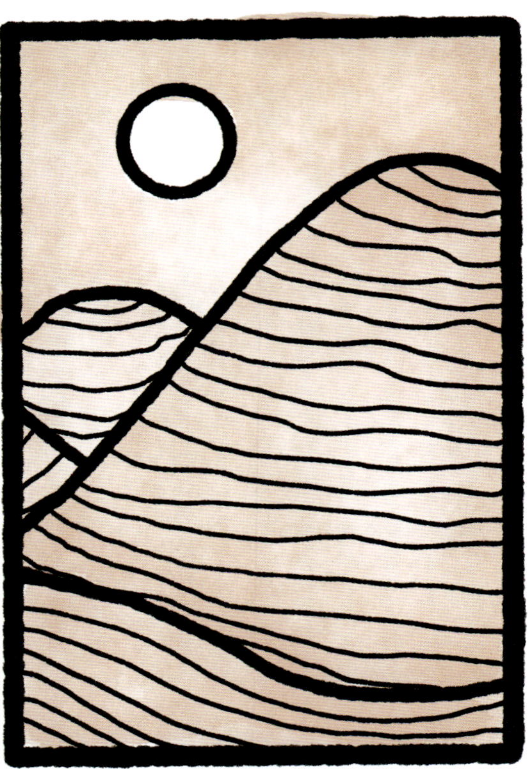

WHAT YOU NEED

Watercolor or mixed-media paper

Black pens in three sizes: 1.5, 05 and 01

Ruler

Watercolor or ink wash of your choice (optional)

Medium round brush (size 3) (optional)

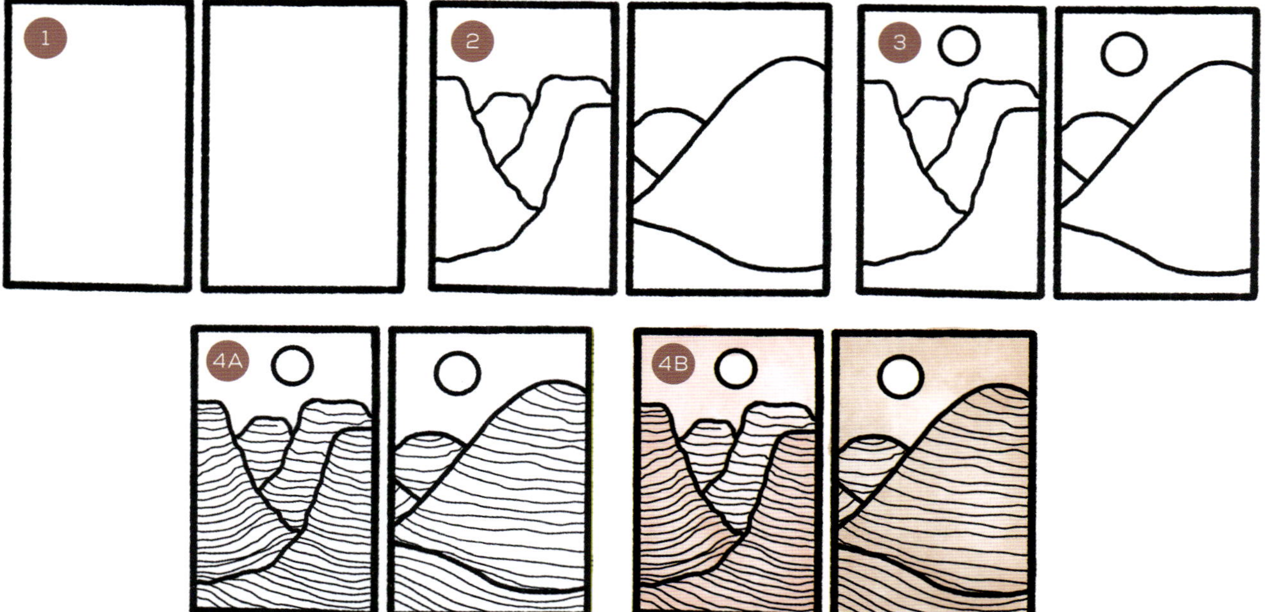

STEP 1

With your ruler and thicker (1.5) pen, draw two rectangles of the same size next to each other.

STEP 2

Draw the outlines for your landscape in 05 pen. You can shape them in different ways or make them all similar. I went with a rounder hill-shaped outline on the right and flat tops and steeper side slopes on the left.

STEP 3

Draw a circle for the sun in each sky and you are 70 percent done with this project!

STEP 4

Draw cross-contour lines within your mountain outlines with your thin (01) pen. Follow the shape with your lines intentionally. I usually start at the bottom of a shape and work my way upward. Don't worry if your lines aren't perfect. With this technique, they don't have to be. When you've finished drawing all the lines, you should have something like the above illustration in front of you.

OPTIONAL: Add color. I chose some earthy tones here that I tried to match to one of my favorite pictures. It does work with any color though. You could even create day and night variations if you choose a darker wash for one rectangle and a very light one for the other. (Hint: A full chapter of day and night designs can be found on page 145.)

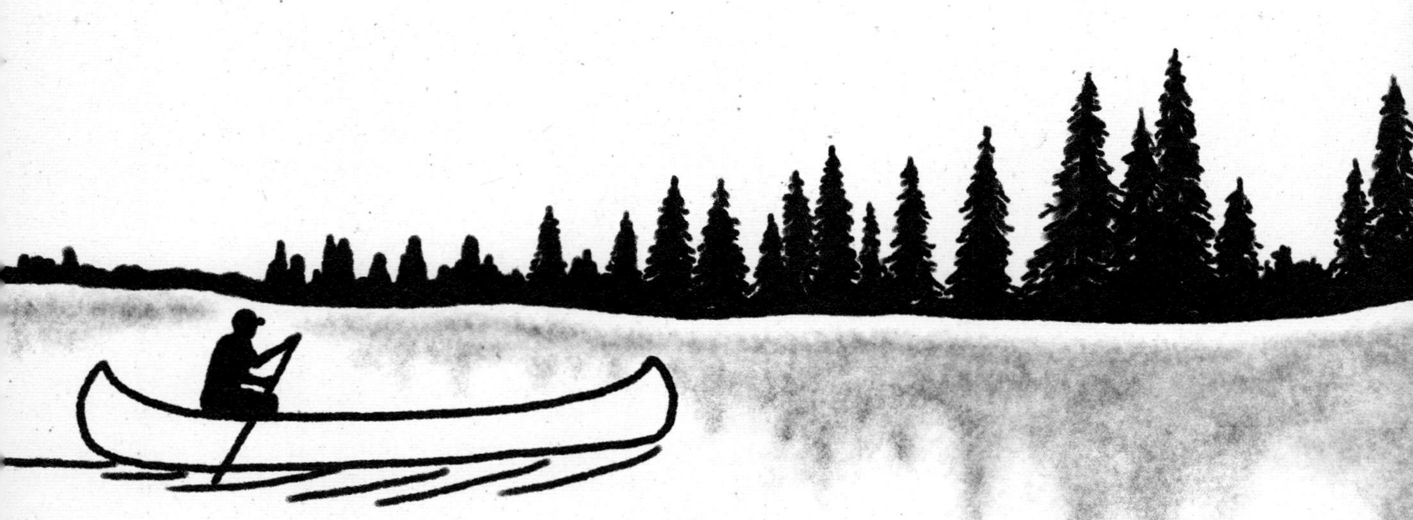

LAKES, RIVERS AND WATERFALLS

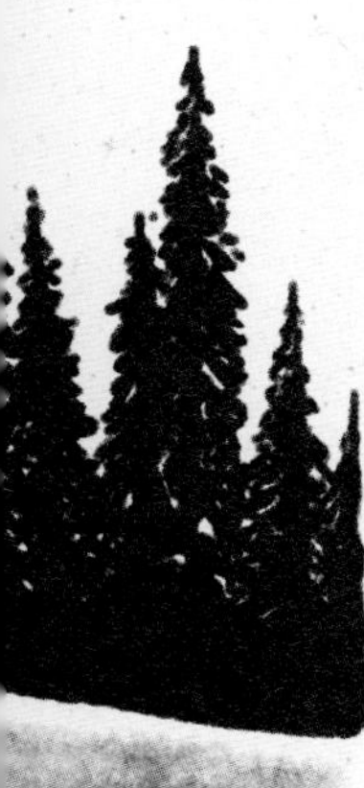

After our trips to the beach (page 33), the underwater world (page 55) and the desert (page 71), let's head back to the mountains. To me, there is only one thing that can make a mountain landscape even more stunning: water! It brings movement to the calm, solid rocks, plays with light and shadow or mirrors its surroundings. A lake at the foot of a mountain can change the atmosphere of a mountain scene every hour!

Like most things that are interesting and beautiful, water isn't easy to draw in black and white. Leaving it a blank white space doesn't do its beauty justice, same if you paint it black. But don't worry: I'm here to show you some tricks in the next projects, which mainly involve expressing the texture and setting the overall scene.

They include a lake with the wind rippling over the surface and a cabin on the shore (page 88)—and, in contrast, a perfectly still lake with a fisherman (page 91). You can work on showing water through the reflections of the surroundings (page 93) and by drawing movement lines on a high waterfall (page 95) and a small stream (page 98). After completing this chapter, your toolbox will hold plenty of water interpretations for you to use in your own designs.

SMALL WOOD CABIN ON THE LAKE

A small cabin by the water surrounded by mountains is such a perfect hideaway. When I am old and gray, this is where I want to spend most of my time. I will sit on the porch all day and watch the reflection of the sky in the water and the mountains in the distance. While I am still sitting in my big-city apartment, I wanted to visualize this dream in a drawing. In this project, you will learn how to show the wind on the water with just a few lines or by including the plants that would grow alongside your lake.

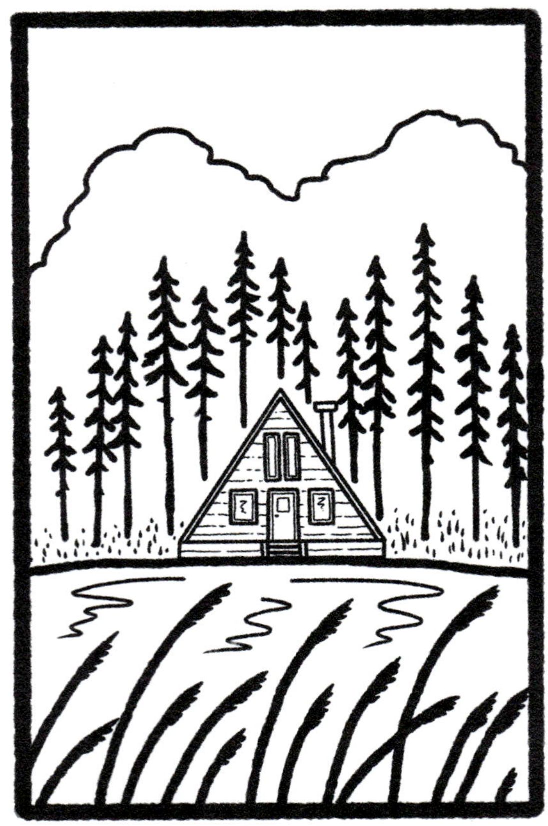

WHAT YOU NEED

Paper of your choice

Black pens in four sizes: 1.5, 05, 01 and 005

Ruler

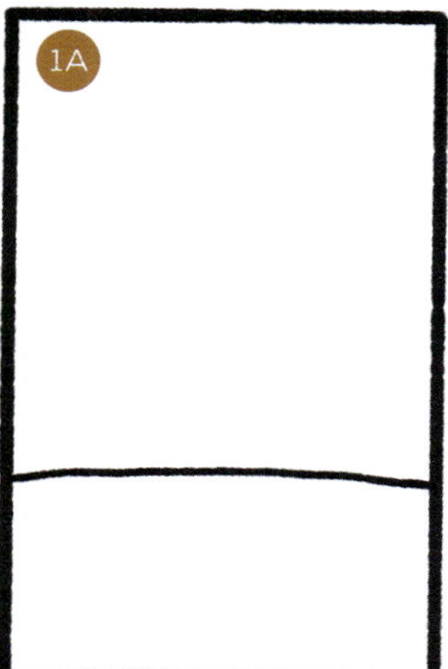

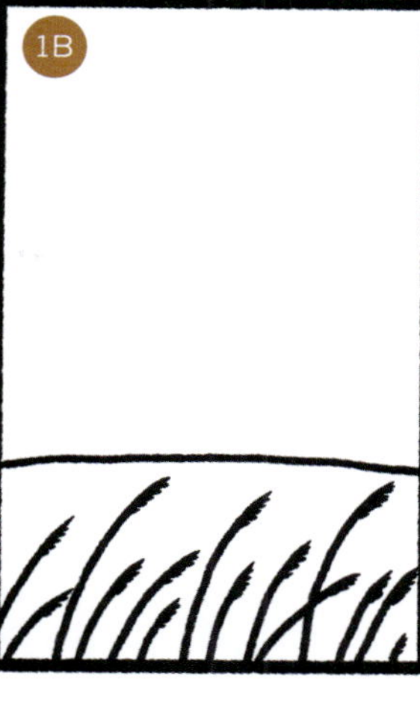

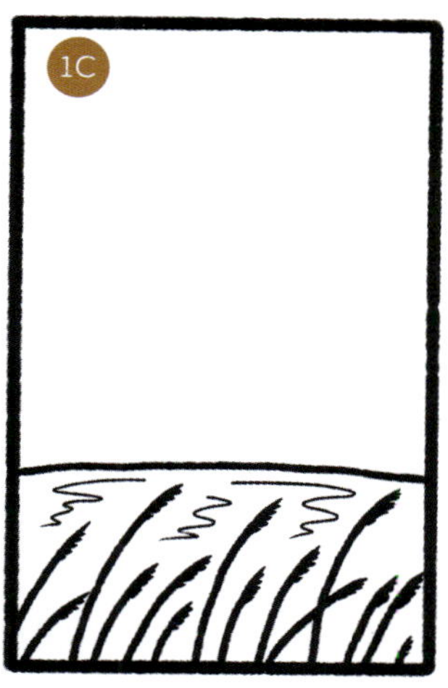

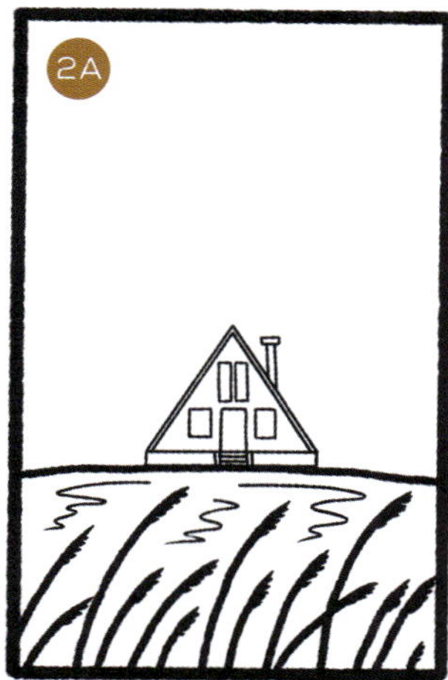

STEP 1

Start out with a rectangle shape with your thick (1.5) pen. About one-third from the bottom, draw the bank of the lake with your medium (05) pen.

In the foreground, there are the tops of some reeds bowing toward the right. I imagine there is a breeze blowing in that direction.

With a thin (01) nib, I also added some curvy lines to the surface of the water that would be moved by the wind too.

STEP 2

Move on to the cabin. I used a ruler here to draw the outlines because I wanted them sharp and mostly used my thin (01) pen. Then, I filled in the wood texture and some details on windows and door with a fine (005) pen and freehand.

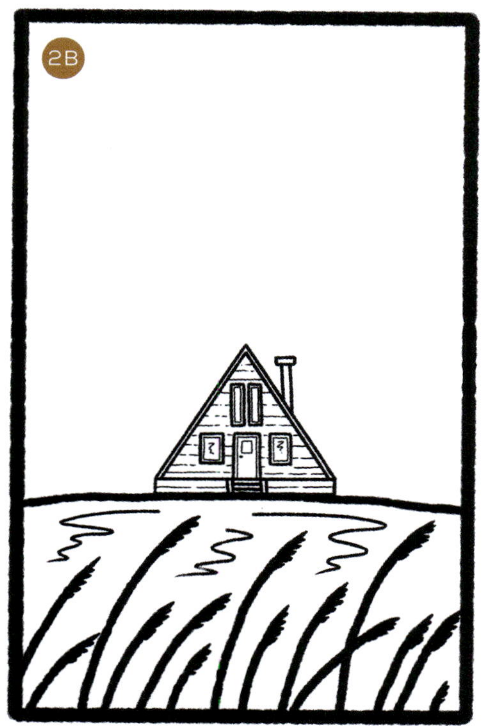

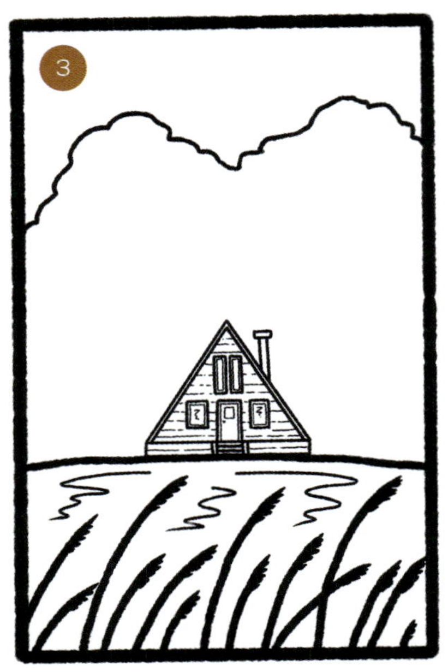

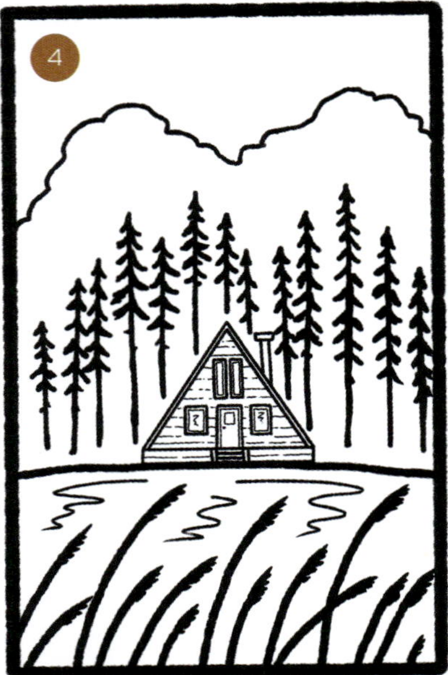

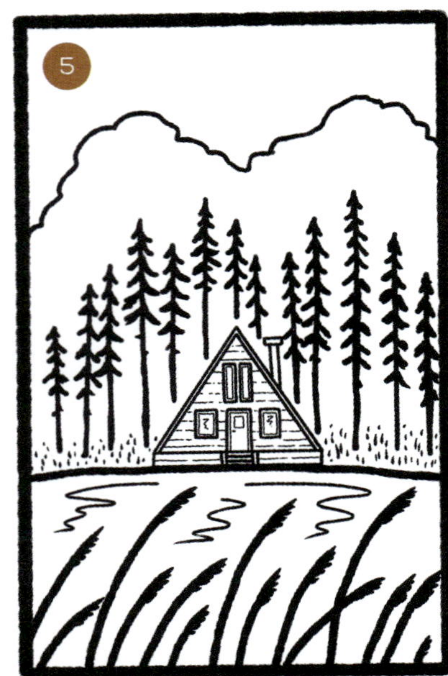

STEP 3

Add the cloud in the background as an uneven line in thin (01) pen.

STEP 4

Now, add the trees with your medium (05) pen. In contrast to the tidy and sharp linework of the cabin, I kept them a bit messy and uneven. That way, the viewer will focus on the cabin more.

STEP 5

As the final touch, add grass blades between the tree stems around the cabin in thin (01) pen.

FISHING ON A MOUNTAIN LAKE

Have you ever noticed that there is a special kind of stillness on the water in the morning? Without even the slightest breeze, the water would be perfectly still. To convey this image, we will use a totally blank space. Remember how on page 87 I told you that blank or black spaces don't make interesting drawings? To counteract that, we will put a small boat with a fisherman on the water and focus on adding more details to the mountains in the background or the design of the frame of the drawing.

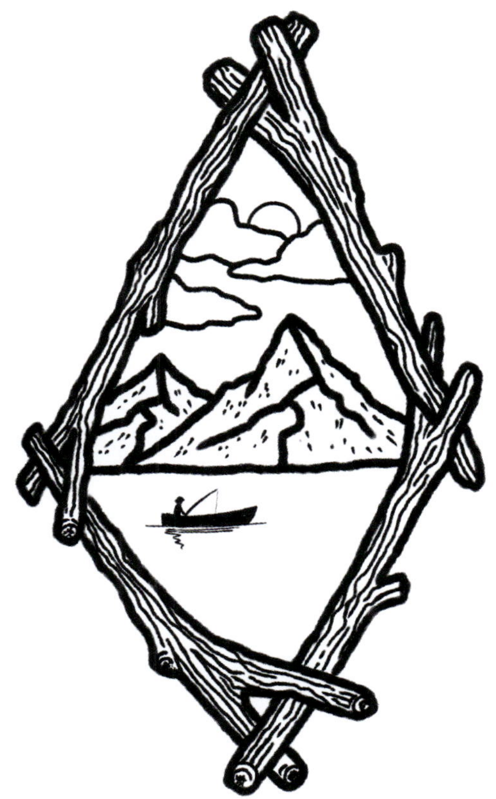

WHAT YOU NEED

Paper of your choice

Black pens in four sizes: 1.5, 05, 01 and 003

Optional: ruler, pencil and eraser

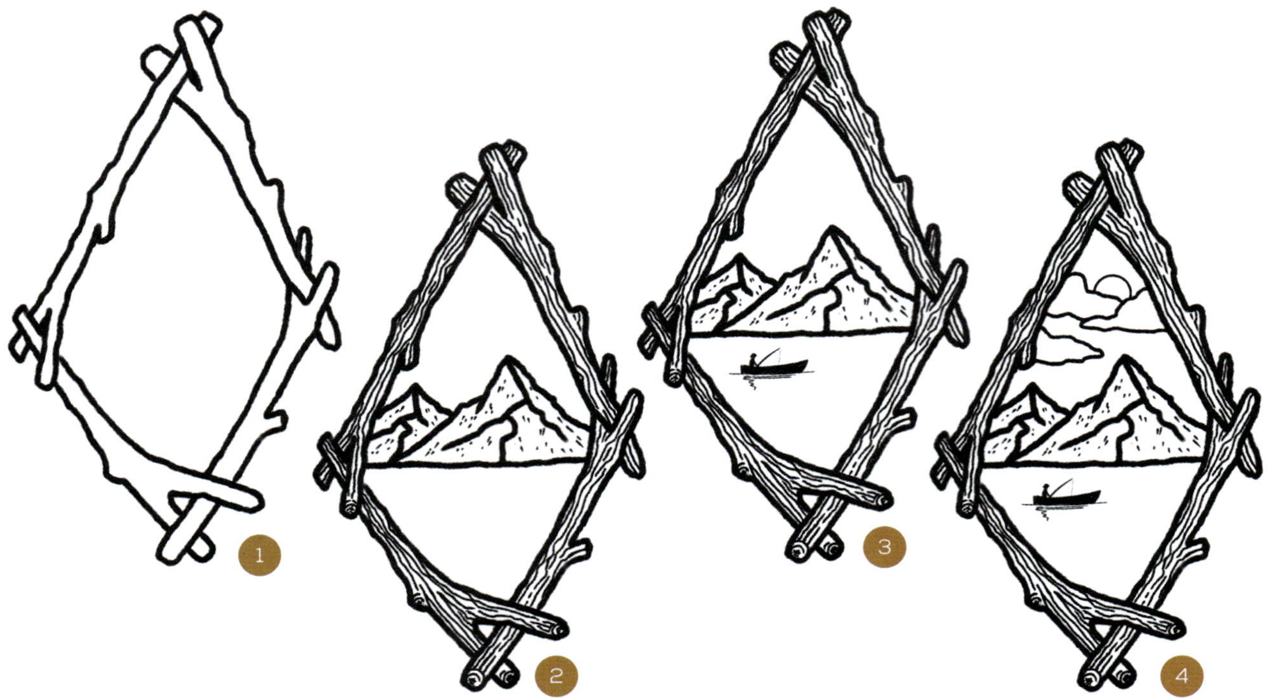

STEP 1

If you want, draw yourself a diamond in pencil as a guide. The Cable Car over the Mountains project (page 19) has a step-by-step instruction. Draw outlines for four twigs in thick (1.5) pen arranged in a diamond shape. Pay attention to the ends where they overlap. You will have to complete the twig ends in stages to create this.

STEP 2

When the outlines are done, use uneven lines in thin (01) pen to create the wood structure. Break the lines from time to time to make it look natural.

Now, it's time to draw the mountains in the upper part of our diamond shape in thick (1.5) pen. You've done this before in several projects, like in The Way to the Mountaintop (page 16) so I'll keep this brief. Start with a triangle shape in medium (05) pen and draw a jagged line down the middle. Add some details for a rocky texture with your fine (01) pen.

STEP 3

Place the silhouette of the fisherman in his boat on the surface of the water. For the fishing line, I used the finest (003) nib (you could also use a sharpened pencil). I also added some lines behind and in front of the boat to show the waterline and a few lines to hint at a reflection.

STEP 4

Final touches: clouds and a half-hidden sun in the sky in medium (05) pen.

CANOEING ALONG THE RIVER

With the perfect weather and light, water can act like a mirror. Small movements in the water slightly modify the image on the surface. This is another option for you to avoid showing water in drawings simply as a blank space. You mirror whatever you put beside the water but change it a bit and make it less detailed to show the blurred image you would see on the surface. Of course, you can also choose a kayak—or any boat really—for this project.

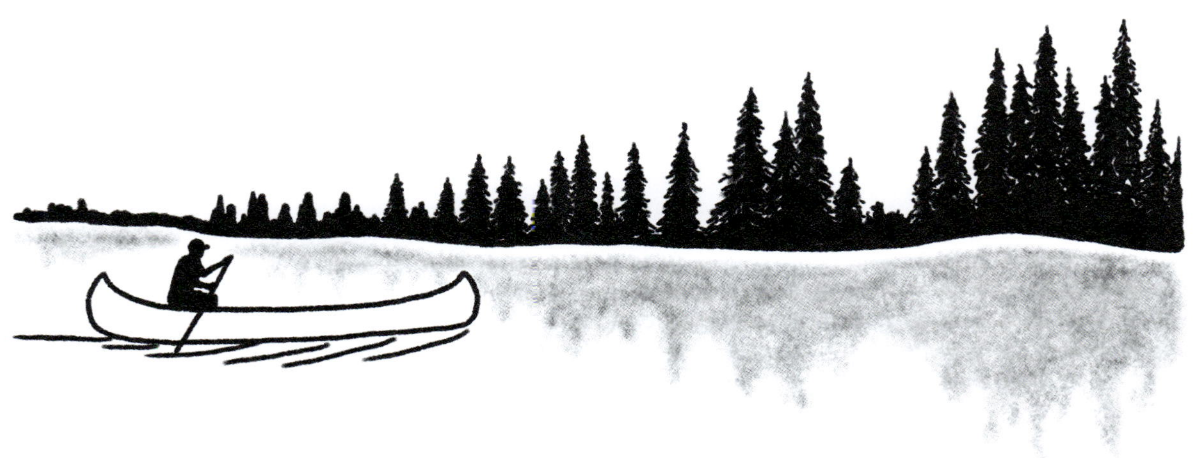

WHAT YOU NEED

Paper of your choice

Black pens in three sizes: 1.5, 05 and 01

Pencil, the softer the better

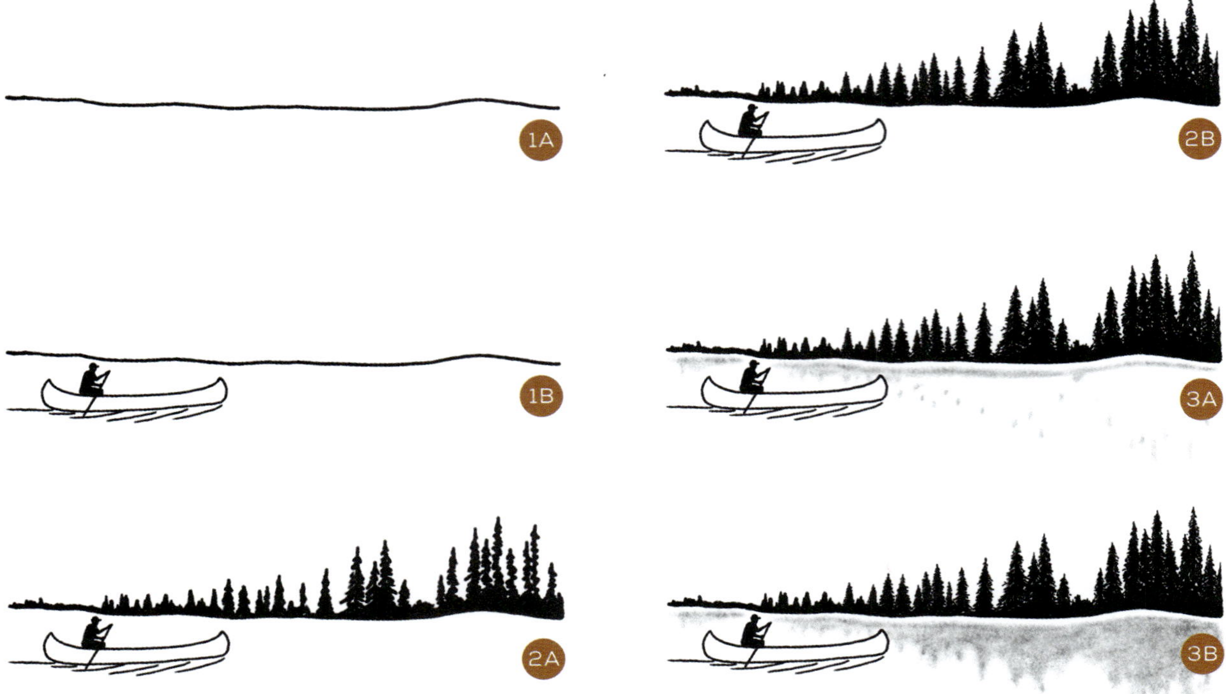

STEP 1

Draw a line for the riverbank in medium (05) pen and add the canoe, including the guy in it. You could go for a full silhouette and also color in the canoe black.

STEP 2

On the riverbank, roughly block in your trees in medium (05) pen. This doesn't have to be tidy; in fact, it's better if it's not. Space the trees unevenly and vary their size to avoid an unnatural look.

Then, switch to your thin (01) pen and carefully add branches to the trees. Do this in a very detailed manner on the right-hand side of the riverbank. Gradually decrease the amount of detail moving toward the left. This part is farther away from the viewer and gets more blurry.

STEP 3

Use a similar process in pencil for the tree reflection in the water. Establish where the tips of your trees will reflect and make marks. Also, I put down a line parallel to the ink line of the riverbank and left a bit of space between my ink and pencil lines. It separates both areas more clearly.

Now, shade the reflection of the trees. The water reflection is not a mirror image of the tree line and the edges are a little fuzzy. Toward the left faraway side or the riverbank it's gradually less visible. Move your pencil at a very flat angle over the paper. It's more the side of the pencil lead you are drawing with rather than the tip.

HIGH WATERFALL

In this project, you are working with a technique called framing. The actual motif—our waterfall—is far in the distance. In the foreground, the canyon walls frame the waterfall and are composed in a way that supports drawing the eye to the waterfall in the distance.

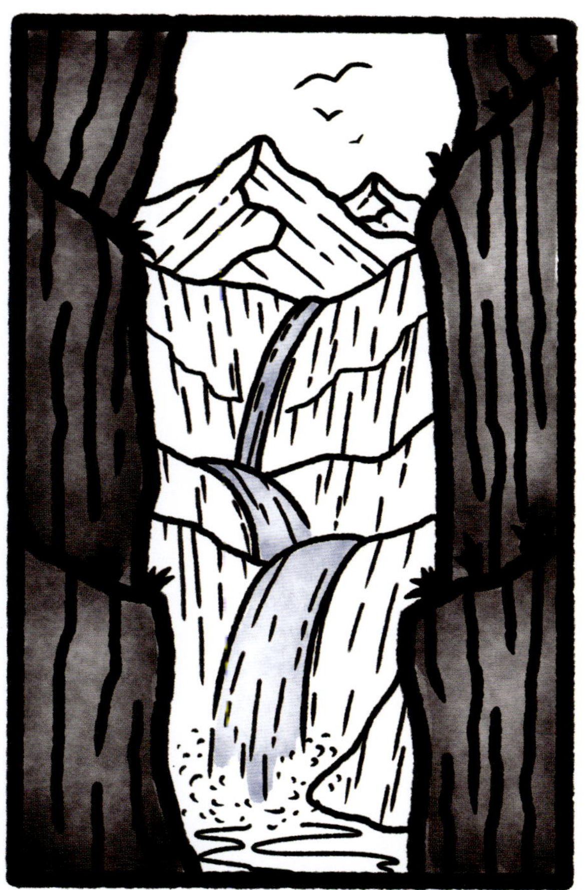

WHAT YOU NEED

Watercolor or mixed-media paper

Black pens in three sizes: 1.5, 05 and 01

Ruler

Ink wash or watercolors in tones of blue and gray (optional)

Medium round brush (size 3) (optional)

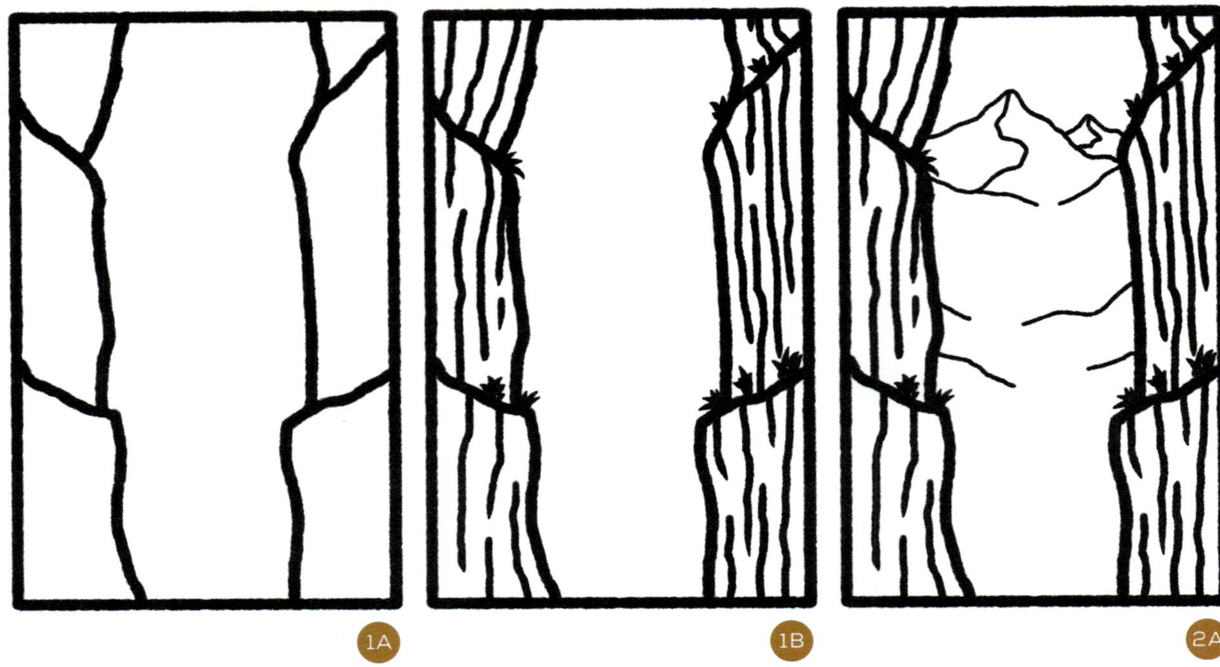

STEP 1

Draw a long rectangle with your ruler and the thick (1.5) pen. On both sides, draw wall rock outlines—imagine you are in a canyon of sorts. Then add lines for crevices. I also added a little grass on the ledges.

STEP 2

A little below the highest ledge, start the baseline for your background mountains. Add two more lines farther below. Use your medium (05) pen for this step. Note that in each line, there is a little gap—this is where the waterfall will come down. Also note that the gap gets larger from top to bottom where the waterfall is closer to the viewer. Then, draw the mountain outlines by roughly following a triangle shape. Then, draw a jagged line down the middle of the triangle to make the mountains look three-dimensional.

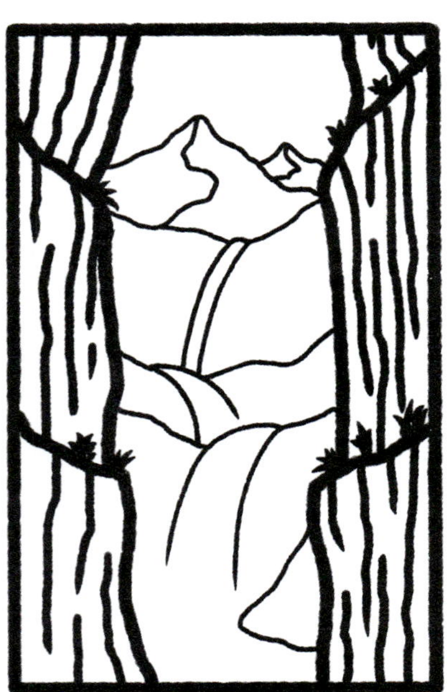

Draw the waterfall with your medium (05) pen by connecting the horizontal lines with smooth curves. I arranged my waterfall in a zigzag shape because I think this makes for an interesting look.

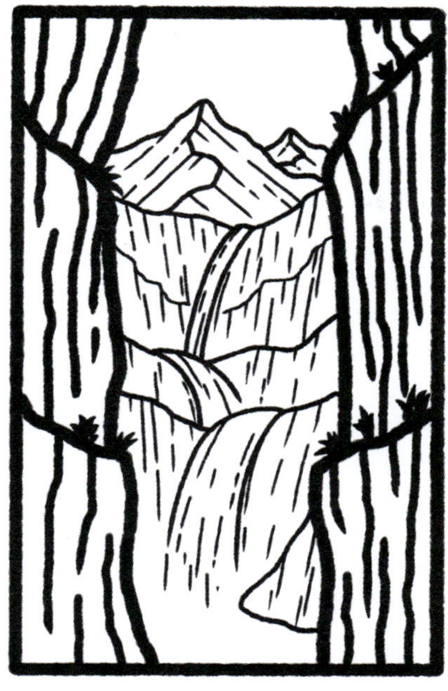

3

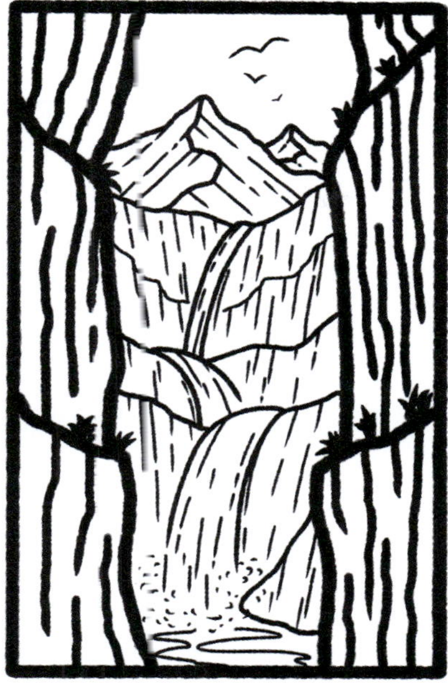

4

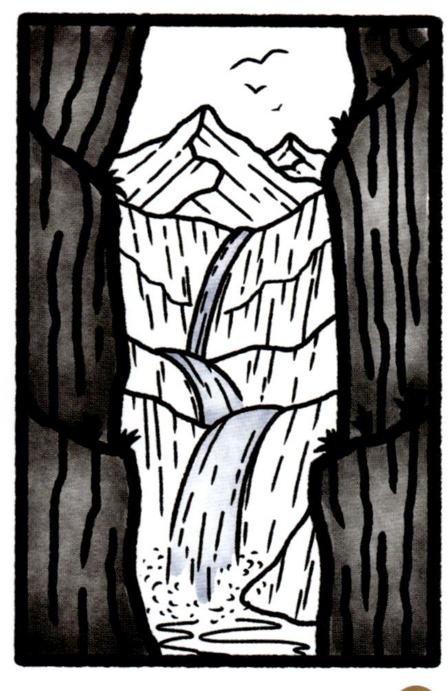

5

STEP 3

With the thin (01) pen, create the downward movement of the water by adding some smaller lines on the surface of the water. Still using your medium (05) pen, we will add one more rock edge under the waterfall at the top. Draw two lines from the rectangle outline and slope downward the closer you get to the waterfall. Switch back to your thin (01) pen. To make the rock face more interesting and to imitate cracks and crevices in the surface, draw smaller lines from the rock edges downward and upward. Lastly, draw some lines on the mountain slopes to imitate the cracks and crevices of the rock surface there as well.

STEP 4

Create some spray at the bottom of the waterfall with dots and small curves. Then, add a few wavy lines on the surface of the bottom pool. You're almost done now—on to the last details! As a last touch, add a few flying birds in the sky. If you're not a fan of birds, you could also draw a sun instead, clouds, an airplane or a hot-air balloon.

STEP 5

This is the optional color part: Cover the canyon rock face on both sides in a gray tone. I like it because it draws the eye to the far view of the waterfall. I also added a little blue on the waterfall to highlight it. Sit back and admire your work, then go show it to someone else and fish for compliments!

BRIDGE OVER A SMALL FOREST STREAM

This drawing is inspired by one of my favorite hiking paths. A big part of the way is next to this little stream that eventually turns into a gorge when the terrain gets steeper. In the farther course of the path, there are several small bridges that cross the gorge back and forth until you leave the gorge behind you. In addition to working from a sketch, we will be using different kinds of brushes to depict the different elements—from brush pens to ink pens of various sizes.

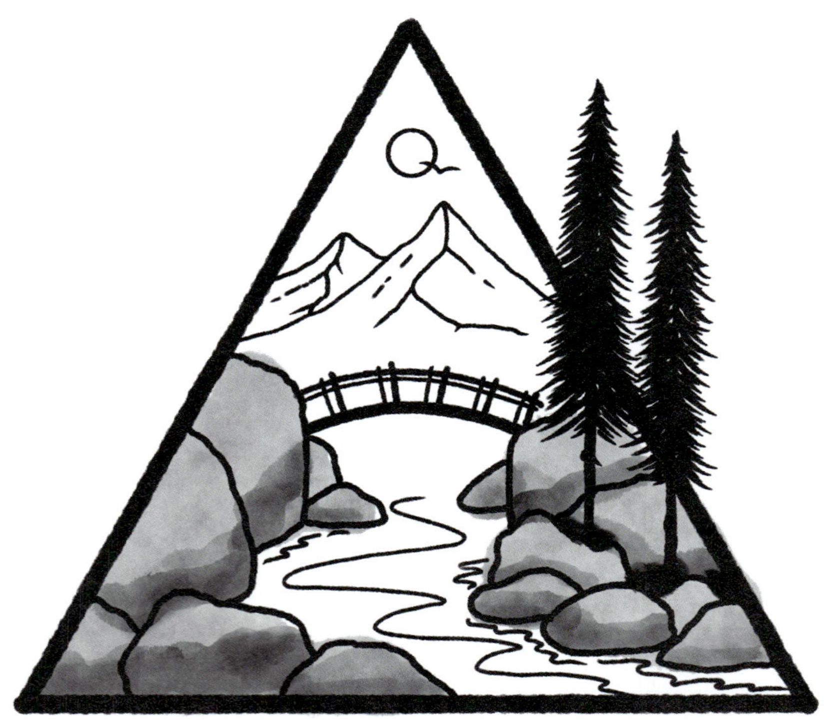

WHAT YOU NEED

Watercolor or mixed-media paper

Black pens in three sizes: 1.5, 05 and 01

Brush pen

Ink wash or watercolor in tones of gray (optional)

Medium round brush (size 3) (optional)

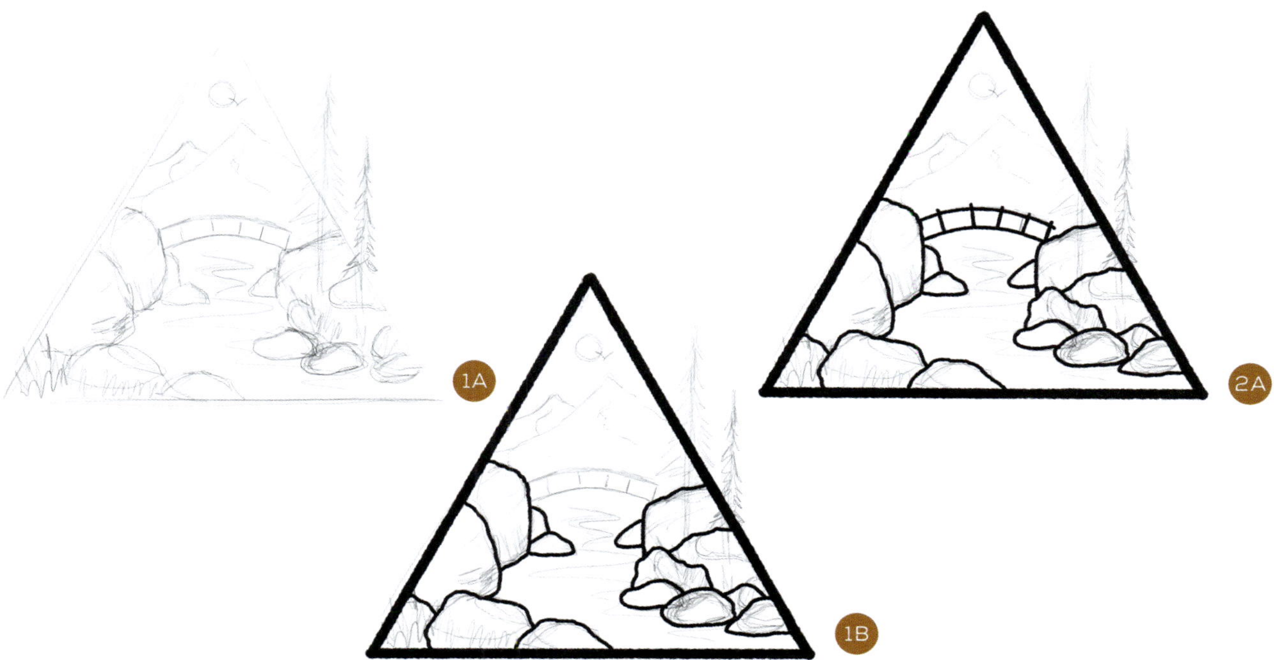

STEP 1

Because there are more elements here than in most other drawings, I'm working on the base of my rough pencil sketch in this one. Normally, I would dab my kneadable eraser on the sketch so the underdrawing would be very light and nearly invisible. In this case, I left it in its original state so you can see it better.

Draw the triangle frame with your thick (1.5) pen (refer to the Rock Formation Landscape project on page 72 for more detailed steps). Start with the rocks in the foreground in medium (05) pen. As mentioned before, begin with the one closest to the viewer and work your way backward.

STEP 2

The next element is the bridge. It's composed of two parallel curved lines for the planks and the handrail, and straight lines for the posts.

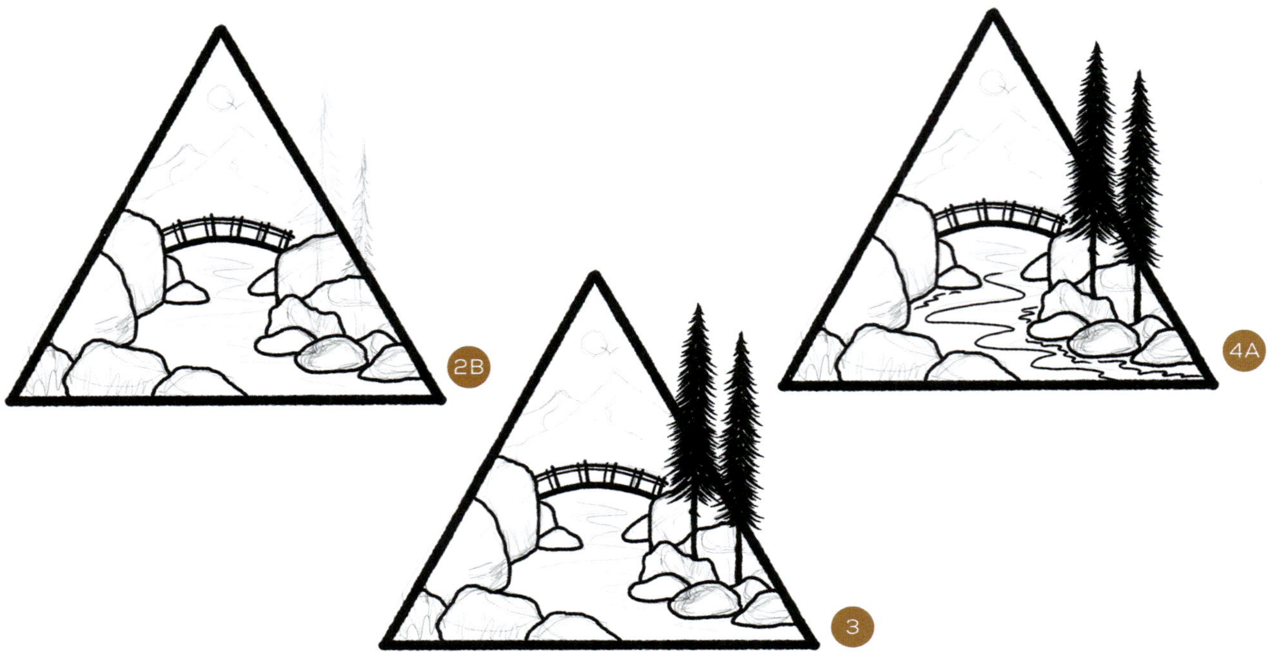

To give the bridge a bit of perspective, think about what you would see if you were standing in that drawing. Your viewpoint is below the level of the bridge, so you are looking upward. This means that you would see more of the bottom of the bridge. Just switch to your thin (01) pen and draw a curved line below the bottom of the bridge, then fill in the space between the two bottom lines to get a bigger solid line. This is the plank bottom you can see from where you stand. Now, add another curve for the handrail. Between the lines for the handrail, you want some space. For the posts, draw more solid lines with a bit of space between the posts you've already drawn.

STEP 3

Ready for the brush pen trees? Refer to the Linework Basics chapter (page 8) for a more detailed description of how to draw the branches. Use your brush pen for most of them and also add some branches with your medium (05) pen. I also made the tips of the trees a little sharper and more detailed with my medium (05) and small (01) nibs.

STEP 4

At this stage, you are ready to add some movement lines to the water surface with your thin (01) pen. Note how I put smaller wiggly lines on the edges of the stream close to the rocks? It's my interpretation of how the water hits the rocks there and the movement as well as the reflection of the rocks in the water.

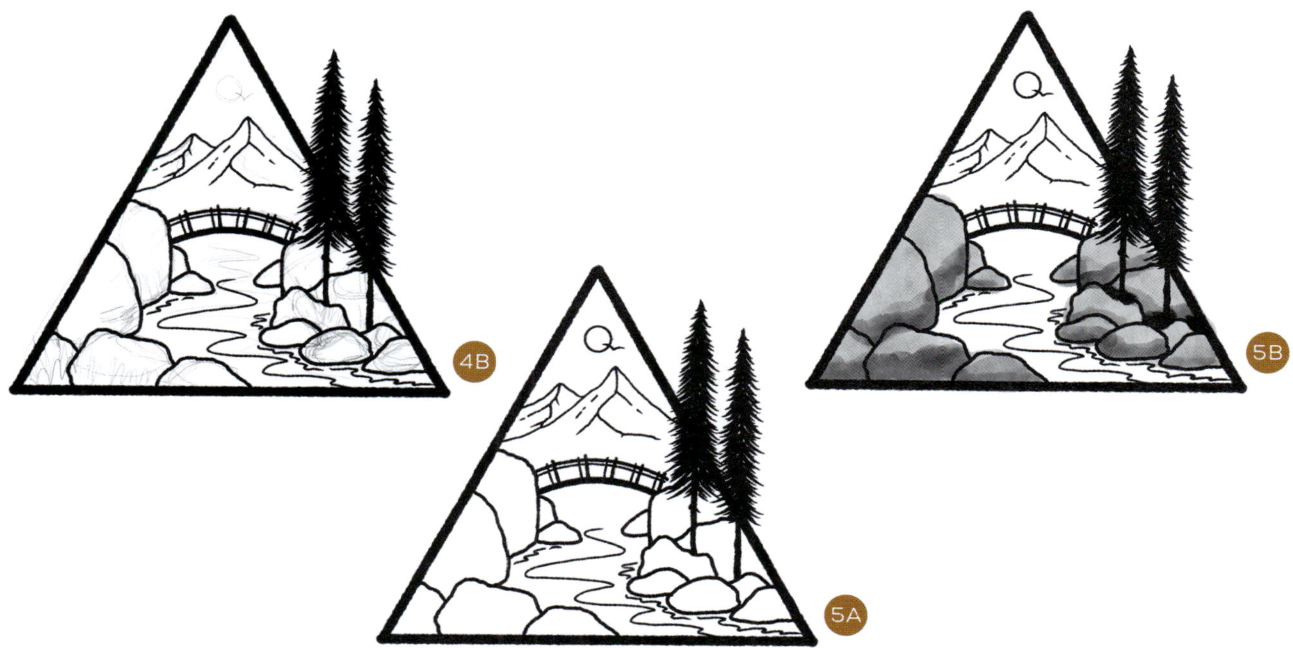

Add the mountain outlines in the distance with the thin (01) pen. As usual, first draw a triangle shape and then a zigzag line down the center. As they are far away, there is not much detail needed and the zigzag should be fairly light.

Once all your ink is completely dry, gently erase the pencil sketch.

STEP 5

The finishing touches here are the sun and the bird in the sky. This is a very complex piece. If you made it to the end, you rock!

If you want to go for the optional color, I suggest painting the rocks in gray tones. Make each one a little darker toward the bottom to give them the same subtle three-dimensional effect as the rest of the drawing.

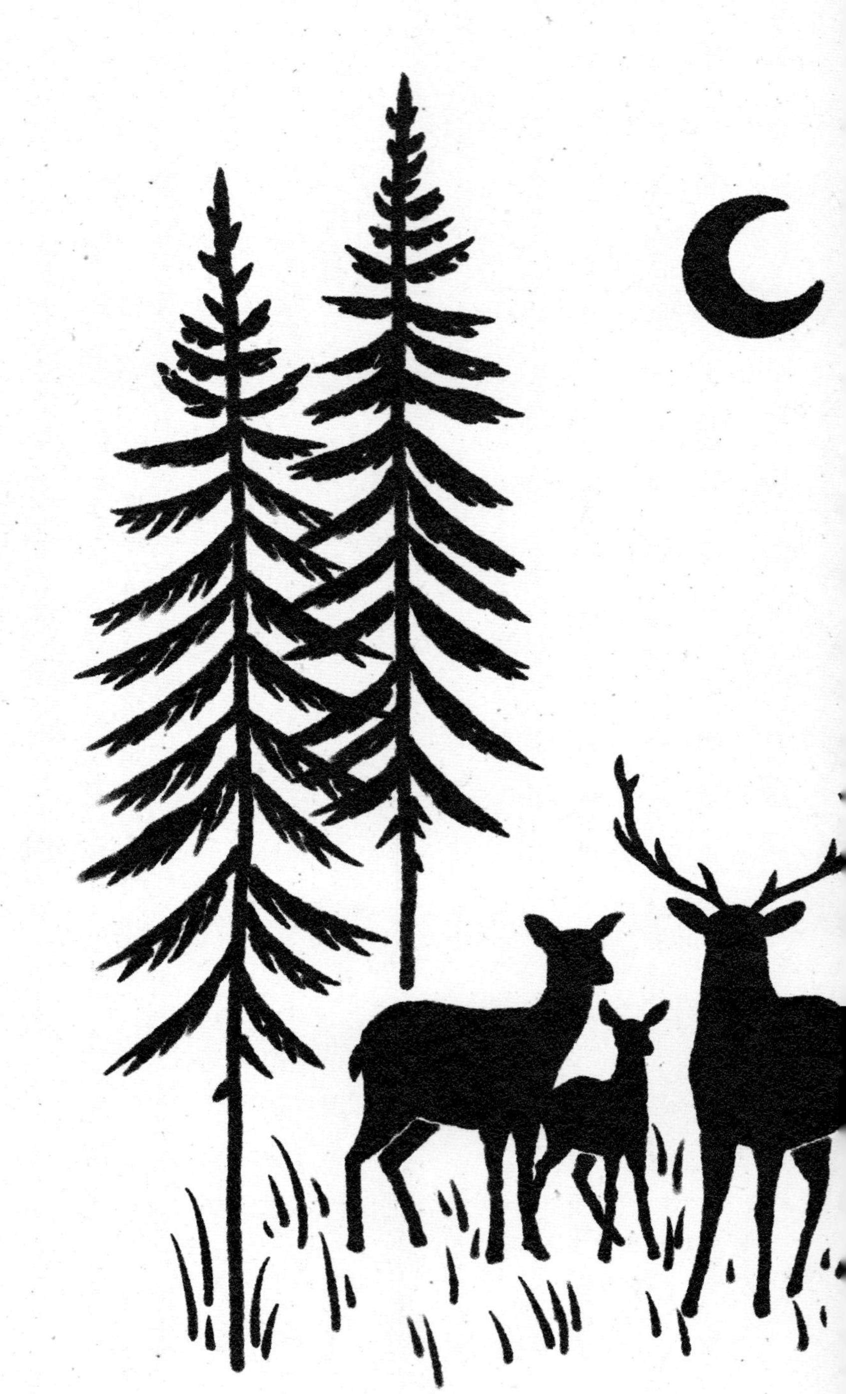

FOREST SCENES

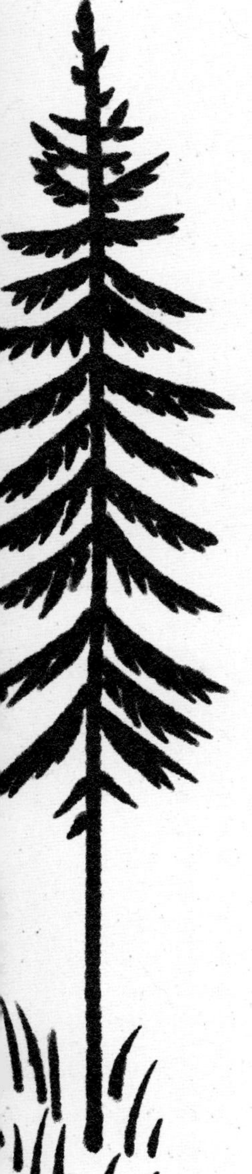

Have you ever felt like a hike through the woods calms your mind? Studies show that the sights, smells and sounds of the woods are good for our health. If you live in a big city like me, a walk underneath pine trees might not always be an option when you need peace and quiet.

So, how about this . . . let's bring the forest to us! The next projects will teach you how to draw trees, how to convey different kinds of silhouettes and, once you're happy with your results, you can even close your eyes and try to smell the pine trees.

Trees are often prominent in nature scenes and you can practice your skills in the following projects. You can fill your tree interpretation toolbox with abstract pines (page 104), tree silhouettes (page 106), brush pen trees (page 112) and fir trees (page 109) in delicate linework.

CABIN IN THE WOODS

Don't take this project too seriously: It's mostly meant as a relaxing exercise to improve your linework. That said, even though it's very accessible, you'll work on creating a stunning borderless composition using smartly placed trees.

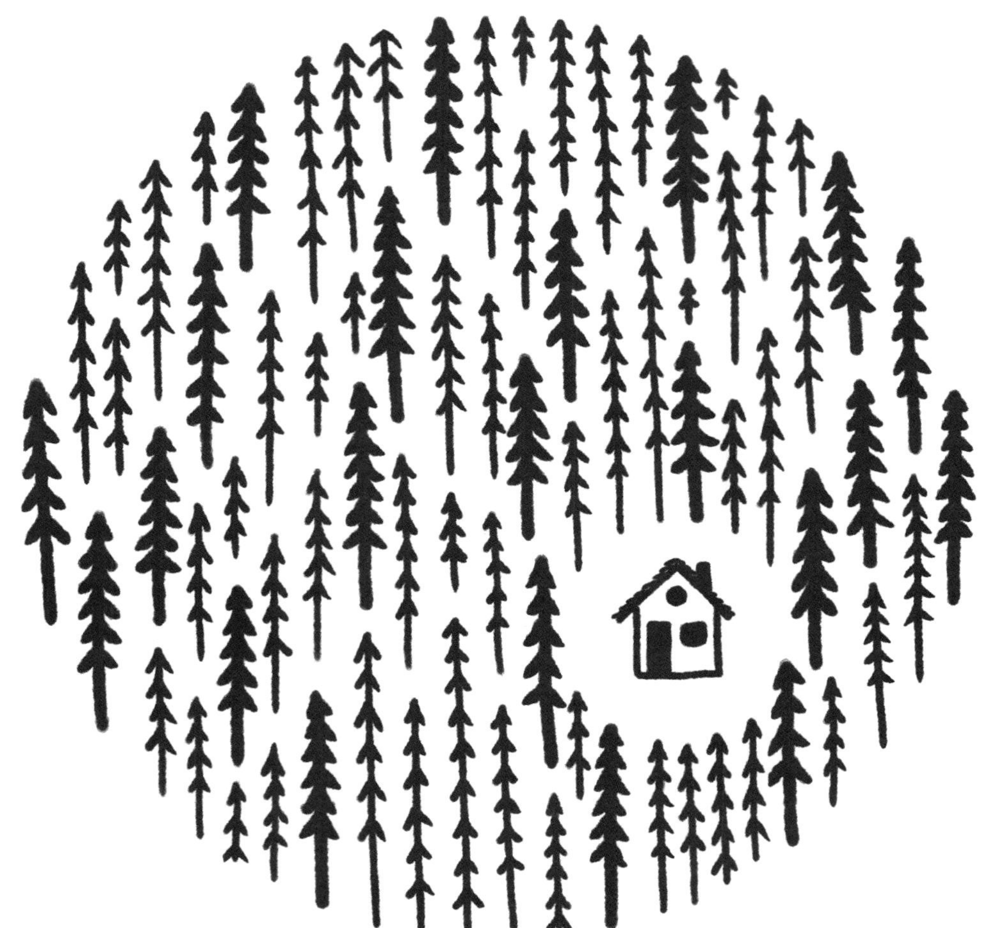

WHAT YOU NEED

Paper of your choice

Compass, circle tool or round object to trace

Pencil and eraser

Black pens in three sizes: 1.5, 05 and 01

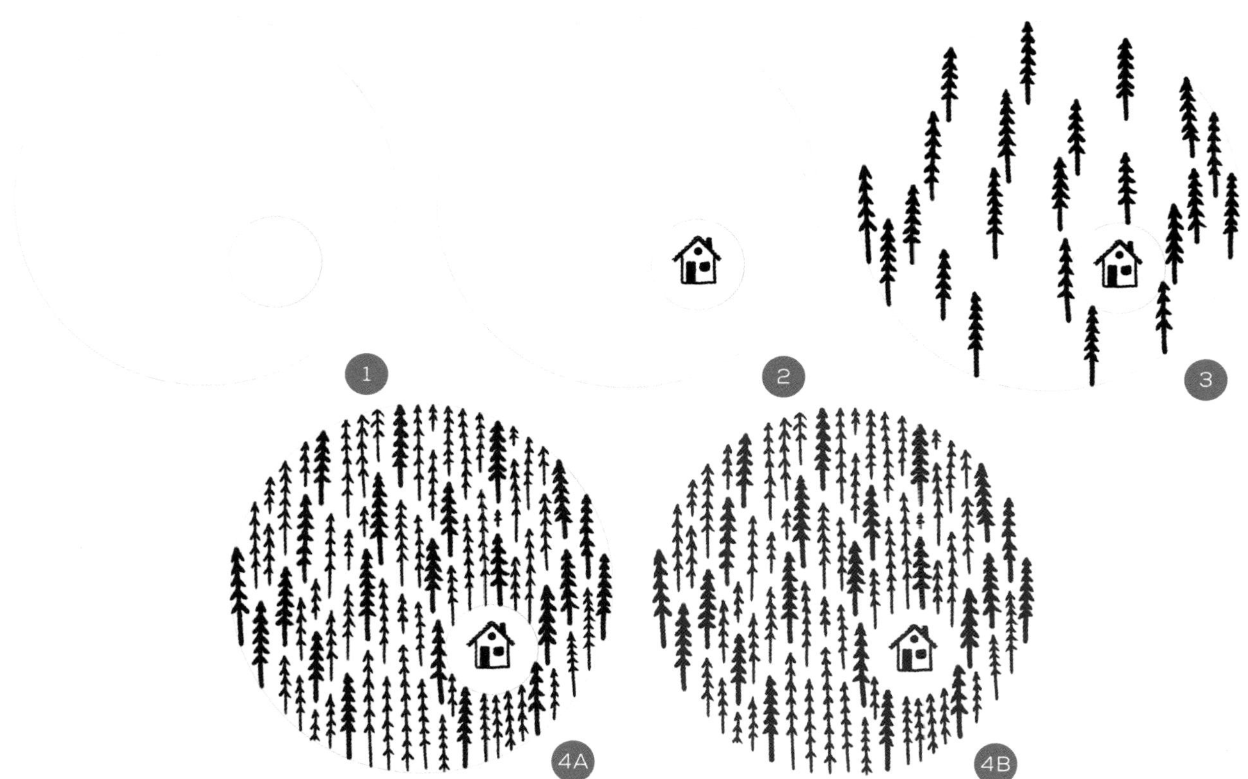

STEP 1

This project starts with a pencil circle you can create with your compass. Then, draw a second smaller circle inside the first. Place it wherever you want. I went toward the bottom right.

STEP 2

Inside the smaller circle, place a small cabin in a medium (05) and a thin (01) pen. You can do that with the level of detail that looks good to you. I kept it fairly simple with a door, two windows, a chimney and some tiny shingles on the roof outline.

STEP 3

Now comes the actual drawing exercise. With your thick (1.5) pen, draw a bunch of trees within the big circle. Make sure the lines are straight and even. Do not draw outside the pencil line of the big circle or inside the small circle.

STEP 4

With your thin (01) pen, fill in the gaps with more trees, again remembering to stay inside the pencil lines. Make sure your inkwork is dry and you won't smudge anything before carefully erasing the pencil lines.

WOLF HOWLING AT THE MOON

Natural-looking, detailed trees are difficult. Silhouettes are much easier and provide nice contrast too. With a bit of practice, you will be able to draw silhouettes in no time. You can use them to put interesting scenes together, like this project here. All you need is a bright source of light to balance the black areas.

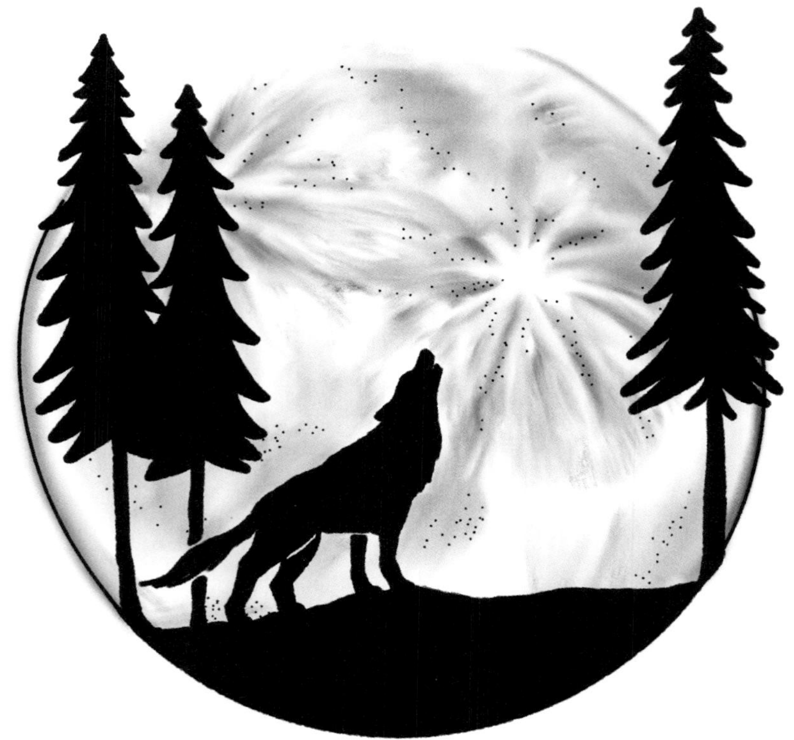

WHAT YOU NEED

Paper of your choice

Pencil and eraser

Compass, circle tool or round object to trace

Black pens in three sizes: 1.5, 05 and 01

Brush pen or liquid ink

Medium and fine round brushes (sizes 3 and 4)

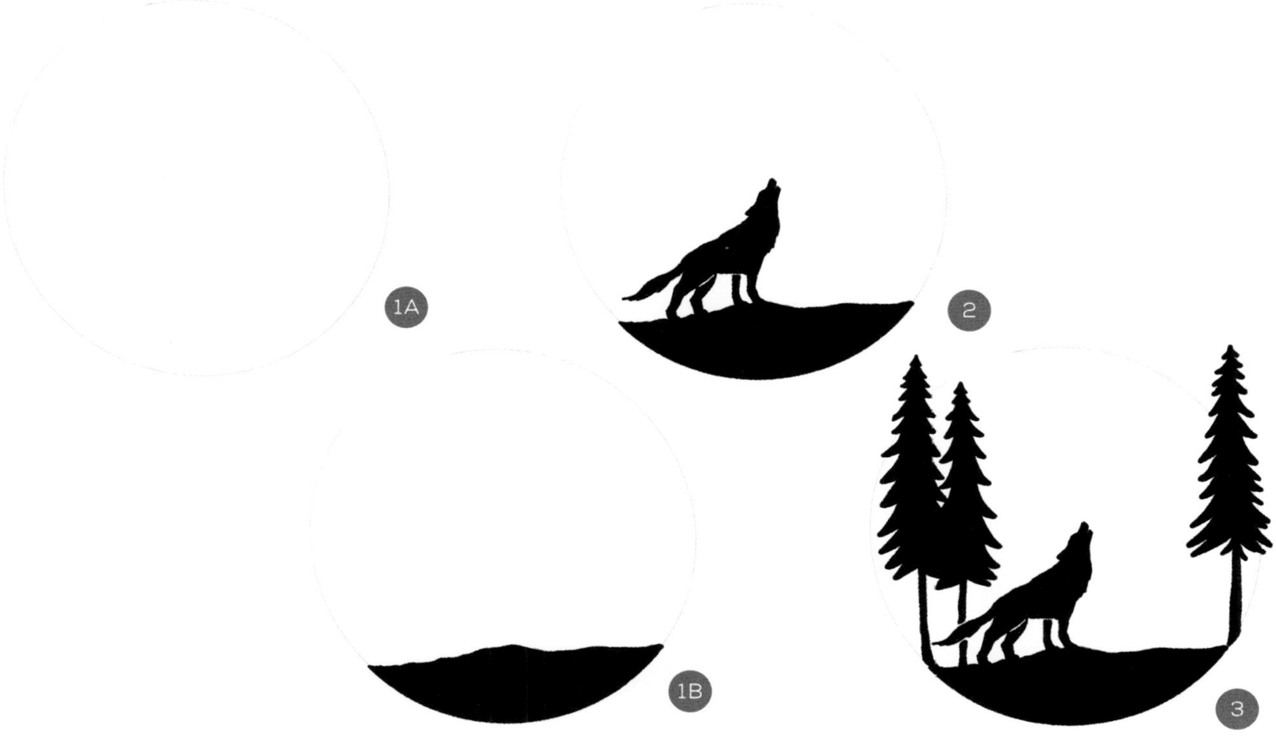

1A

2

1B

3

STEP 1

Using your compass, start with a circle in pencil and fill in the bottom with black using your brush pen, so we have a forest floor to place the wolf on.

STEP 2

And here comes the wolf silhouette. Can you hear it howl? Awooooo! Focus on the overall proportions and the shape of the head (in the Deer Family in a Forest Meadow project on page 109, I talk about how I draw silhouettes in more detail).

STEP 3

Surround the wolf with tree silhouettes in solid black. I created some overlap on the left to make one tree look farther away and behind the wolf.

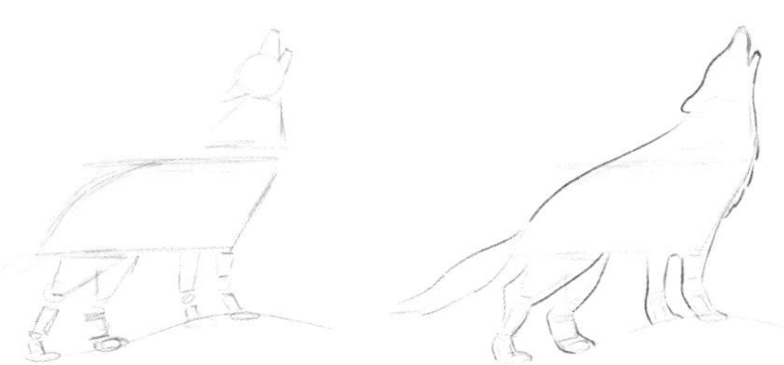

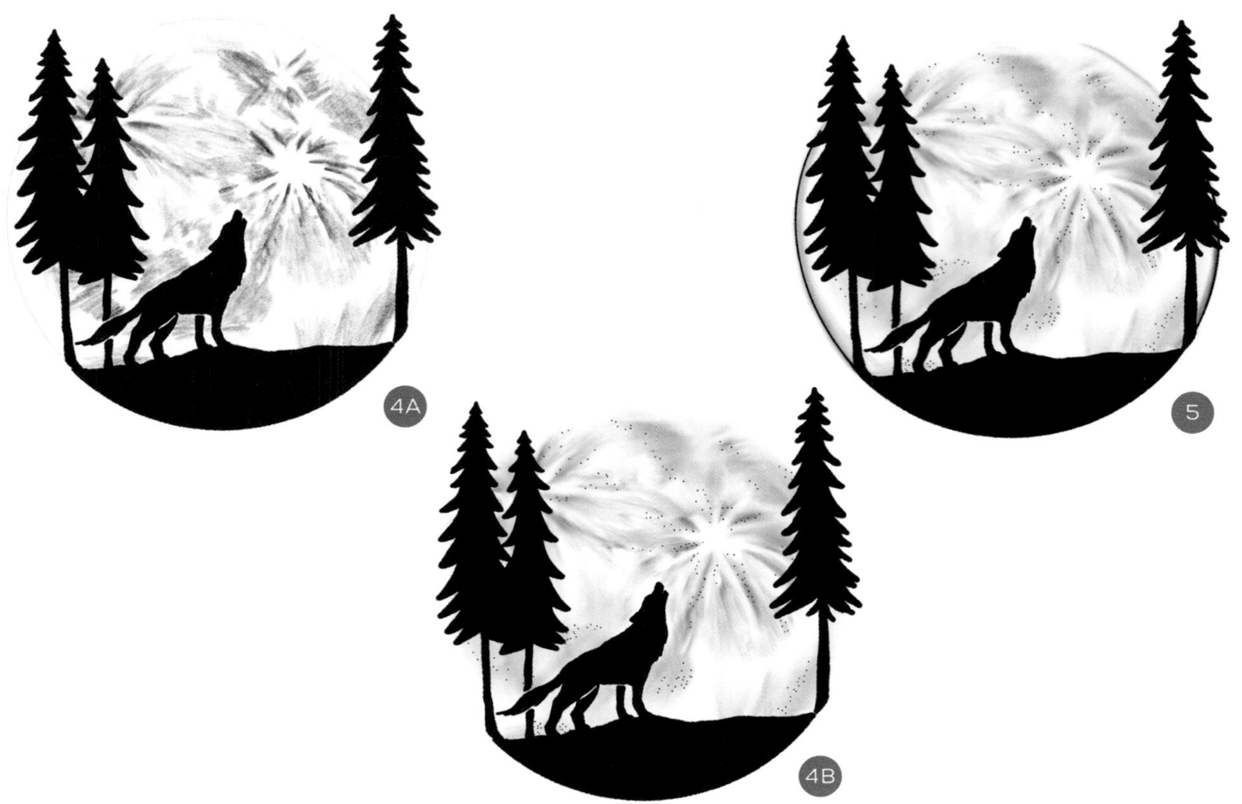

STEP 4

The hard work is done. The rest of this piece is pencil and shading work. Within the circle outline, lay down pencil strokes in different layers to imitate the craters on the moon surface. Mostly hold your pencil at a very flat angle so you get broad and soft marks on the paper.

Now, use your finger or a tissue to smudge the pencil into a softer look. You might have to layer more pencil and blend it again until the contrast looks good. Whenever you blend, you rub some of the pencil off in the process and the gray turns out lighter than anticipated. I also added some random dotwork with my thin (01) pen. (By the way, there are blending tools you can buy for pencils if you want to keep your fingers clean.)

STEP 5

Final touch: Work on the outline of the moon with more smudged pencil and ink lines on the left and the right side of the trees. Another great artwork! *Awooooo!*

DEER FAMILY IN A FOREST MEADOW

In the last project, I showed you some strong silhouettes for the trees. In this one, the focus is on a more delicate linework for the trees. Plus, you can say hi to Bambi!

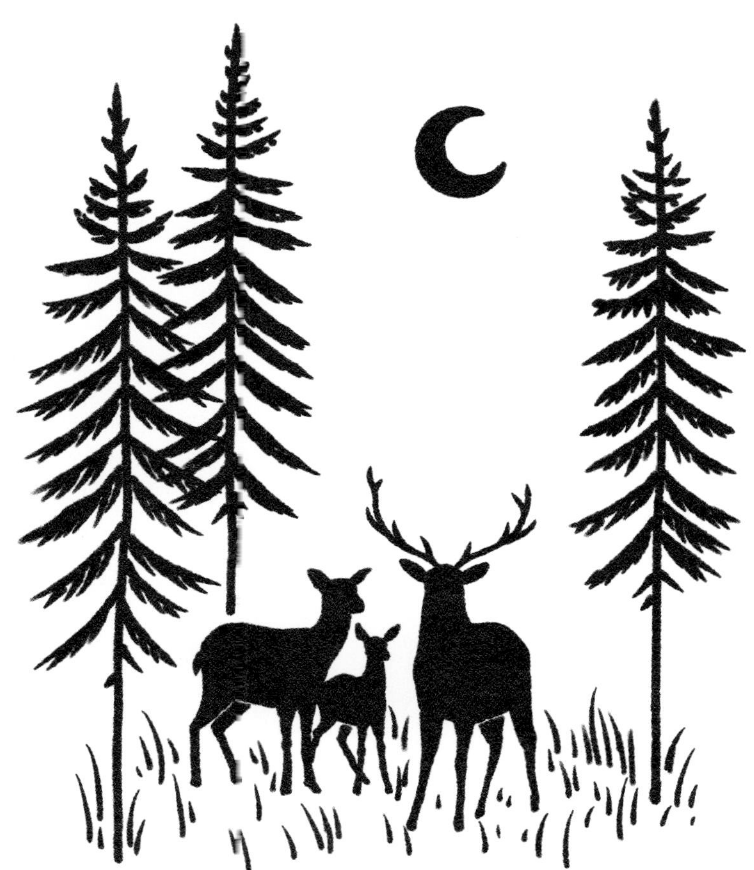

WHAT YOU NEED

Paper of your choice

Black pens in three sizes: 1.5, 05 and 01

Brush pen or liquid ink

Fine round brush

Pencil and eraser

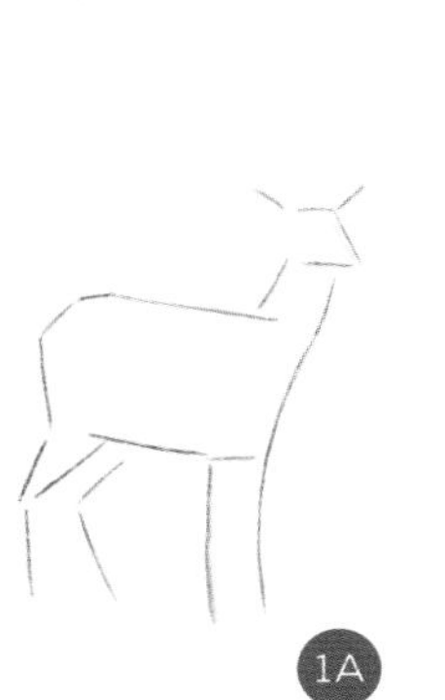

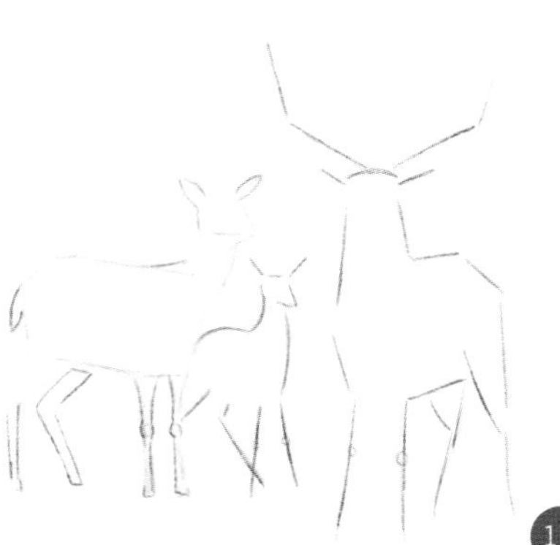

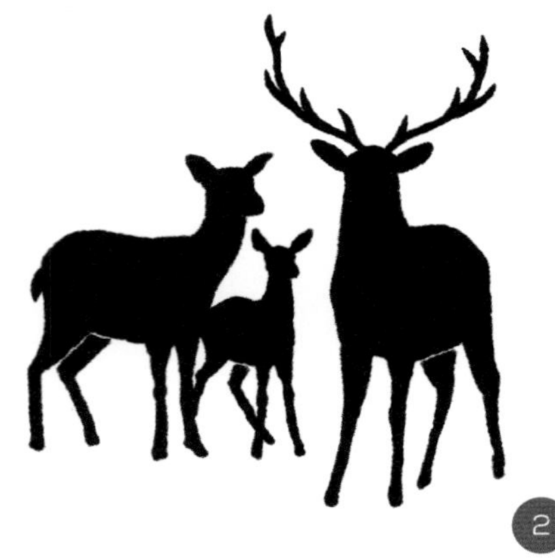

STEP 1

The first step in this project is to draw the silhouettes of the deer family. I would like to show you how I approach this. You can try it like that and see if it works for you or you can always develop your own technique. I usually tell you to focus on the main characteristics and not the details. So, my first step is to do a very simple shape sketch of my subject.

For the doe, I find the shape of the head and neck and its hindquarters important. That's why I worked with shape here. The rest of the elements (legs, ears, etc.) that I find less important are just lines at this point or not there at all. At this stage, I also pay attention to the proportions because you can still adjust them easily. If you are not sure you have the proportions right, turn your sketch facedown for a minute and do something else. Then, turn it back over and look at it again. You will see immediately if everything is okay.

My second step is to flesh out the form some more. For the doe, you can see that I worked out the ears and the legs in more detail and then defined the connections between the head, the neck and the backside better. I also added a tail. This is the basis for filling in the silhouette with black ink.

Bambi and his father are still in the first stage of sketching, to show you the difference side-by-side.

STEP 2

Dab off most of the pencil so only very fine lines remain and outline your silhouettes with the thin (01) pen and fill them in with black. Once the ink is dry, carefully erase any pencil lines that might still be visible.

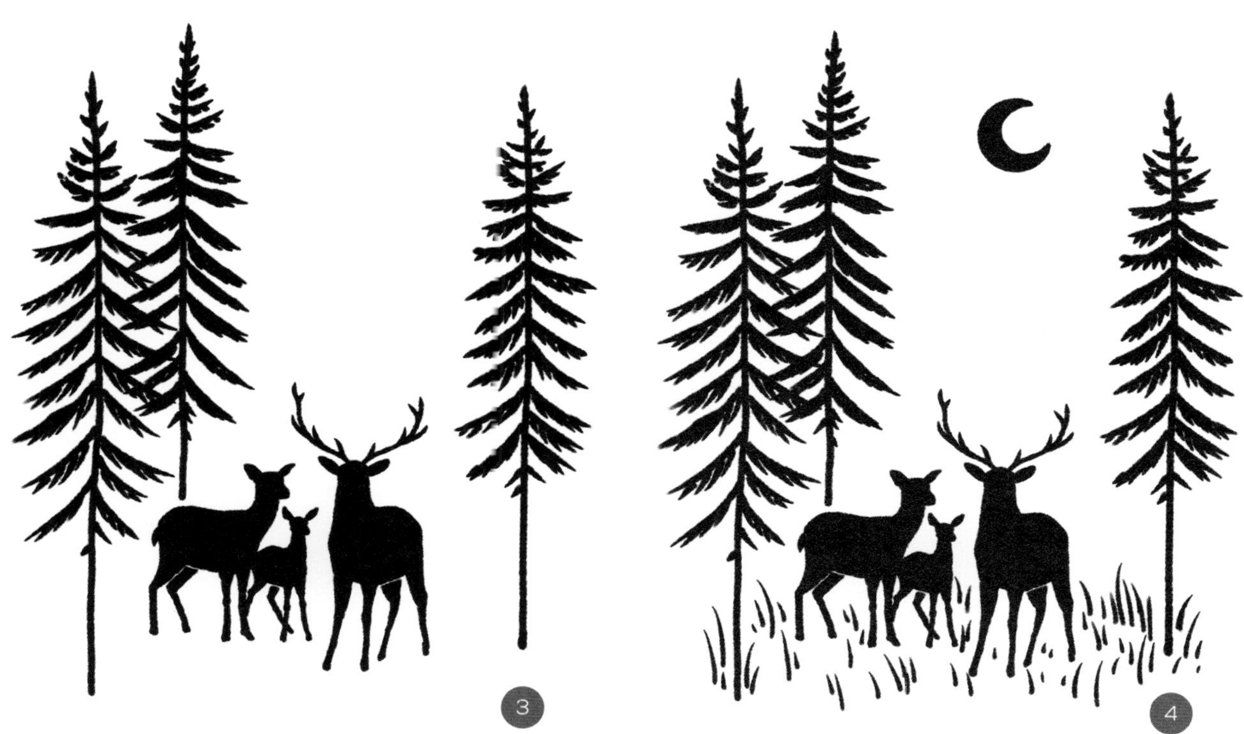

STEP 3

Ready for the trees? Use your medium (C5) pen. (You will need the fine nib for the grass in the next step.) Draw the horizontal lines for the tree trunks first. Next come the lines for the branches. Last are the needles. They are drawn in a similar way to the palm leaves in the Chill-Out Hammock Between Palm Trees project (page 50), just with less curve and spaced a little wider apart.

STEP 4

The trees and deer are currently all suspended on a large, white space. You want to avoid that unnatural look and ground your subjects. Here, you can add some grass between the deer and trees, for example. I also added a crescent moon because I like it and deer are more active in twilight.

Great work on the detailed trees! Now, you deserve a break and a treat before moving on to the next project.

MISTY WINTER FOREST

This piece is a little different than most of the other projects as it's not really line art. It's compiled through layering ink wash. (No ink wash or watercolor on hand? You can do this in pencil layers as well, with or without blending.) I thought this would be a fun break from the line art. At the same time, it's a good technique if you want to achieve a spooky or misty vibe.

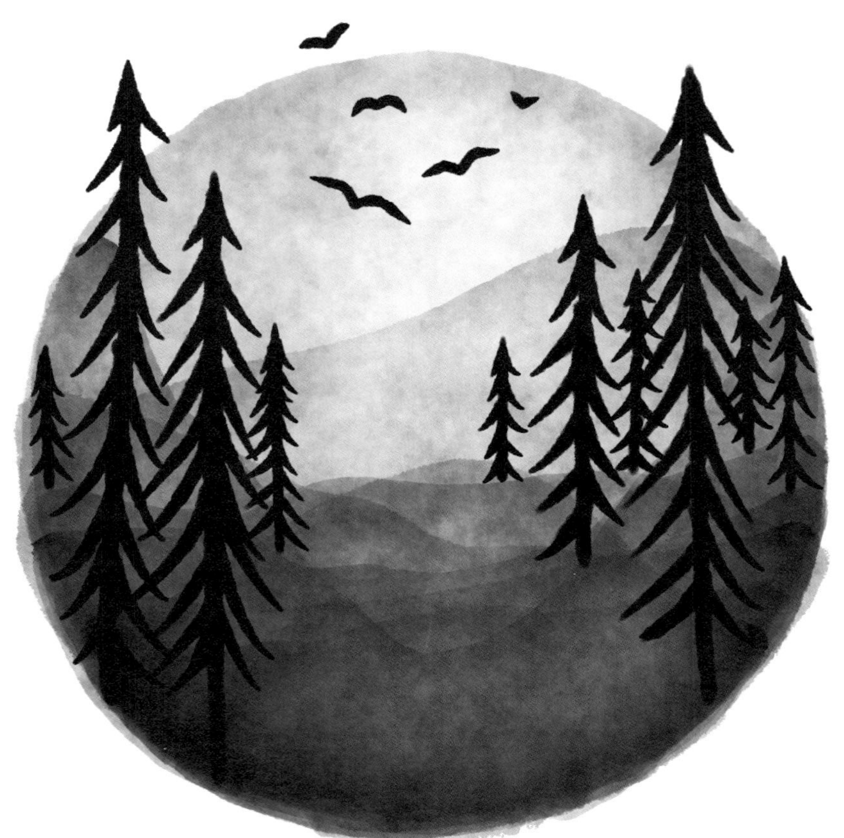

WHAT YOU NEED

Watercolor or mixed-media paper

Ink wash or watercolor in a soft gray tone

Medium round brush (size 3)

Brush pen

Black pen in one size: 05

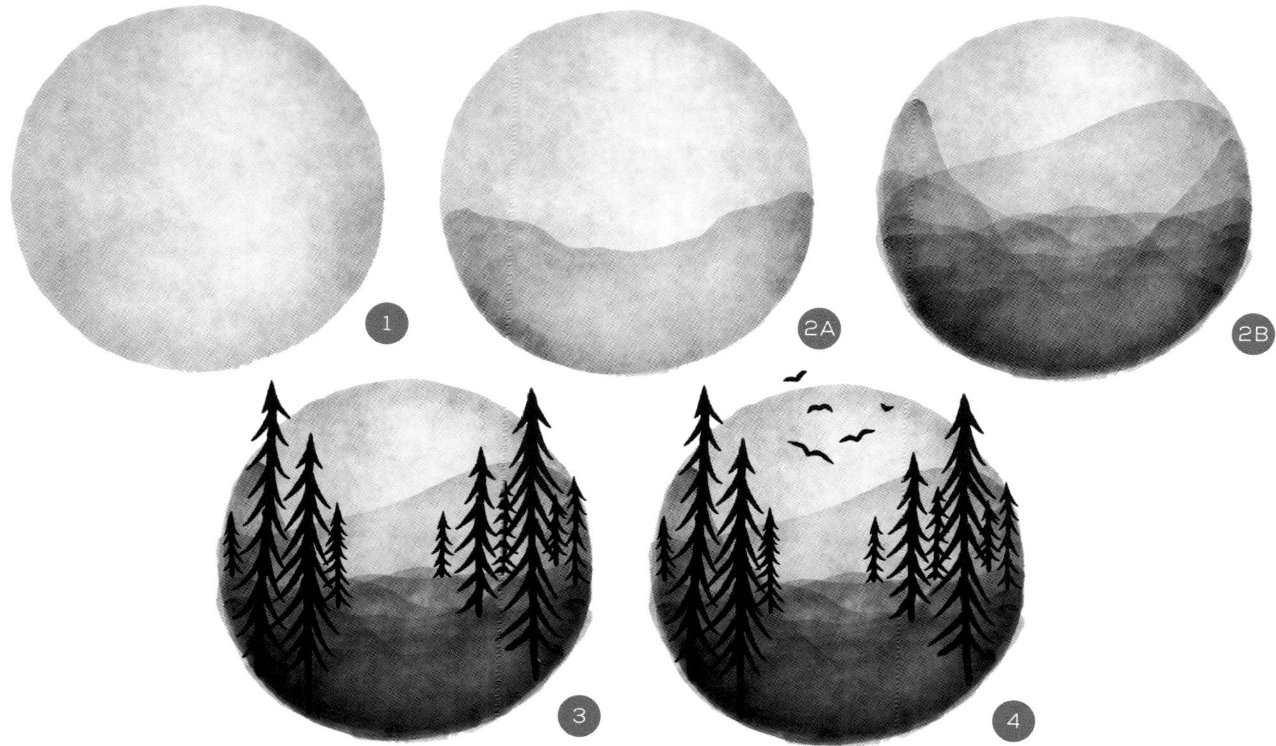

STEP 1

Paint a circle in a transparent soft gray tone (the circle can be done freehand, but you can use a pencil outline if you'd like). To mix the tone, use lots of water with very little black color mixed in. If you use a bit more water than you need, so that you leave a small puddle on your paper, it will dry with the edges a bit darker like it did here. If you use just enough ink wash on your brush to paint the circle, you will get a smoother coat without darker edges. Let it dry completely before going on to the next step.

STEP 2

Put a second layer over the first in the bottom of the circle. Let it dry again.

Keep adding more layers in different shapes, each time letting them dry completely before adding the next. Stop when you think it looks dark enough in the bottom. You should now have something like this.

STEP 3

Once your drawing is completely dry, use your brush pen to add the trees. They should overlap each other and become smaller where they are farther away.

STEP 4

As a final touch, add a few birds in the sky with the black pen.

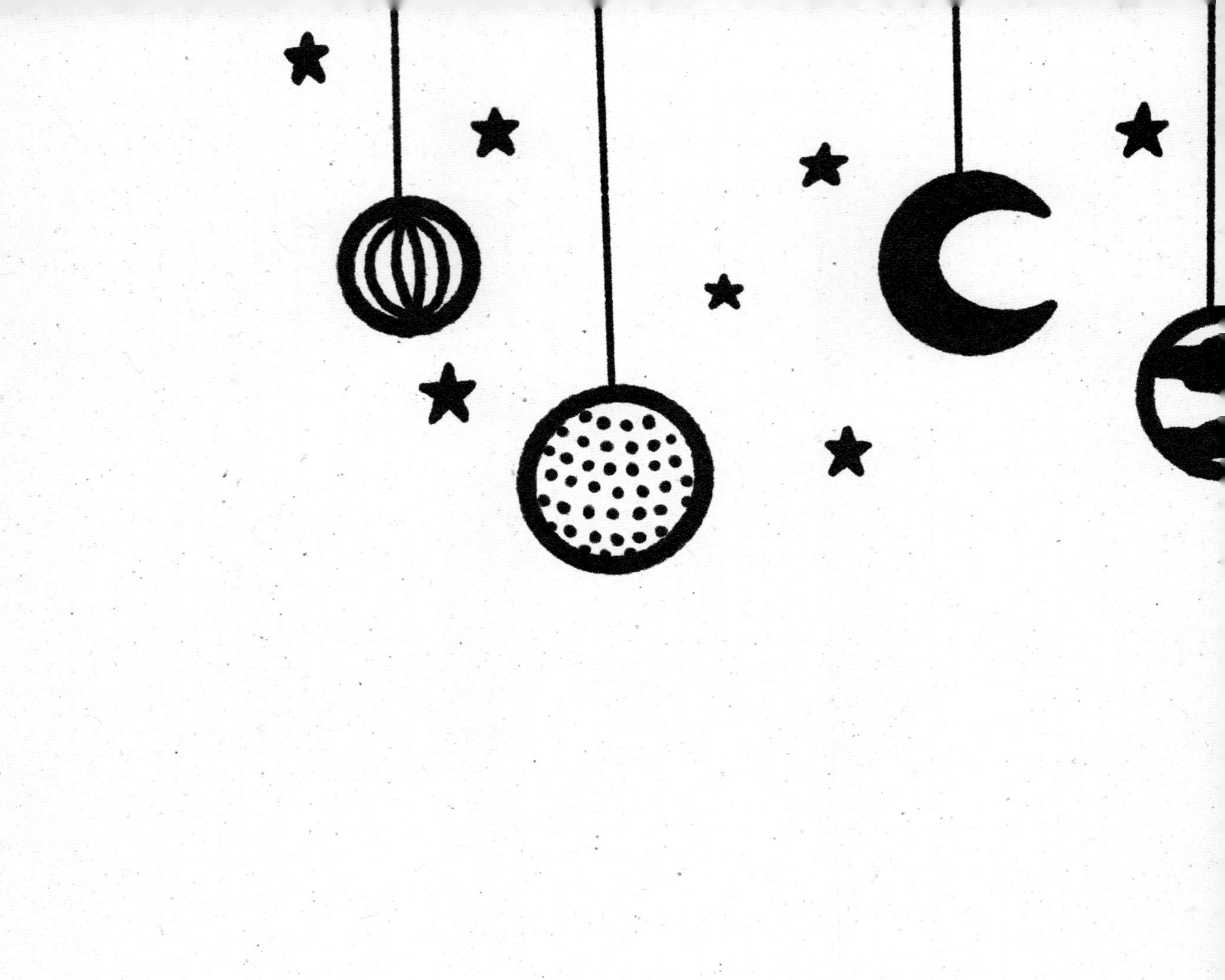

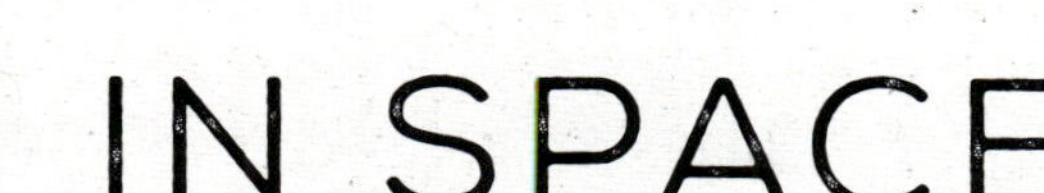

IN SPACE

When I camp during my hikes, I don't think about the dark night around me. Instead, I think about the sky above me and all the beautiful, real and magical fantasy world things that are up there in space.

You will learn how to put some of these things on paper in the next few projects. As space is mostly black, this is the perfect opportunity to learn more about leaving negative space, which requires careful planning of your composition. Once an area is painted black, you cannot go back and erase. A side effect of this will be getting a lot of practice with fixing errors and drawing white on black.

The projects kick off with a secret planet (page 116) and continue on to galaxies (page 122)—you will even draw an astronaut or two!

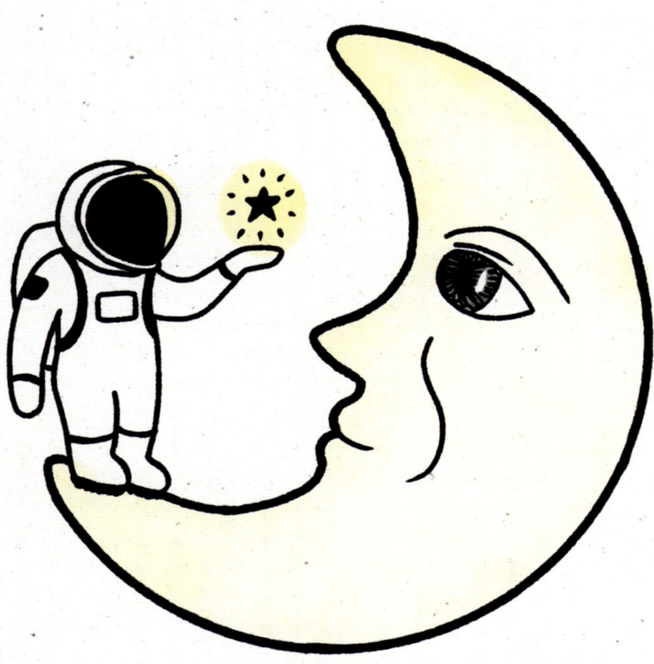

SECRET PLANET LANDSCAPE

One of the things I hope to bring across in this book is that, with drawing, you can keep arranging the same elements in different ways and each time you will get different artwork out of it. It's part of the creative process. In some of the other projects in this book, such as the Van Life Night Scene on page 22, you have drawn circle scenes before. This one is essentially the same thing, you just put a ring around it to make a planet.

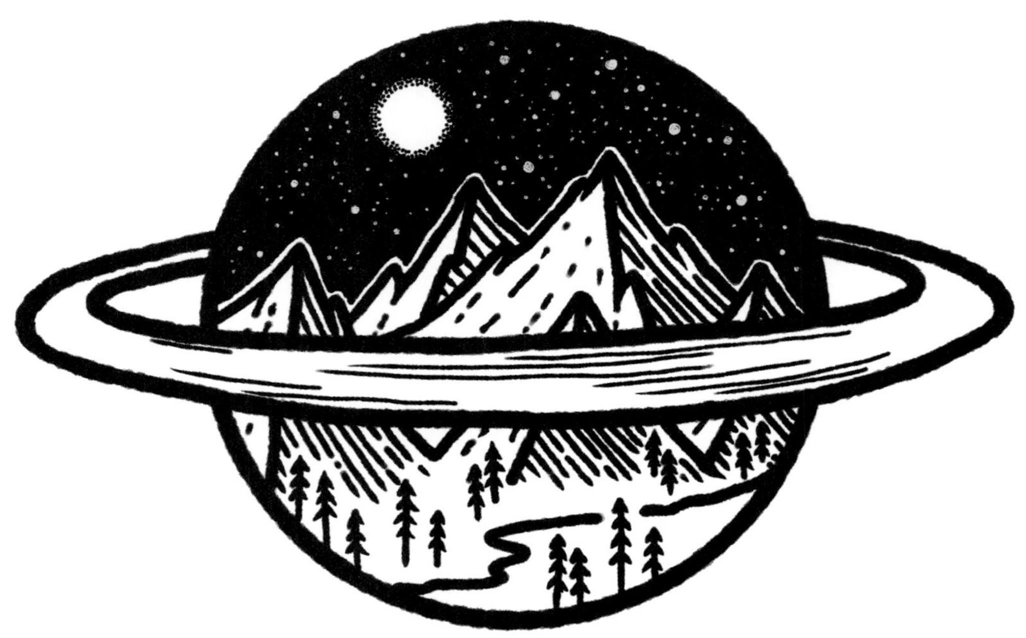

WHAT YOU NEED

Paper of your choice

Compass, circle tool or round object to trace

Pencil and eraser

Black pens in three sizes: 1.5, 05 and 01

Brush pen

White pens in two sizes: 10 and 08

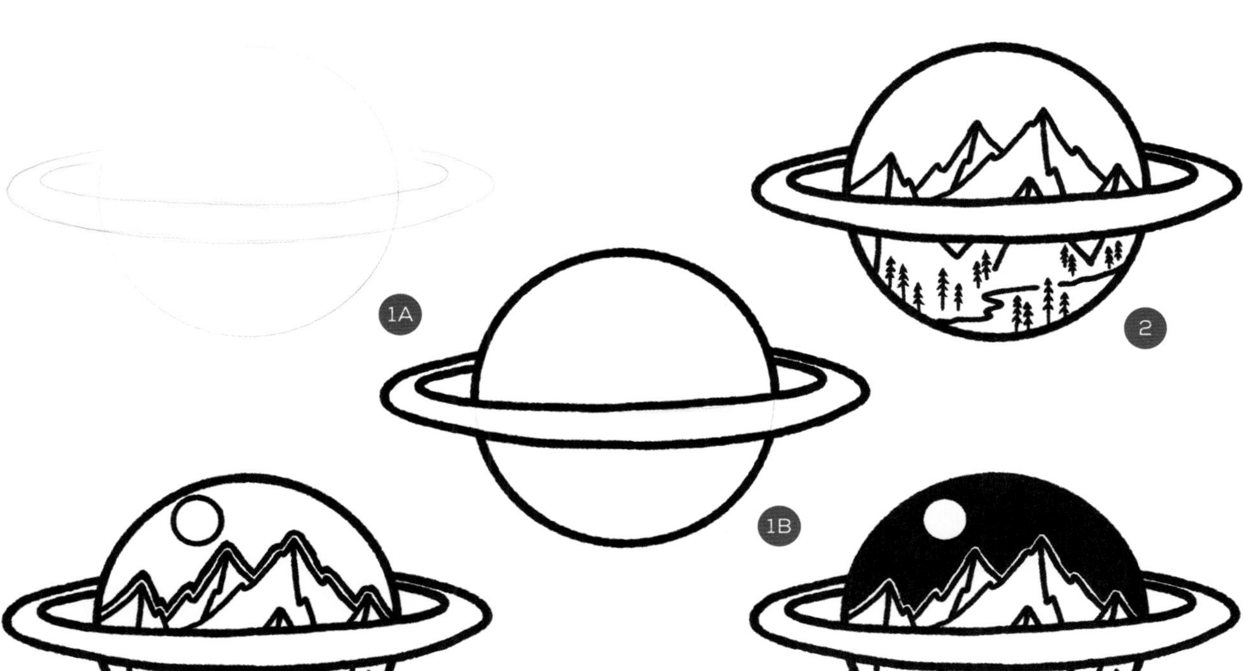

STEP 1

To get the line intersections for the ring and the circle of the planet just right, I made a little sketch to guide me, using my compass. I used that as a basis to ink the outlines in the thicker (1.5) pen and then erased it.

STEP 2

The next part is adding the outlines for the landscape in medium (05) pen on the inside of the planet. I chose mountains, a small river and some trees. You could go with anything you like instead. Just make sure that you connect the pieces above and below the ring correctly so it looks like one landscape.

STEP 3

Next come some familiar steps. A second mountain outline above the peaks to set it off against the dark later. A small circle for the full moon. Then, filling in the black background creates the night sky.

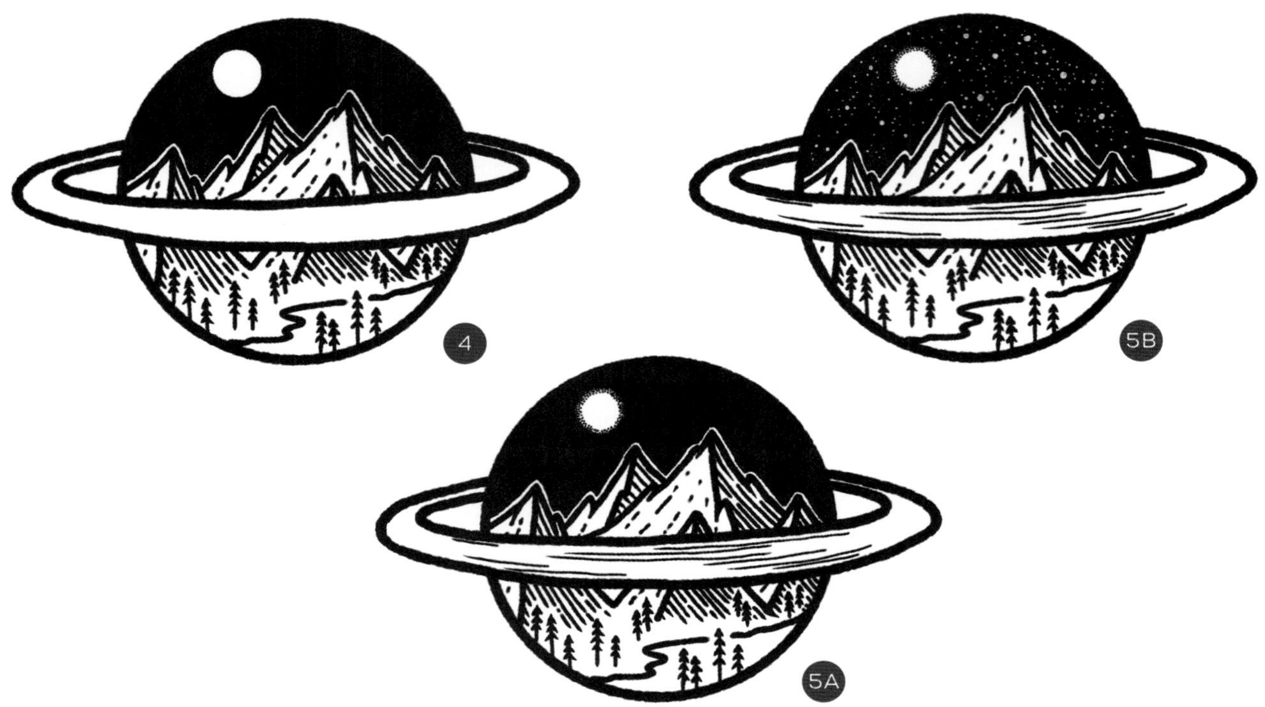

STEP 4

As the next step, move on to the surface texture on mountains in your thin (01) pen. Create a darker side that faces away from the moon by using more lines and drawing them closer together. The lighter side faces the moon and is only accented with a few short strokes.

STEP 5

For the moon glow effect, use your (01) pen and draw many small dots close together around the edge of the moon. To finish this piece, draw curving lines on the ring and add white dots for a starry sky.

A CLOUD OF PLANETS

Not all drawings have to depict a full scene. I often do small doodles as a pick-me-up when drawing a landscape scene isn't going the way I wanted. It takes away the limit of thinking about perspectives or difficult shapes and you can return to your other drawing with a fresh mind and new motivation. Get creative and let your mind run free on this one!

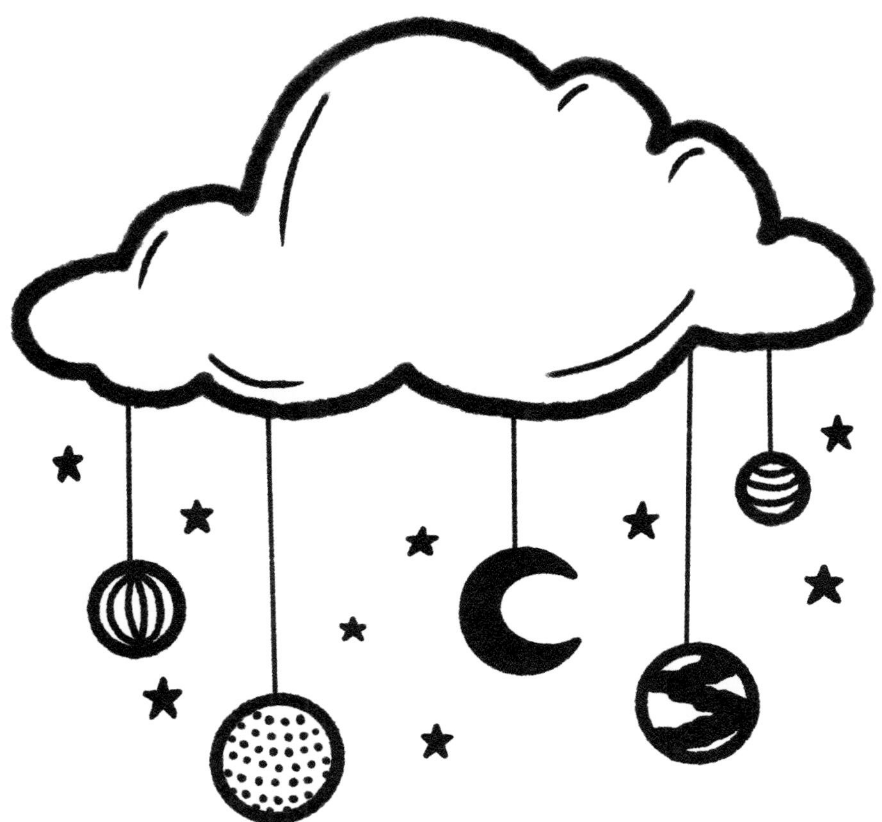

WHAT YOU NEED

Paper of your choice

Black pens in three sizes: 1.5, 05 and 01

Compass, circle tool or small round objects to trace (I recommend small buttons here)

Ruler

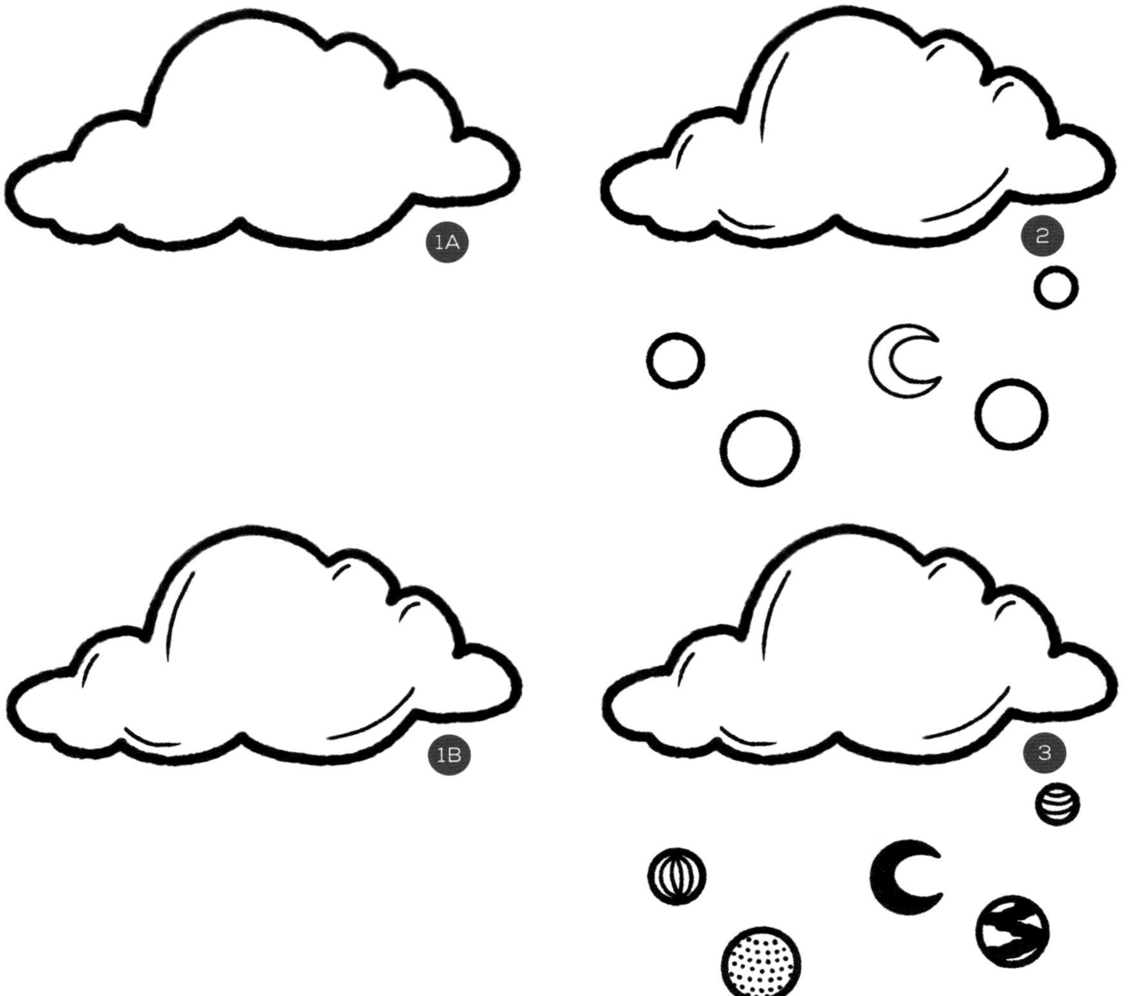

STEP 1

Draw a cloud outline with your thick (1.5) pen and some thinner lines as accents on the inside with—you probably guessed—your thin (01) pen.

STEP 2

Then, with the help of your compass, draw the outlines for the planets in your medium (05) pen, with the details inside done in your (01) pen and a crescent moon outline also in your (01) pen.

STEP 3

Decorate the planets with random patterns and color in the crescent moon with black.

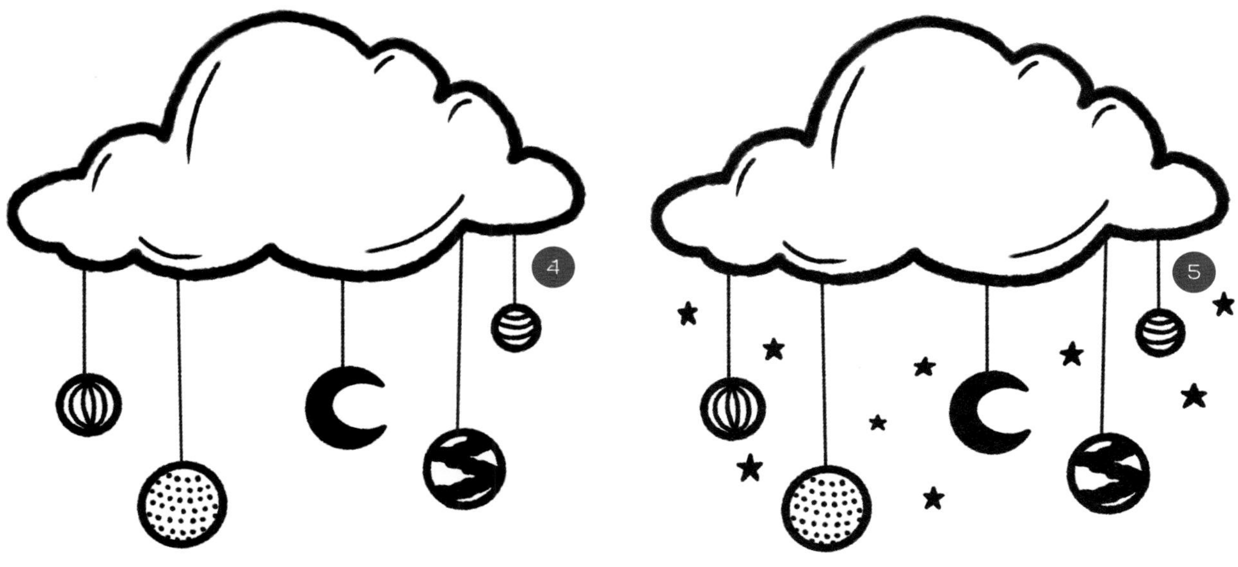

STEP 4

Draw lines to connect the planets and the cloud in thin (01) pen. I used my ruler here.

STEP 5

Draw some five-point stars around the planets. That's easier than you think. Just follow the steps shown here:

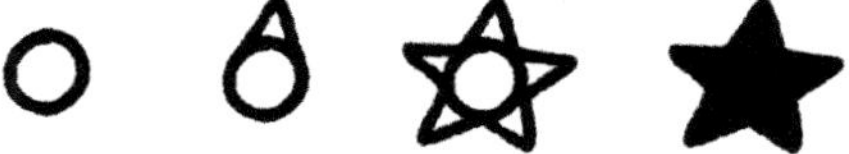

Aaaaand . . . you finished your cloud doodle. You're a star!

GALAXY IN A JAR

Small galaxy drawings like this one are Instagram gold—they always get a lot of likes. Maybe what appeals to everyone is the idea of confining the vastness of space in a really small space. It's almost as if you could carry a small piece of space with you this way. I used a jar in this project. Whatever you choose as a frame or its content, make sure to have one item that the viewer will instantly recognize from space—like, in my case, Saturn.

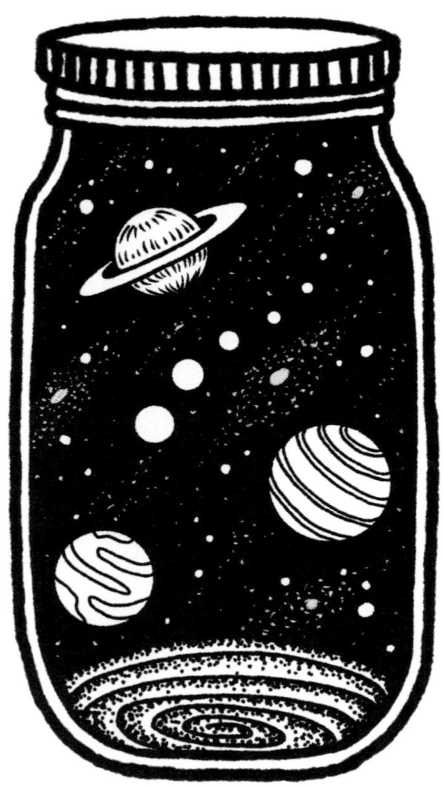

WHAT YOU NEED

Paper of your choice

Black pens in two sizes: 1.5 and 05

Compass, circle tool or round objects to trace

Brush pen or liquid ink

Medium round brush (size 3)

White pens in two sizes: 10 and 08

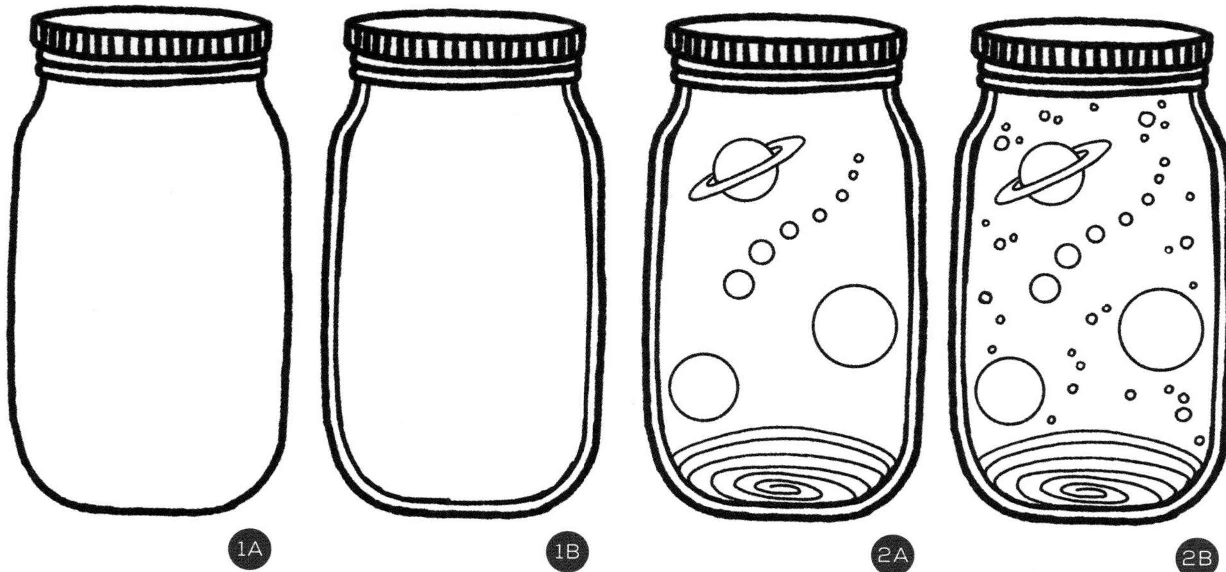

STEP 1

Use your medium (05) pen. The top of the jar lid is a flat oval. A line with exactly the same curve just below that oval creates the bottom edge of the jar lid. Two more that are a bit shorter show the edge of the thread. Add some downward-facing short lines on the side of the jar lid. Now, draw the jar body.

Switch to the thin (01) pen and draw a line inside that is parallel to the jar body to show the thick glass of the jar.

STEP 2

Use your thin (01) pen and your compass to add round objects for planet outlines. I did a Saurn-style planet and kept the rest simple circles. Also, draw a spiral on the bottom of the jar—this will become a black hole later on.

Once you have your main space elements in place, add more small circles. These are the bigger stars. (You could skip this step and also add those in white pen later. I do think that they pop more when the paper white shows, that's why I make the effort.)

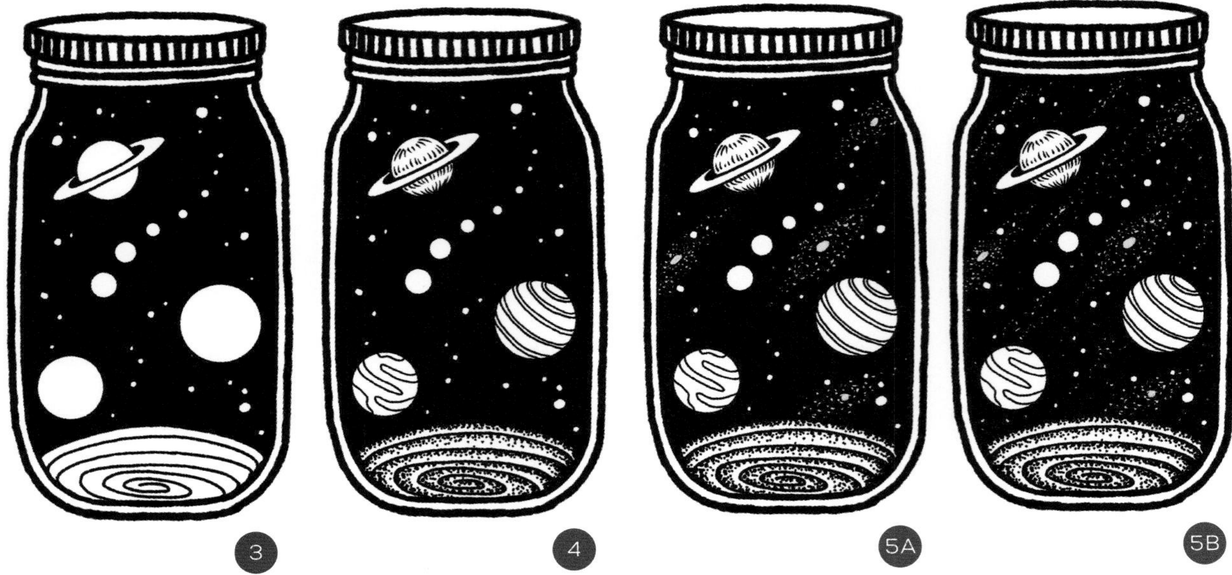

STEP 3

Fill in the background with black, leaving the inside of your circles uncovered, as well as the spiral for the black hole. Note that I carefully filled a small area on each side between the planet and its ring with black too.

STEP 4

Pick up your thin (01) pen and draw details on your planets. To form the black hole, put many small dots close to the spiral line you drew earlier.

STEP 5

Let's switch to the white pen and take care of the final touches. Add small white circles and dots in different sizes for more stars. I like to do small circles and big dots first and make sure I distribute them nicely over the area, then add many smaller ones around those. Here, I also clustered them closer together than I normally would to imitate galaxies.

ASTRONAUT FLOATING THROUGH OUTER SPACE

I don't recall the name of the movie, but the story started with an astronaut getting separated from the spaceship. Naturally, it's a bit dicey to be floating around in space with a limited amount of oxygen and it's not clear if a rescue is even possible—not going to spoil the rest of the movie plot. Just pointing out: In addition to playing with white details on black backgrounds, the astronaut in our drawing is still tied to the spaceship, hence the cable. The spaceship just did not fit into the drawing space-wise (I'm bad with puns, ignore it).

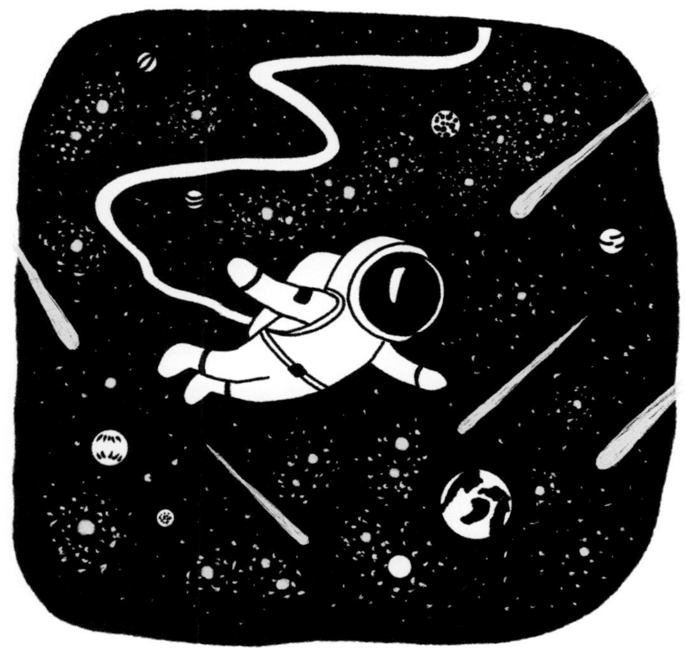

WHAT YOU NEED

Paper of your choice

Black pens in three sizes: 1.5, 05 and 01

Brush pen or liquid ink

Medium round brush (size 3)

White pens in two sizes: 10 and 08

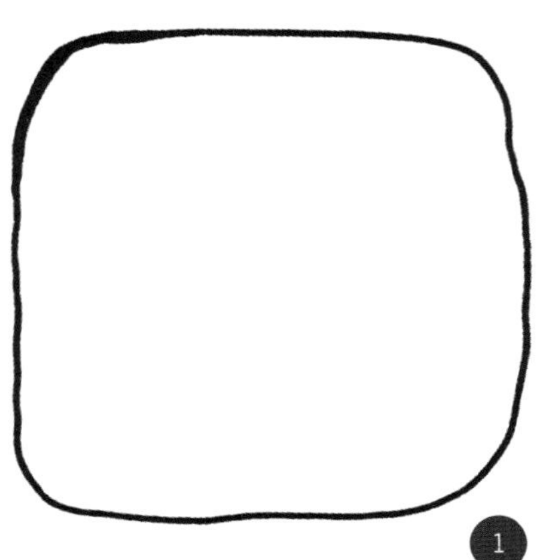

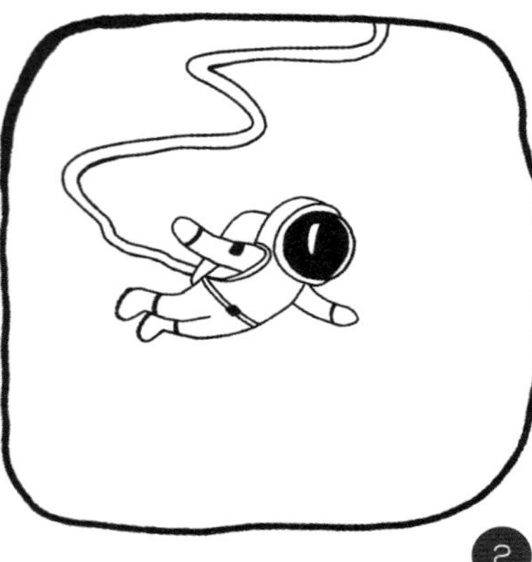

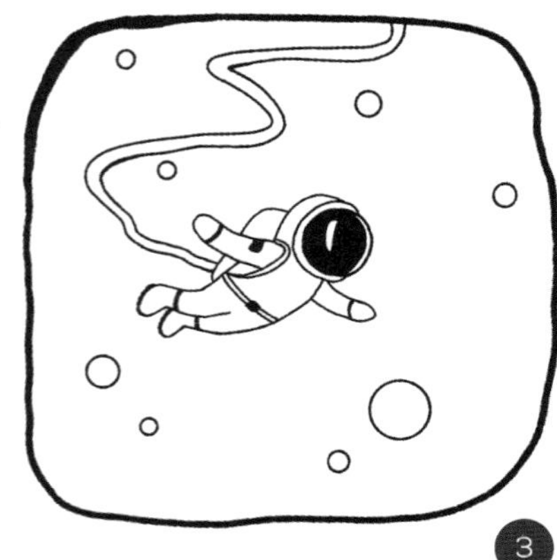

STEP 1

Draw a square-shaped line as a frame with your medium (05) pen.

STEP 2

Now, draw your astronaut in thin (01) pen and the important connecting line to his spaceship. Fill in his helmet visor with black, but leave a sliver of white on the upper left as a highlight and also a thin white space at the right edge of the visor. The white line at the edge ensures it clearly separates from the black background later on.

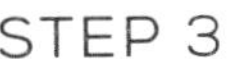

STEP 3

Draw different-sized circles in the space around the astronaut. These will become stars and planets, so draw as many as you want. (More planets mean less work filling in the background with black, but more work on the planet details and vice versa.)

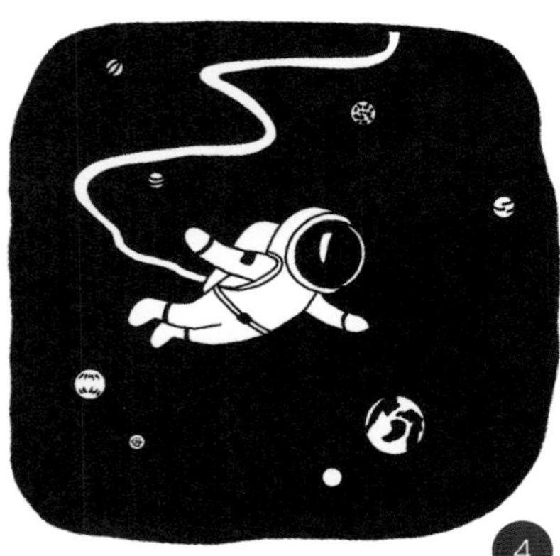

STEP 4

Fill in the background with black ink and add details to the planets. Example:

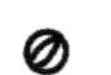     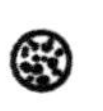 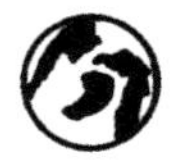

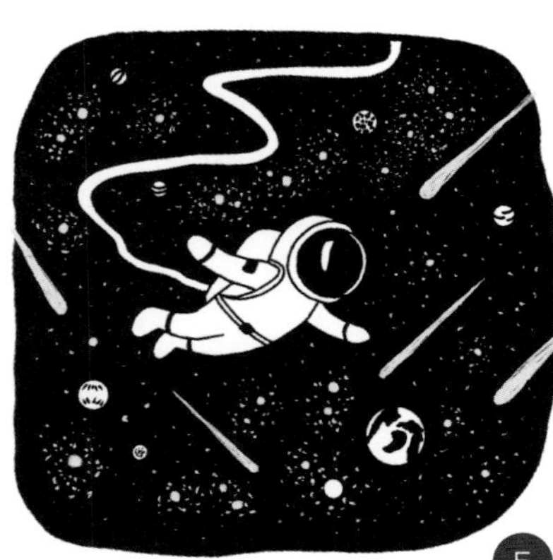

STEP 5

With your thick (10) white pen, add the bigger end of the falling stars. Switch to the thin (08) white pen where they taper off, and dot stars and small circles into space.

You finished your space drawing—bravo!

THE ASTRONAUT AND THE MOON

Bringing two characters together in an unusual way can create great drawings. In this piece, I wanted to combine the moon and an astronaut. I feel like I created the beginning of a cute children's book where the astronaut gifts a star to the moon and they become friends. To bring two characters together, it's important to include an element that connects them—in this case, the star. An element like this takes a little more planning and might require you to start with pencil first.

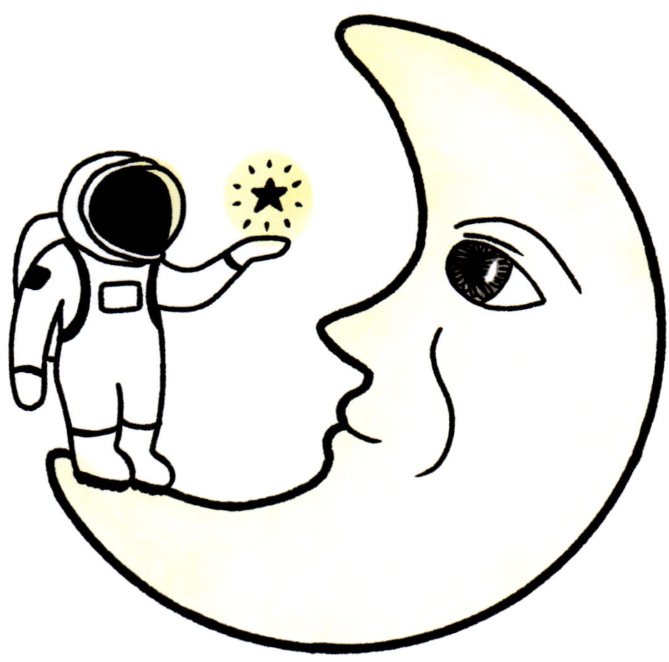

WHAT YOU NEED

Watercolor or mixed-media paper

Black pens in three sizes: 1.5, 05 and 01

Pencil and eraser

Watercolors in tones of yellow and gray (optional)

Medium round brush (size 3) (optional)

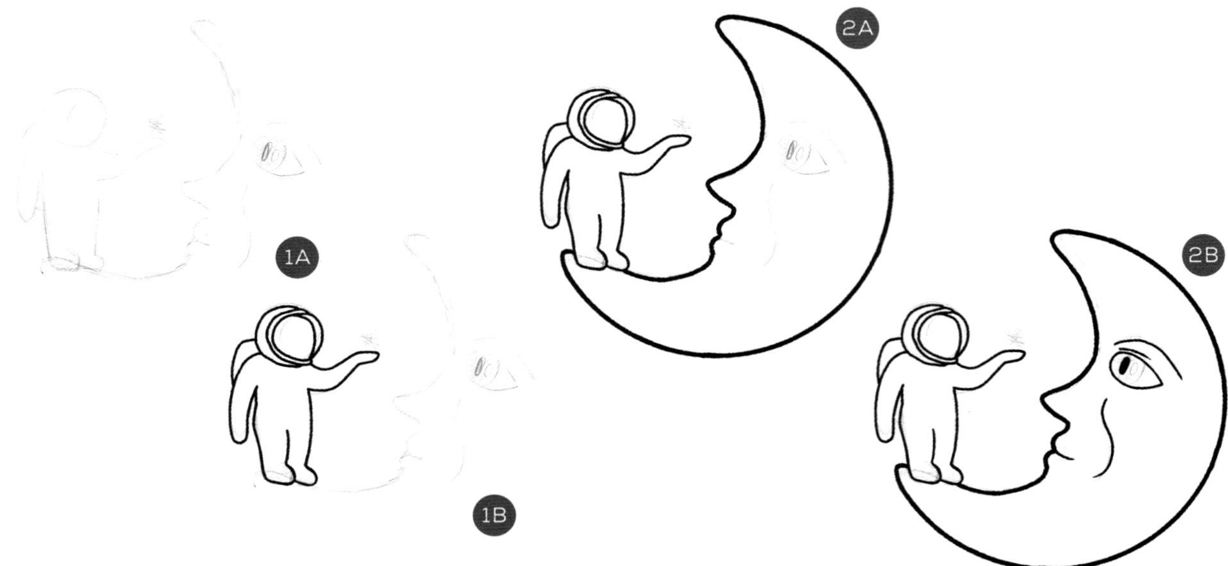

STEP 1

Because there are a few things I wanted to align in this drawing (like the star and the eye of the moon) and keep as white space (the visor reflection and the iris reflection on the moon), I made a pencil underdrawing first. Make the sketch with a very light stroke so it's nearly invisible, which will make it easier to erase later.

Trace the outline for the astronaut with your thin (01) pen. On the right-hand side of the helmet, make sure you draw a double line so you leave a white space for the highlight.

STEP 2

For the outline of the moon, use your medium (05) pen.

Go back to the thin (01) pen for the details of the moon's face. Draw the pupil as a solid black oval. The mouth is smiling just a little.

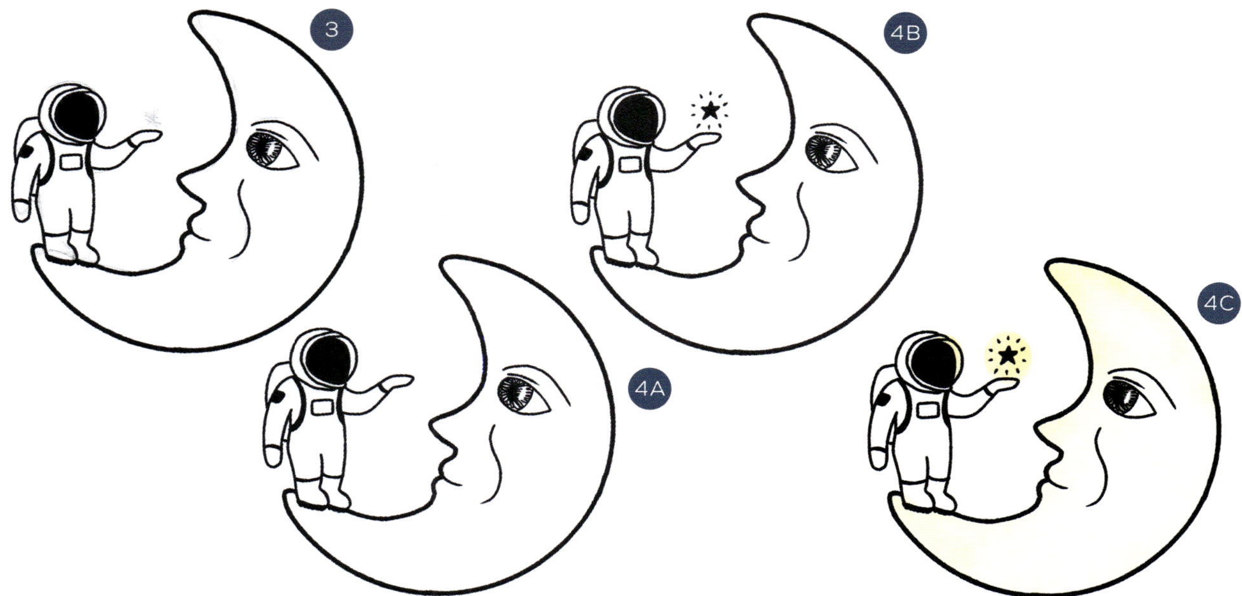

STEP 3

Add the details on the astronaut with a thin (01) pen. Draw the straps for his oxygen backpack, arm and breast patches, then add the edges of his gloves and boots and a thicker line for the sole of his boots. Fill in the visor of the helmet with black. In medium (05) pen, draw curved lines on the iris for the eye of the moon. Spare the highlight that you marked in your sketch with a little oval so it shows the white of the paper. Here is a close-up of the eye:

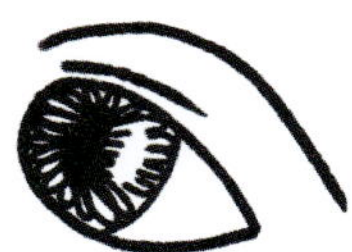

STEP 4

Make sure all your inkwork is dry. Carefully erase the remaining pencil lines.

Draw a star with five points above the hand of the astronaut and aligned with the eye of the moon. Detailed steps for the star drawing can be found in the A Cloud of Planets project on page 119. I also added some short lines around the star for an extra twinkle.

OPTIONAL: Add a bright yellow glow for the star and the reflection of the astronaut's helmet. Paint the moon as well, but make it a yellow that's a bit more transparent. Leave the eye white, and if you want, color the iris with a gray wash (except for the highlight there, of course).

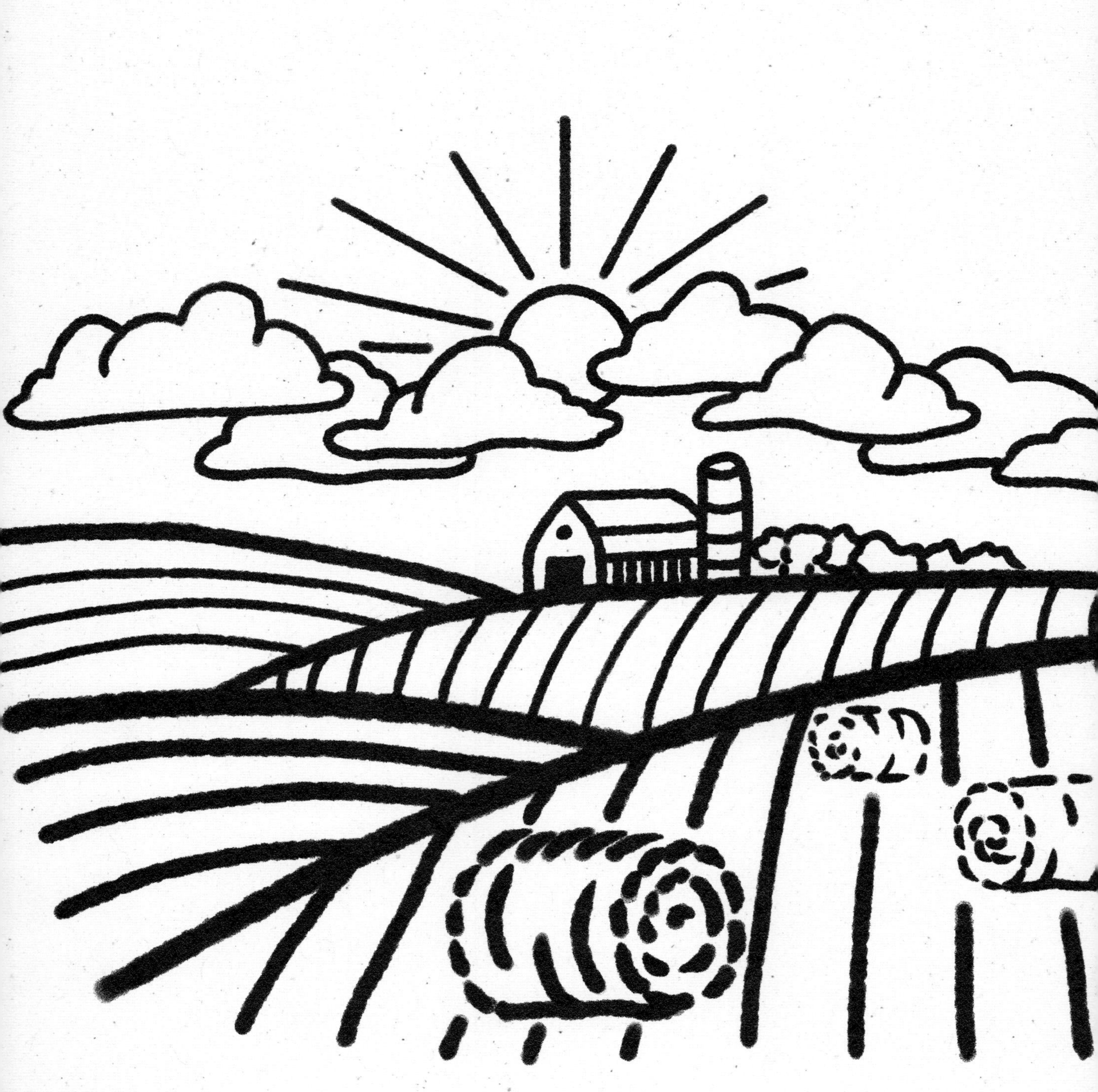

COUNTRY LIFE

Driving through the countryside can give you a lot of inspiration. While the background changes slowly—when you're driving through a hilly landscape, for example—watch out for the things that are different. These are your points of interest.

To illustrate the following projects, Windmills in the Country (page 132) and Small Farm Scene (page 135) will show you how to change a scene by only switching a few elements. In the other projects in this chapter, you can work on your perspective skills once more while drawing power lines (page 138), add to your sun variations (page 135) and doodle mountains of mushrooms (page 142).

WINDMILLS IN THE COUNTRY

The next two projects are similar in their process. The details are not. My goal is to show you once more that you can create a very different drawing by switching out only a few elements.

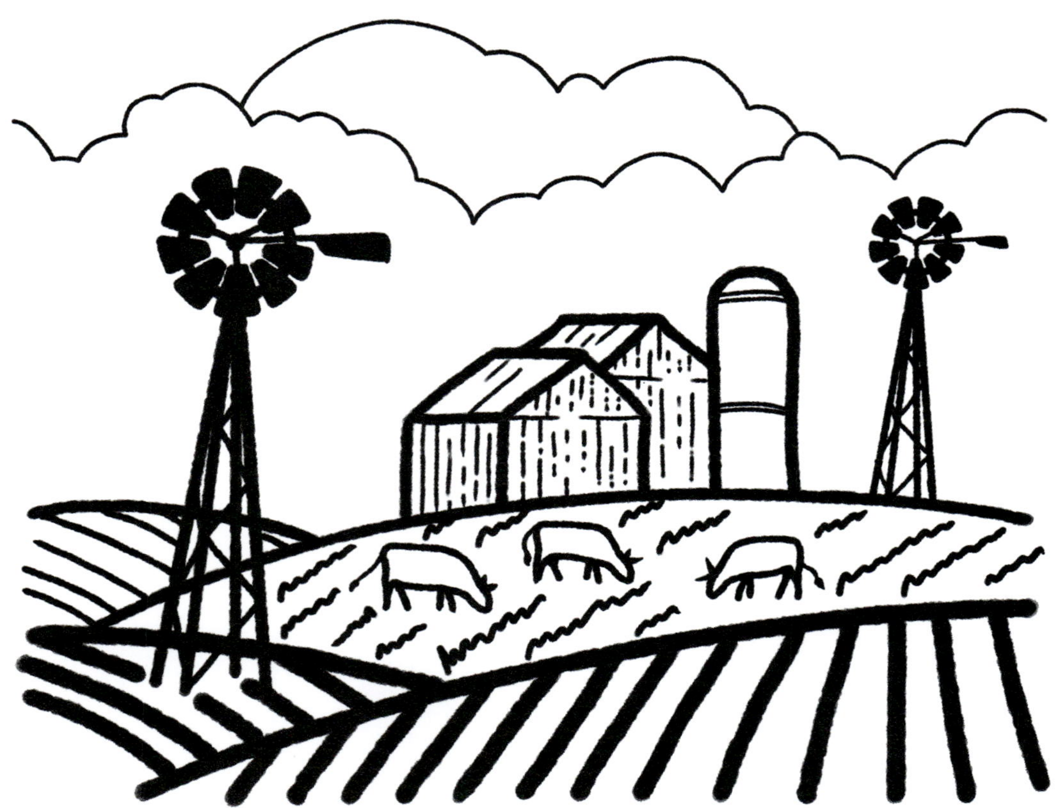

WHAT YOU NEED

Paper of your choice

Black pens in three sizes: 1.5, 05 and 01

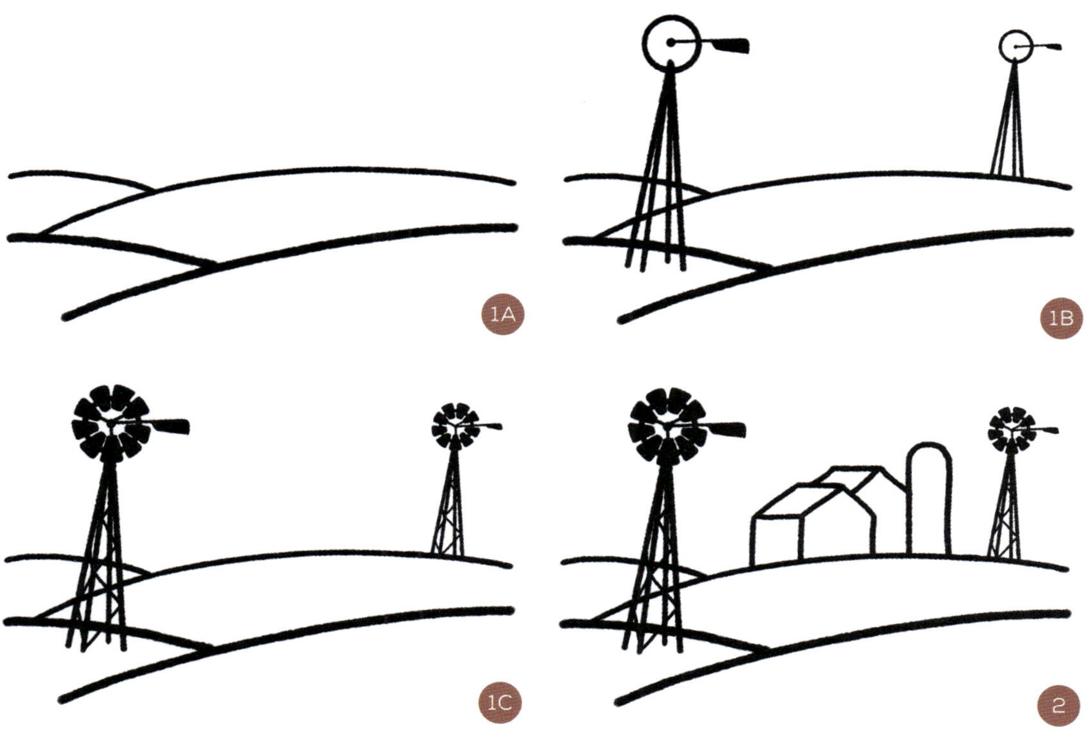

STEP 1

Draw diagonal curved lines to create a hilly landscape: the front in thick (1.5) pen, the back with a medium (05) size.

Place the stilts for two windmills. This means drawing four lines that meet in one point and putting a circle on top. Put a dot in the center of the circle and start drawing the tail from that point. The windmill in the foreground is drawn with a medium (05) nib, the one in the back with the thin (01) pen. Note that the front one is taller.

Now, add the windmill blades and draw some diagonal lines across the stilts to complete the windmills.

STEP 2

Add the outlines of the farm buildings. I used my medium (05) pen, but I think it would look better with the thin (01) nib that I used for the windmill next to it. Make the buildings look three-dimensional. The top of the roof is level (parallel with the top and the bottom paper edge).

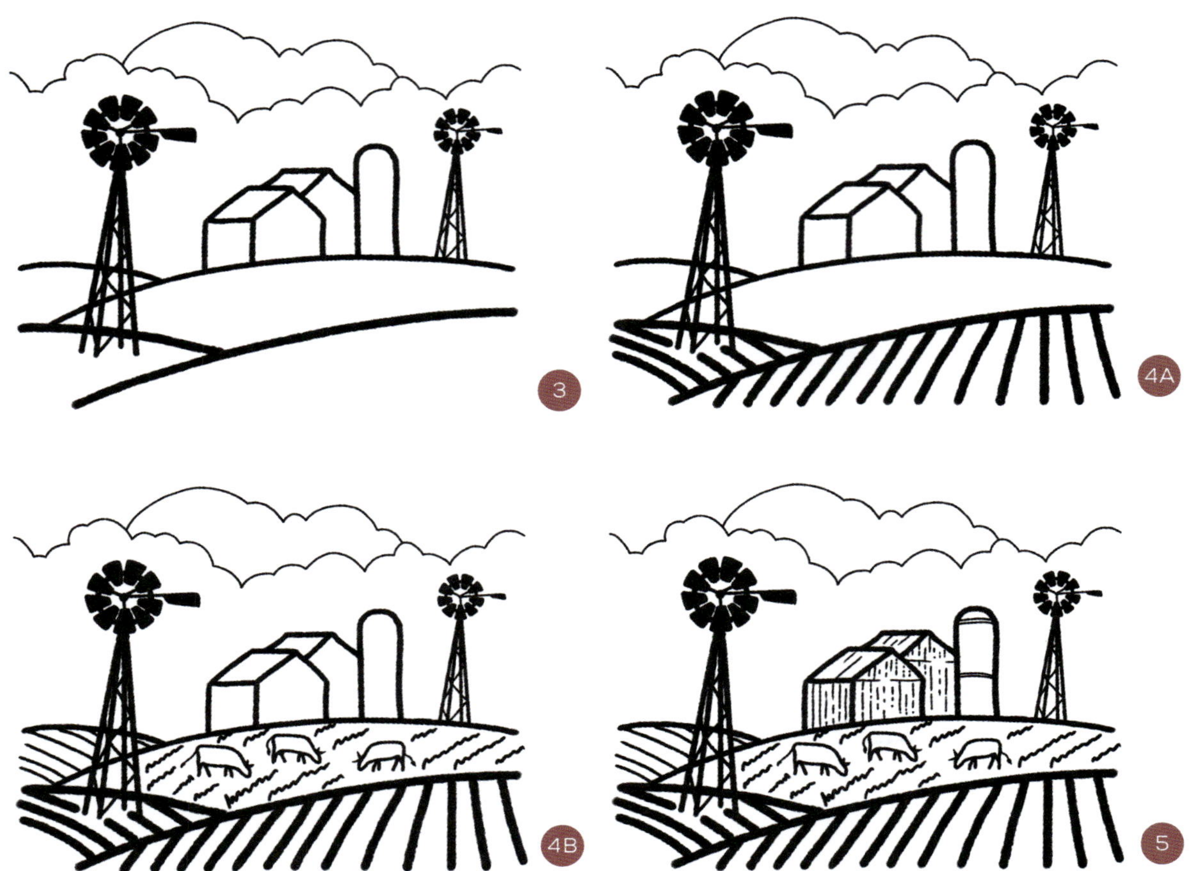

STEP 3

Draw the curved cloud outlines in the background just above your windmills.

STEP 4

Move on to the smaller details and textures in this piece. The fields in front get thick (1.5) pen strokes that create the furrows.

In the middle ground, add a few grazing cattle. Note that they are just a rough cattle-like shape with lines for the legs and the horns. Around them, draw some wiggly lines that might resemble grass.

STEP 5

The last details to be added are on the farm buildings in the background. The barns appear to be built from wood. Break your lines often. As they are far away from the viewer, they would not be able to be seen clearly and broken linework can create that impression.

Nice rural landscape—way to go!

SMALL FARM SCENE

This scene has the same structure as the previous project. I switched out the cows for hay bales and moved them closer to the viewer. The farm buildings are farther away and the weather is different. Can you think of more elements that could be modified to change the visual?

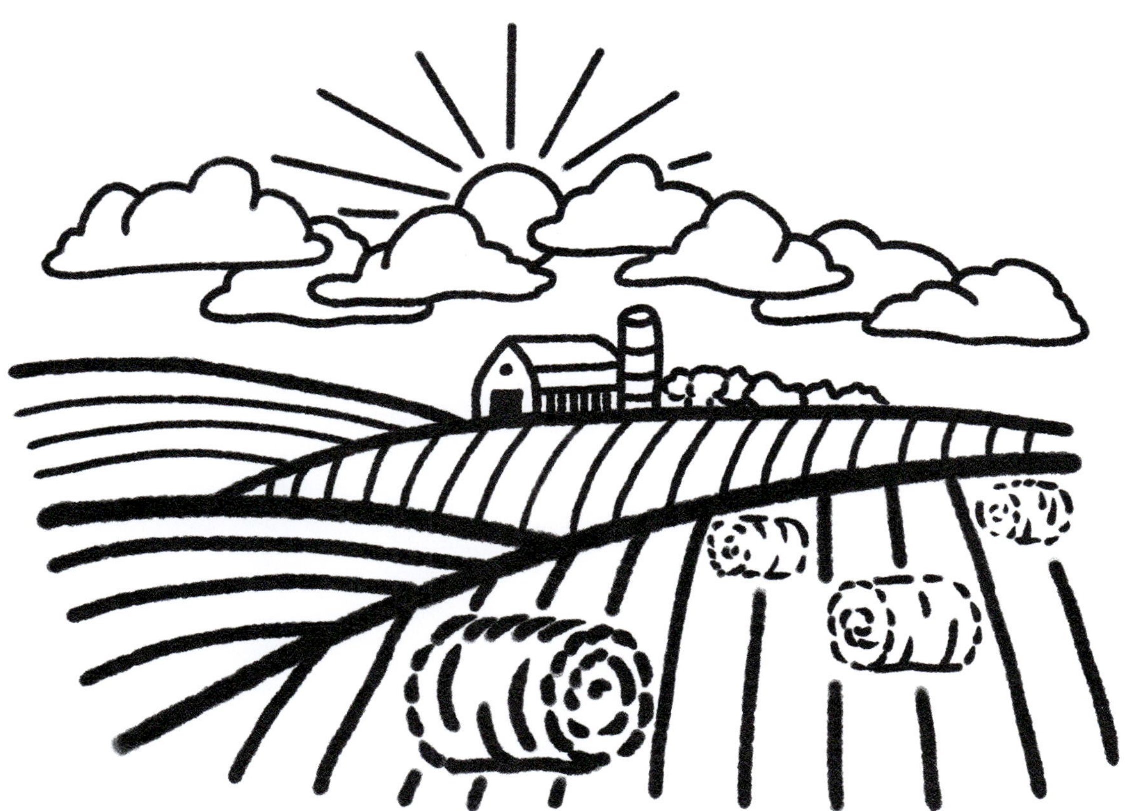

WHAT YOU NEED

Paper of your choice

Black pens in three sizes: 1.5, 05 and 01

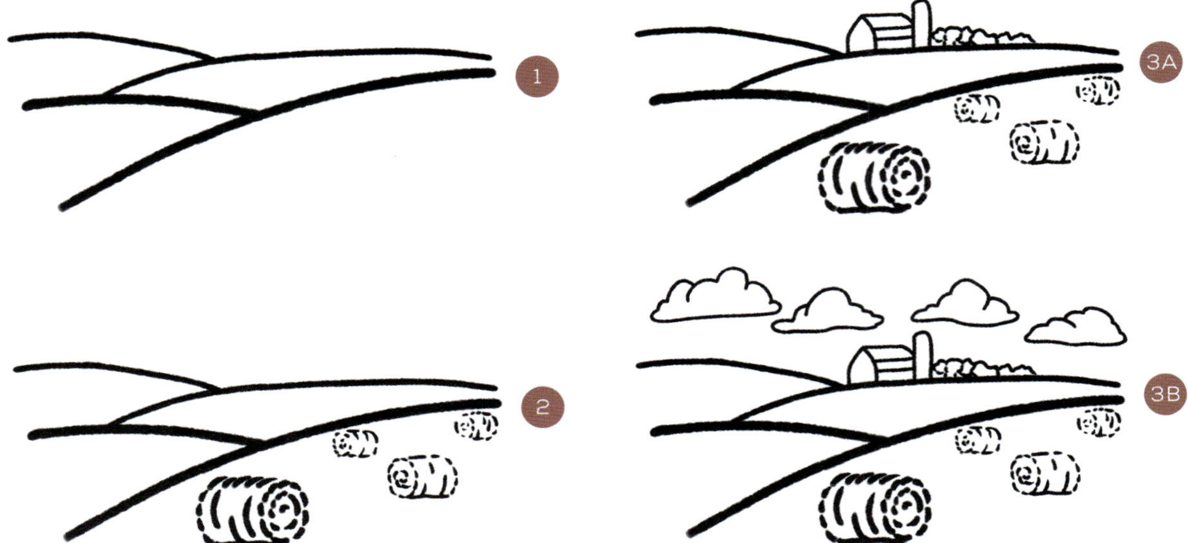

STEP 1

Draw diagonal lines to create a hilly landscape. The front lines should be drawn in thick (1.5) pen, the back in medium (05) pen.

STEP 2

Place the hay bales in the foreground. They were drawn with short curvy lines rather than a full outline to imitate the uneven straw surface. The biggest hay bale up front is done in medium (05) pen, the smaller ones farther back in thin (01) pen.

STEP 3

On to the background elements. Draw the farm buildings in the back with your thin (01) pen as well as the tree line. The trees are very undetailed due to the distance from the viewer. Some fuzzy shapes will totally work to suggest that these are trees—easy!

In the sky, draw the first layer of clouds. This is one of those situations where I tell you to start with the elements in front and work your way backward.

So, add more clouds behind the first layer. None of those clouds are fully visible; they are all partly hidden behind the front layer. All that is left now is the final element: the half-hidden circle for the sun as well as the sunrays. Here is a quick how-to for the sunrays if you want to get them to look nice but don't want to eyeball them:

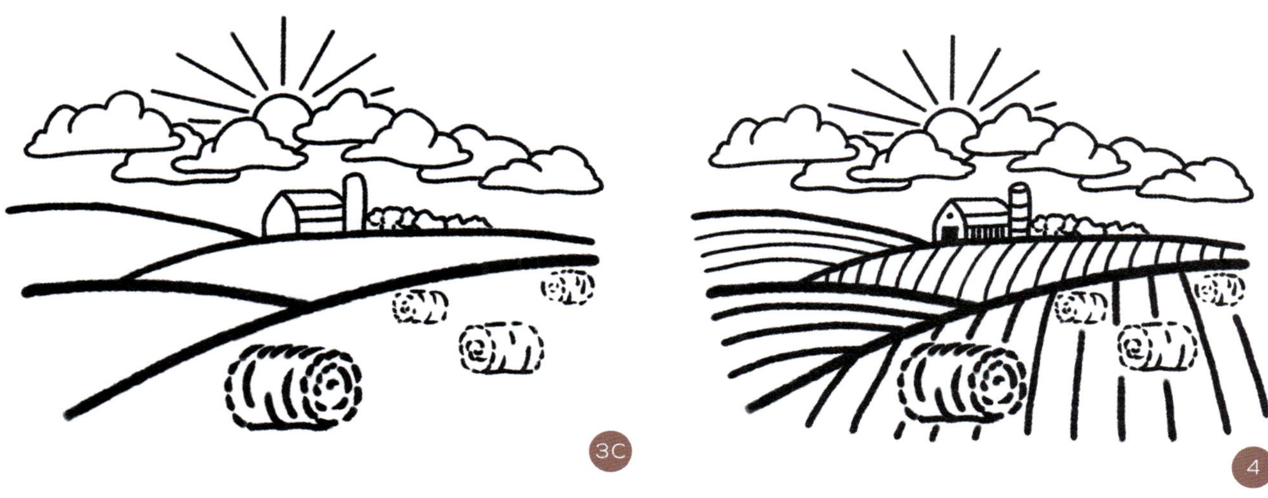

First, you need guidelines. All of the pencil lines intersect in one point; this is the middle of the circle that you draw as sun (that is, where you place the pointy end of your compass).

Around that first circle, draw one more. This is where your sunrays start with an even distance to the sun. (Skip this if you want to start your sunrays directly from the first circle.)

The basic guide would look like this:

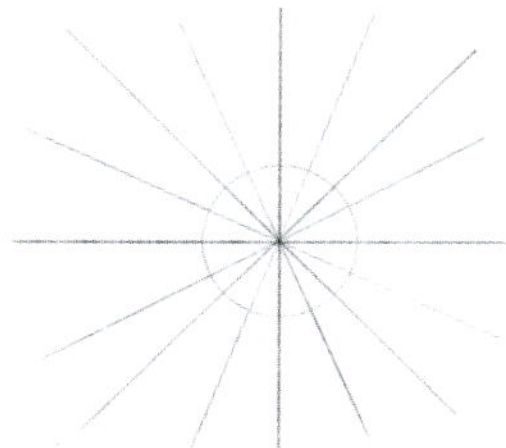

Now, you ink it. Here are some different options for sunrays:

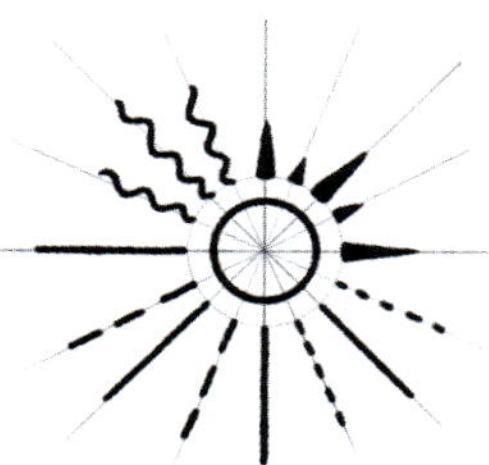

As the sun in the farm scene is only partly visible, so are the sunrays.

STEP 4

You're almost done now. As the last details, add lines for the furrows on the fields. In a medium (05) pen in the front, with a smaller (01) nib farther back. Also, finalize the farm buildings with a few details such as doors, windows and wood textures. Doesn't it look pretty?

FLOCK OF BIRDS SITTING ON POWER LINES

Fall is a beautiful season in the countryside. Nature puts on a good last show before hibernation. One of my favorite parts is watching birds gather to fly south. As the birds will be gone in the blink of an eye, don't bother with details and just paint them super tiny. You can work on your skills for some leafy textures with the greenery underneath the power lines. The power lines themselves will give you the opportunity to work on your perspective drawing skills once more.

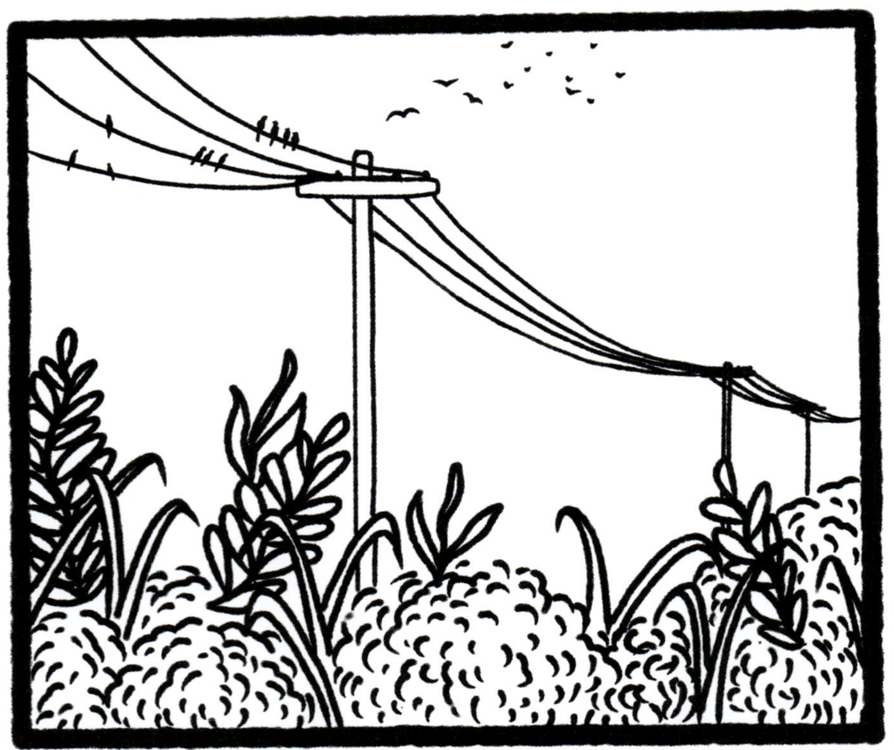

WHAT YOU NEED

Paper of your choice

Black pens in four sizes: 1.5, 05, 01 and 005 (alternative: super-sharp pencil)

Ruler

Pencil and eraser

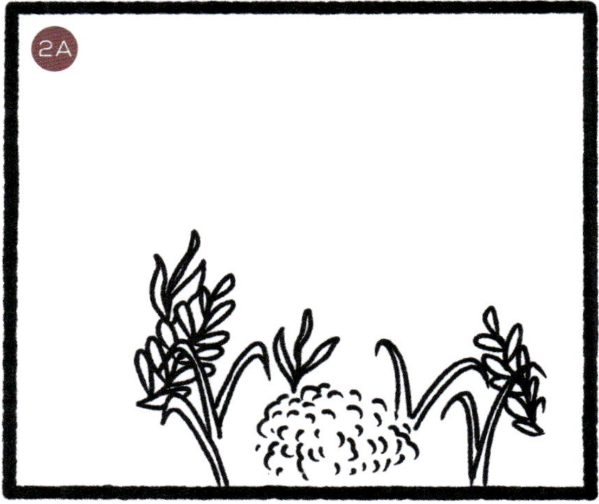

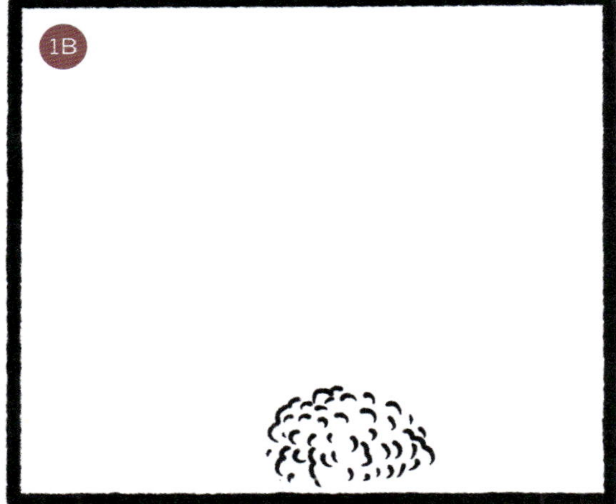

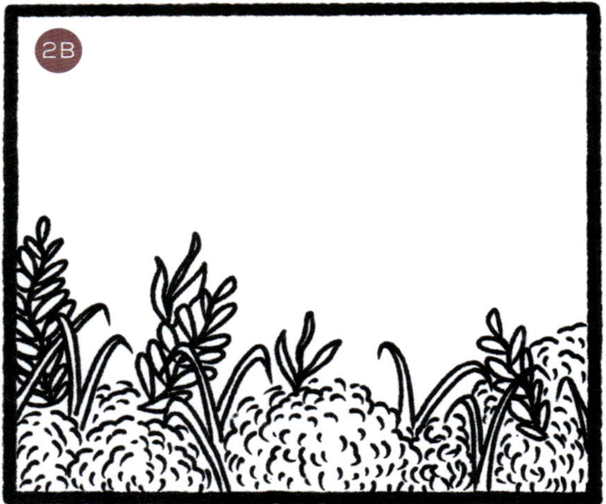

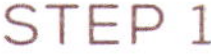

STEP 1

Start with a rectangle shape. Front and center, shape a small bush from short curved lines. From time to time, connect a couple of curves. The irregularity will make it look more natural.

STEP 2

Add more greenery around the bush. You can do some long grass blades and some different forms of leaves. Create some overlap between them to make it look like they are at different distances from the viewer. Refer to the Whale with Small Fish Friends project on page 64 for a more detailed demonstration.

Fill the spaces between the grass and leaves with more short and curved lines for additional bushes. Again, take care to sometimes connect a couple of lines together. In the end, it should look like dense foliage with leaves and grass poking through.

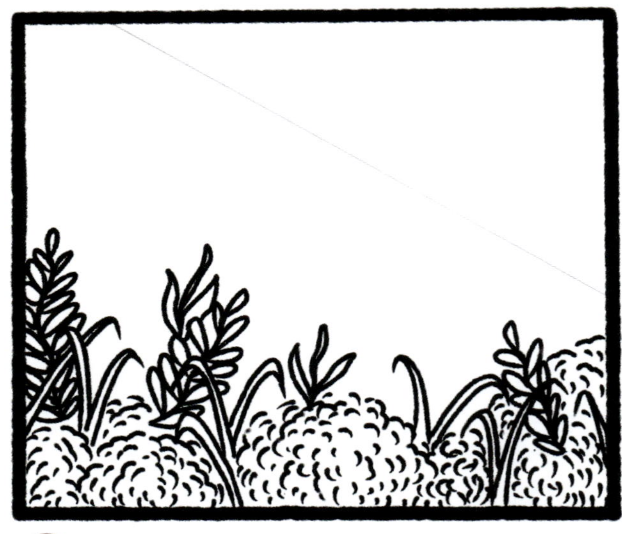

STEP 3

With pencil and ruler, draw the guidelines that will help you with constructing the power lines.

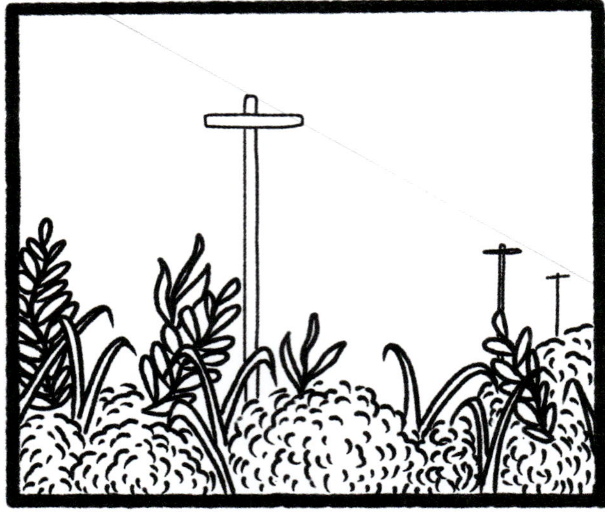

STEP 4

Time to draw the posts. The horizontal lines should be straight and parallel to the frame sides, and the crossbar on top parallel to the frame top and bottom. Make your posts more detailed up front and less detailed going backward. Using a thinner (005) pen nib or super-sharp pencil for the farther-away posts will make drawing them easier too.

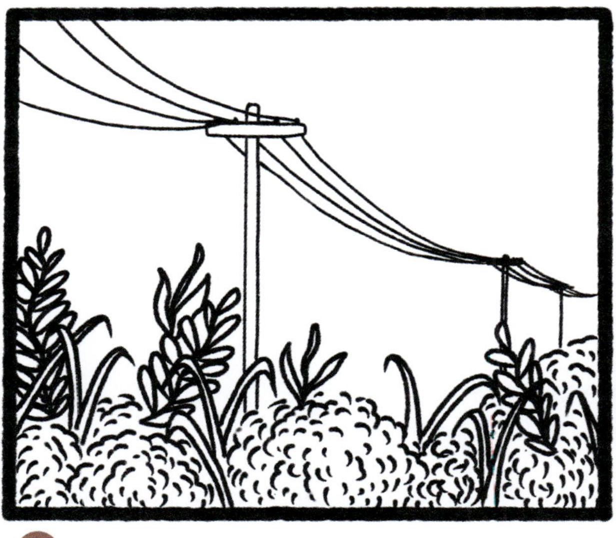

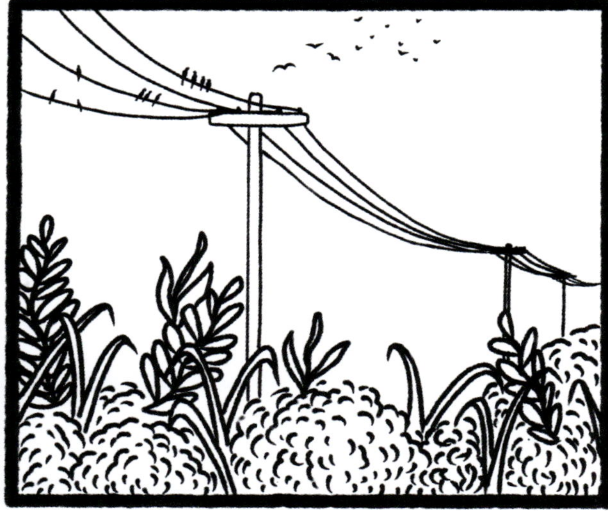

Let's add the cables. There is less space between the individual cables the farther back they are. In the end, it looks more like one entity rather than different cables. Try to create that slightly fuzzy quality that elements have where you can't see them clearly in the far distance.

STEP 5

Place tiny birds on the power line and tiny flying birds in the sky. Use a very fine (005) nib or a very sharp pencil and don't worry too much about details. The birds on the cables are little more than a tiny oval with a short line as a tail. The flying birds are tiny v- and m-shaped forms closer to the front and just dots when they are far away.

This was a difficult drawing. You're an absolute champ for finishing it!

HILLY LANDSCAPE WITH MUSHROOMS

Remember how I told you doodles help increase your creativity and increase the fun in drawing? I feel like we could use a break after that last ambitious drawing. If you have trouble coming up with ideas for your doodle, just pick one object out of your surroundings and draw it in different shapes, sizes and styles.

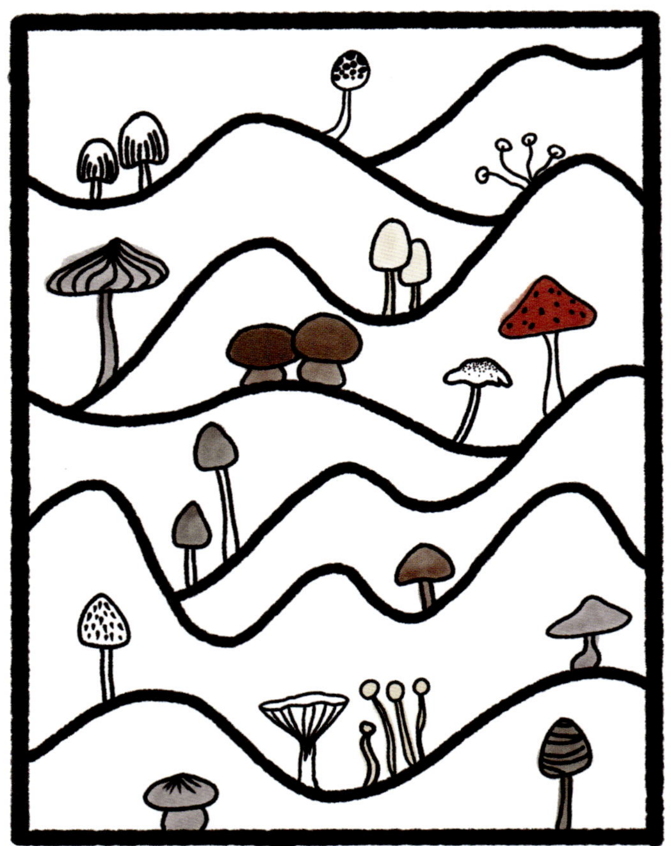

WHAT YOU NEED

Watercolor or mixed-media papers

Black pens in two sizes: 1.5 and 05

Color medium of your choice

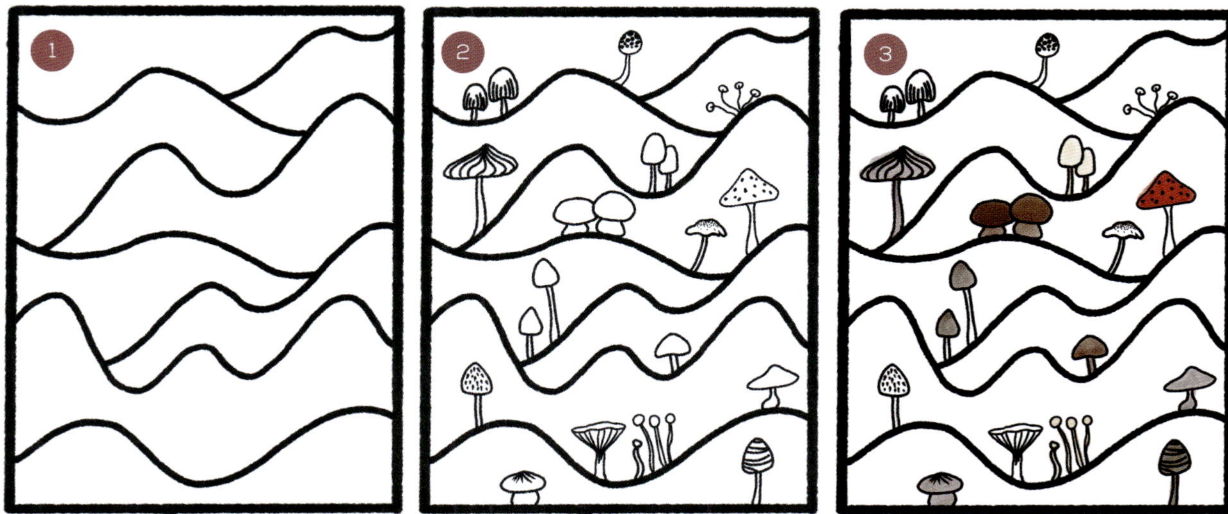

STEP 1

Draw a rectangle in the thick (1.5) pen. Inside your frame, lay down curving lines for the hills. Start at the bottom and work your way upward. There should be places where the lines run close to each other and areas with a bigger distance between them.

STEP 2

Where you have the space, draw different kinds of mushrooms with a thin (05) pen. You can do this in a doodle style, meaning you employ little detail. Here are lots of references for you:

The textures you put on the mushrooms do not need to be realistic. Use your imagination and create some new species if you wish. Note that some of the mushrooms (like the champignons on the third hill from the top) are outlines only.

STEP 3

And you have already reached the optional final step for this artwork! Add color to your liking. You could also add white details on the darker-colored mushrooms with a white pen. A toadstool springs to mind as the perfect species to apply this.

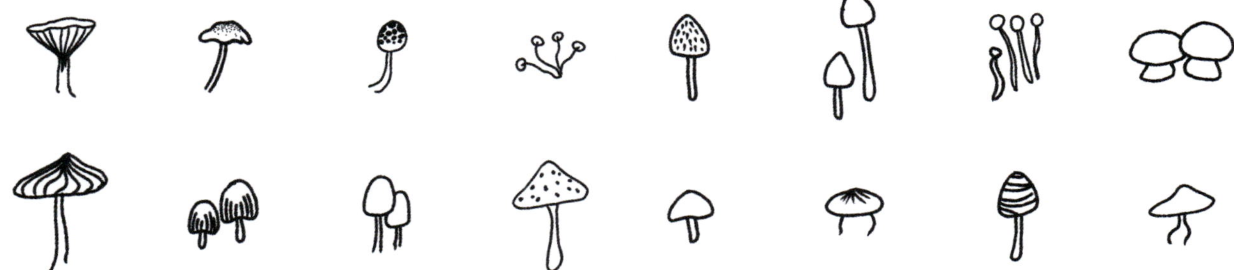

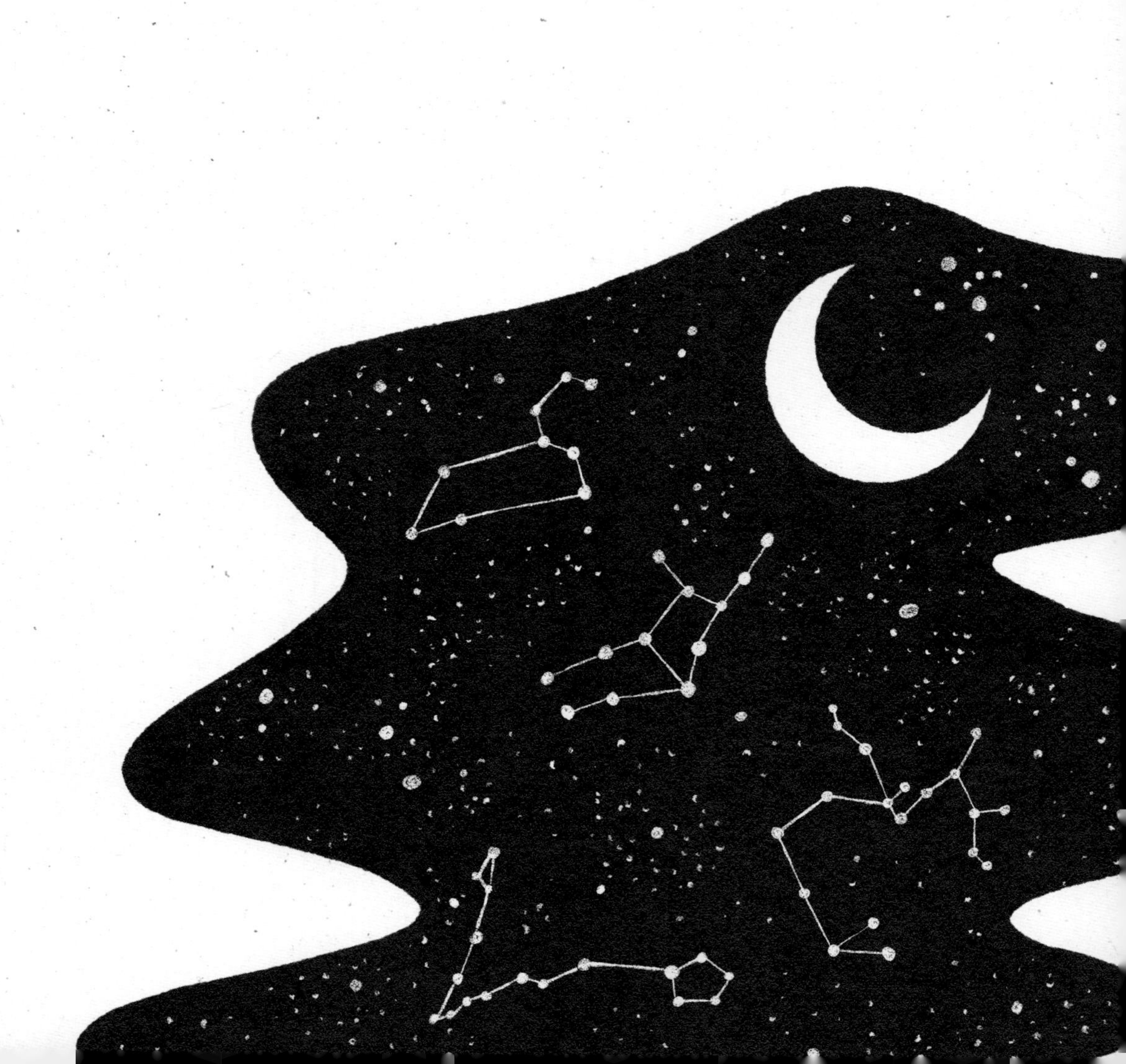

NIGHT AND DAY

Contrast is your friend when drawing in black and white. For the next group of drawing projects, I also chose contrast between day and night as the subject of the artwork. The sun and moon feature prominently and, in different versions, and you can re-create the cover artwork with the Mountain Scene in Day and Night (page 146).

This chapter is a little different than the previous ones. The projects have more than one frame and take about 30 minutes each to complete. They are all broken down into two parts. You can easily stop after 15 minutes and continue another day.

I used 8 x 11–inch (20.25 x 28–cm) sheets of paper for these projects, but the drawings themselves are a little smaller, around 7 inches (17.75 cm) in height.

MOUNTAIN SCENE IN DAY AND NIGHT

With this drawing, make sure you draw the day part on the top half of the paper. When you move on to the night scene part of the project, rotate your paper 180 degrees. With the night part, you want to give subtle hints that the world appears a little darker. Put more texture lines on the mountains and place them closer together to give the viewer an impression of darker surfaces.

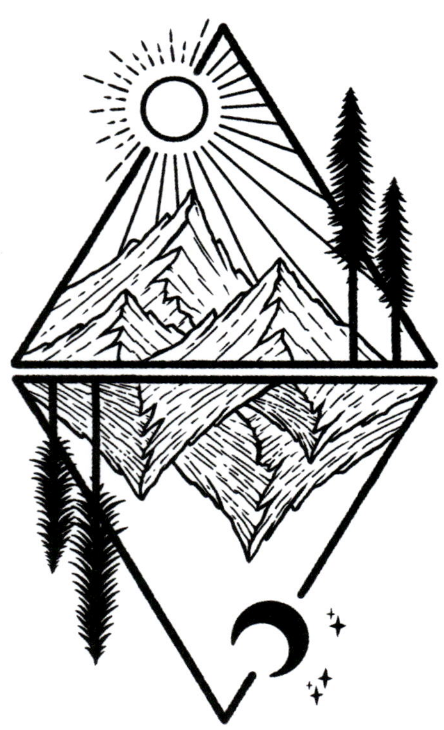

WHAT YOU NEED

Paper of your choice

Black pens in three sizes: 1.5, 05 and 01

Pencil and eraser

Ruler

Circle tool, compass or round objects to trace

Brush pen

White pen size: 08 (optional)

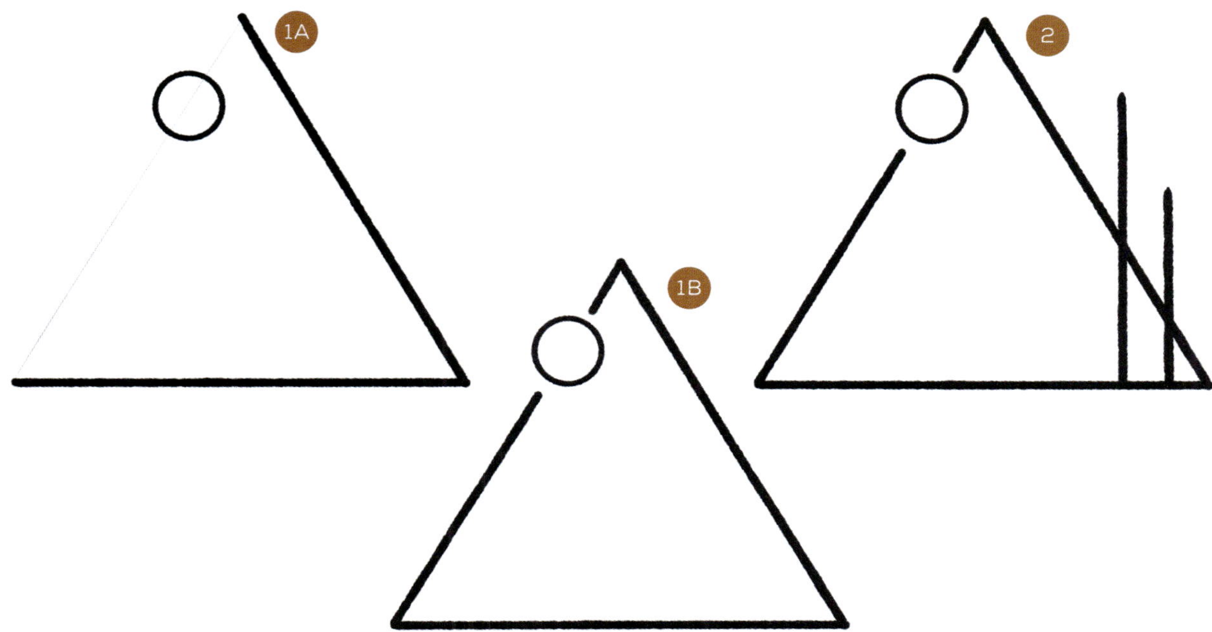

PART ONE: DAY DRAWING

STEP 1

Draw two sides of the triangle with the thick (1.5) pen, the third side in pencil. Using your compass and your medium (05) pen, place the small circle for the sun high up on the pencil line. Then, complete the third side in the thick (1.5) pen, leaving a gap between the line and the sun on both sides. Ensure your linework is dry and erase the pencil line. (For more detailed instructions on constructing a triangle, see the Rock Formation Landscape project on page 72.)

STEP 2

Now, use your thick (1.5) pen and ruler to add the tree trunks on the right-hand side.

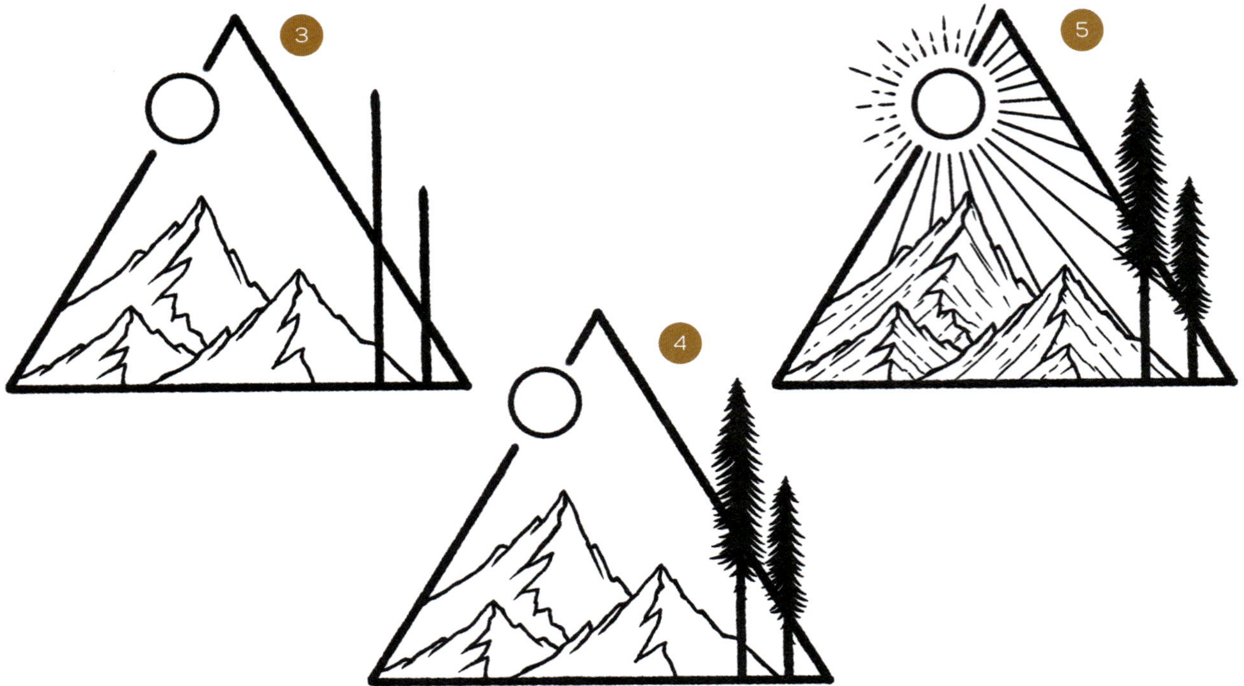

STEP 3

It's time for the mountain outlines in a medium (05) pen. Trace over your lines a second time and create some variation in the line weight. Accent some areas by making the line a bit wider there.

STEP 4

After finishing the mountain outlines, complete the tree branches with the brush pen. I also worked with my medium (05) pen on some of the branch tips. The Linework Basics on page 8 has more information on how to draw trees.

STEP 5

As the second-to-last step, draw the sunrays. You can use your ruler here and draw pencil guidelines in case you don't want to eyeball the distances between the sunrays. In the Small Farm Scene project on page 135, I explain in more detail how to set up pencil guidelines.

To finish the day part of the drawing, take up the thin (01) pen and add a few broken lines to the mountain slopes for a rocky texture. Note how a lot of these texture lines start on the tips of the jagged outline running down the center of the mountain triangles.

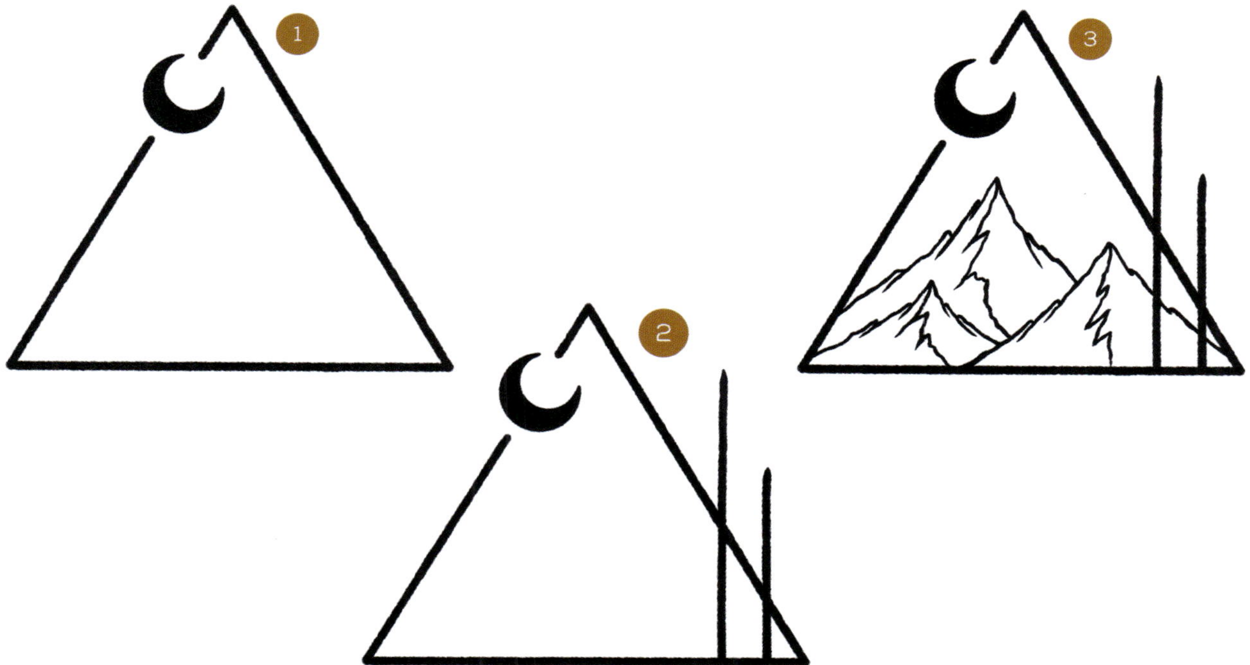

PART TWO: NIGHT DRAWING

Turn the paper with your day drawing 180 degrees. I recommend putting a piece of printer paper over the day part of your project to protect the artwork while you work on the night scene. That way you avoid accidentally smudging your lines. The process for this drawing will be similar to part one, so I'll keep the explanations to a minimum.

STEP 1

Draw the triangle frame and the crescent moon the same way you did in the day drawing.

STEP 2

Add the tree trunks with the help of your ruler.

STEP 3

Next, draw the mountain outlines. Trace over the lines again where you want to broaden the lines for some weight variance.

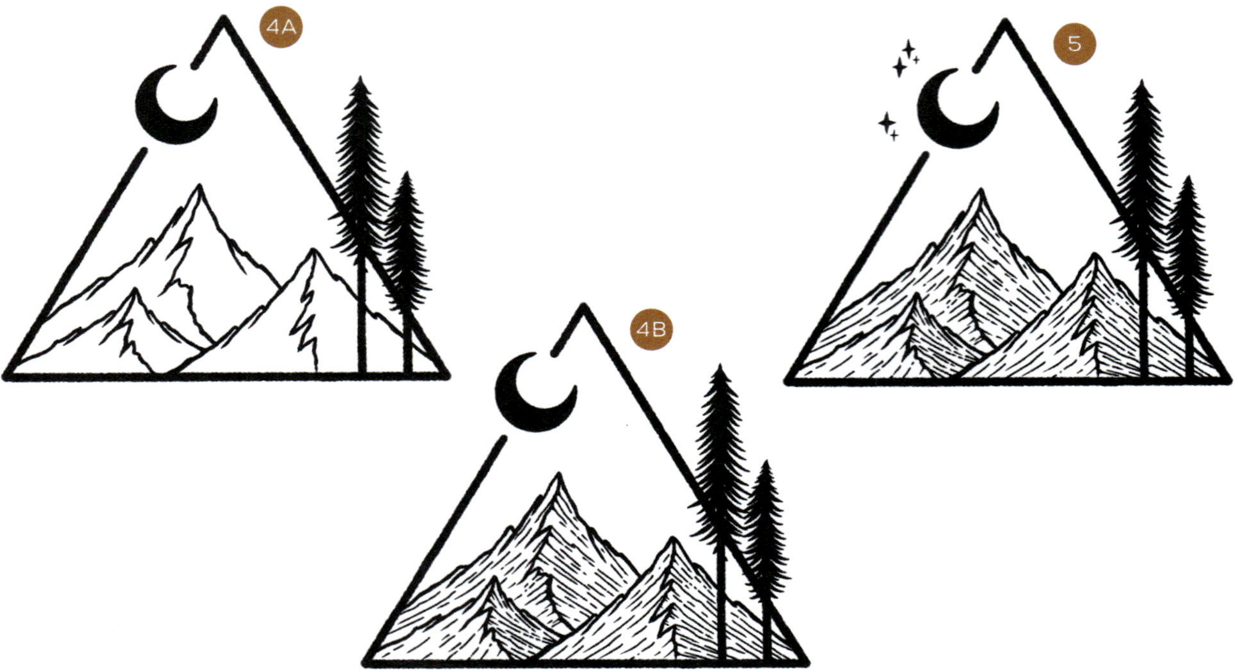

STEP 4

Complete the trees with the brush pen and the medium (05) pen.

Then, add lines to the mountain slopes for texture once more. I used more lines here and also put them closer together because I wanted the mountains to appear darker than the ones in the day drawing.

STEP 5

As the final touch, draw some stars on the outside of the triangle next to the moon.

You completed a large project. You rock!

SUN AND NIGHT SKY OVER A CABIN

The bottom of this drawing is a circle scene that you could also draw without adding the cabin smoke that creates the night part. As constellations for the night sky, I chose my family's star signs (big hint in case you need a last-minute gift for anyone and you can spare the time to draw it!). Once you read the final chapter in this book on how to compose your own landscapes (page 170), you will see all the compositions I stockpiled in this one: diagonal (mountains), as well as an S composition (sky) and radiating lines (sun).

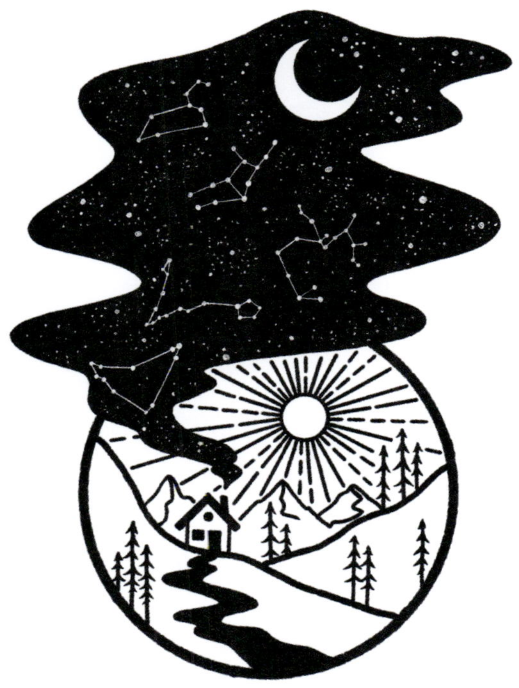

WHAT YOU NEED

Paper of your choice

Black pens in three sizes: 1.5, 05 and 01

Compass, circle tool or round object to trace

Brush pen or liquid ink

Medium round brush (size 3 or 4)

White pen in one size: 08

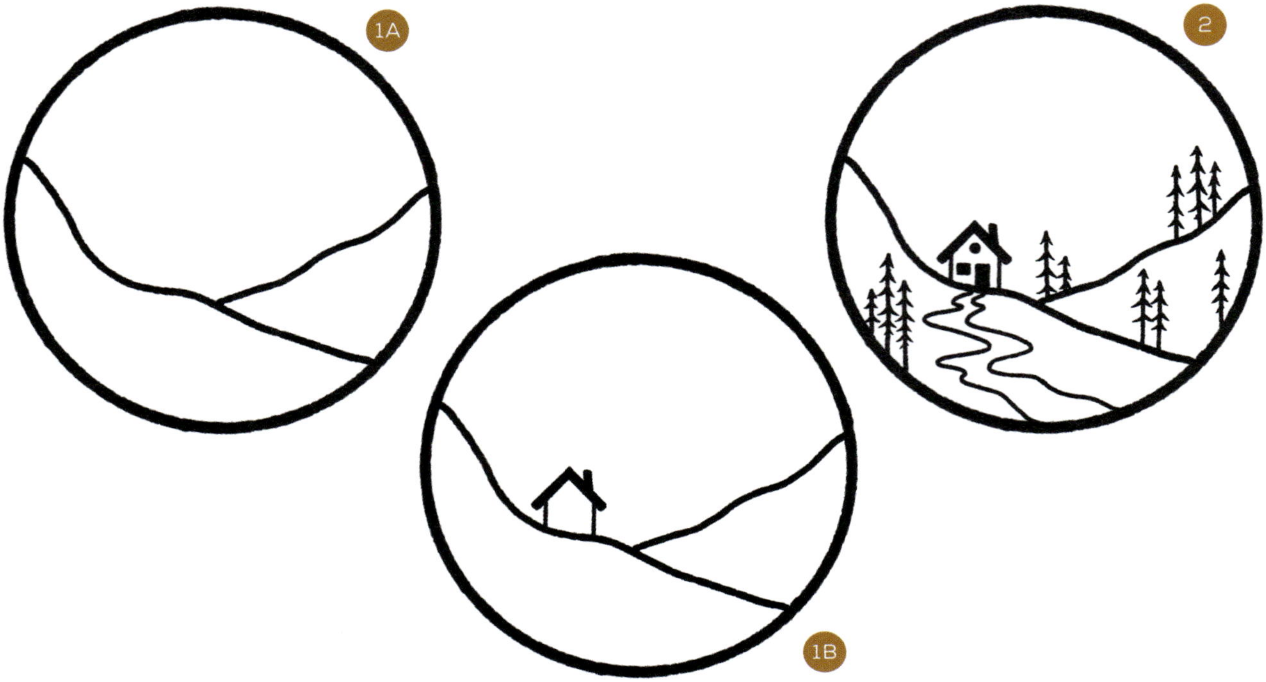

PART ONE: DAY DRAWING

STEP 1

Draw the circle frame in a thick (1.5) pen. Switch to the medium (05) pen to draw diagonal mountain slopes. I left a little "dent" in the left slope to easily place the cabin with the thin (01) pen. Important element of the cabin: the chimney!

STEP 2

Add a door and windows to the cabin and a meandering path leading up to the front door. You can also draw some trees on the mountain slopes at this stage.

Just a small comment on paths, roads or rivers leading into the distance: The way you draw them makes a big difference. Check out this picture:

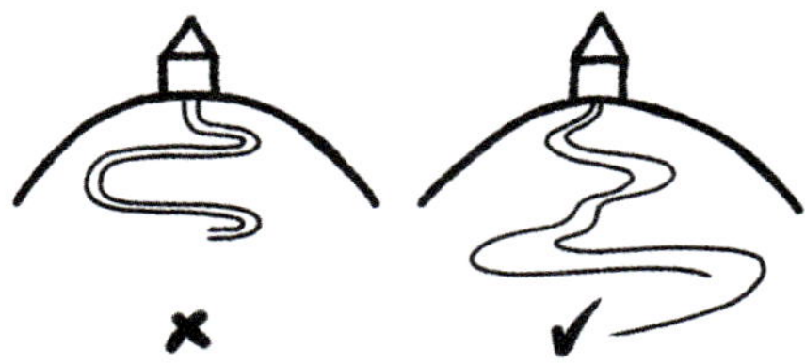

See how the left path looks very static because the lines run parallel to each other with the same distance? The one on the right creates way more interest in the way it leads the eye. It also creates a sense of distance by being wider close to the viewer and narrowing gradually farther away. (As with any drawing rule, there are exceptions and great examples that break them. But unless you are taking an intentional style decision to create a flat drawing, it's usually better to use the second option.)

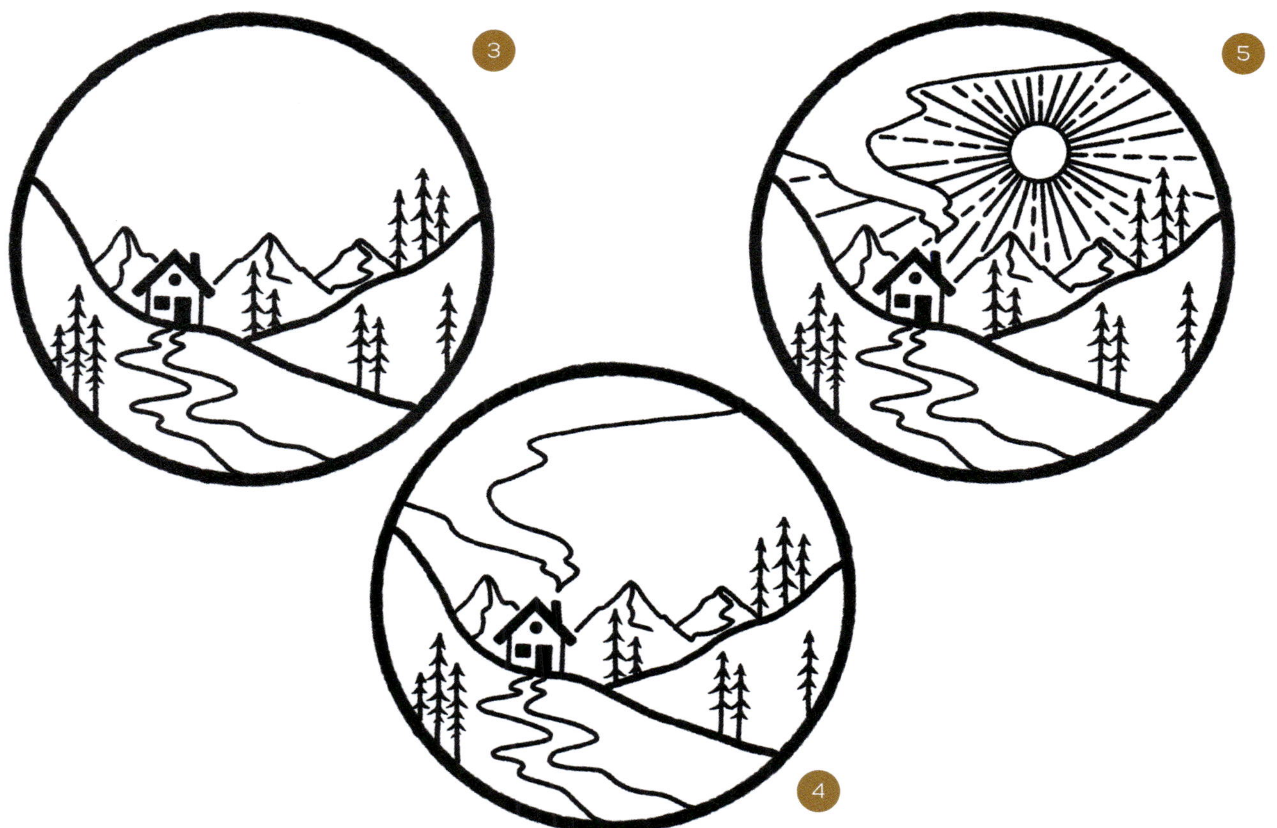

STEP 3

Move on to the background. Draw some mountain outlines in the distance.

STEP 4

You're ready to add the smoke coming from the cabin chimney. For the second part of this drawing to work, connect the smoke outline to the circle frame in two different places.

STEP 5

This is the last step for the day scene. Draw a circle for the sun and then the sunrays.

Check out the Small Farm Scene project on page 135 for help with the sunrays. I explain there how to draw pencil guidelines.

The next step is already part of the night drawing. If you need a break, now is a good time.

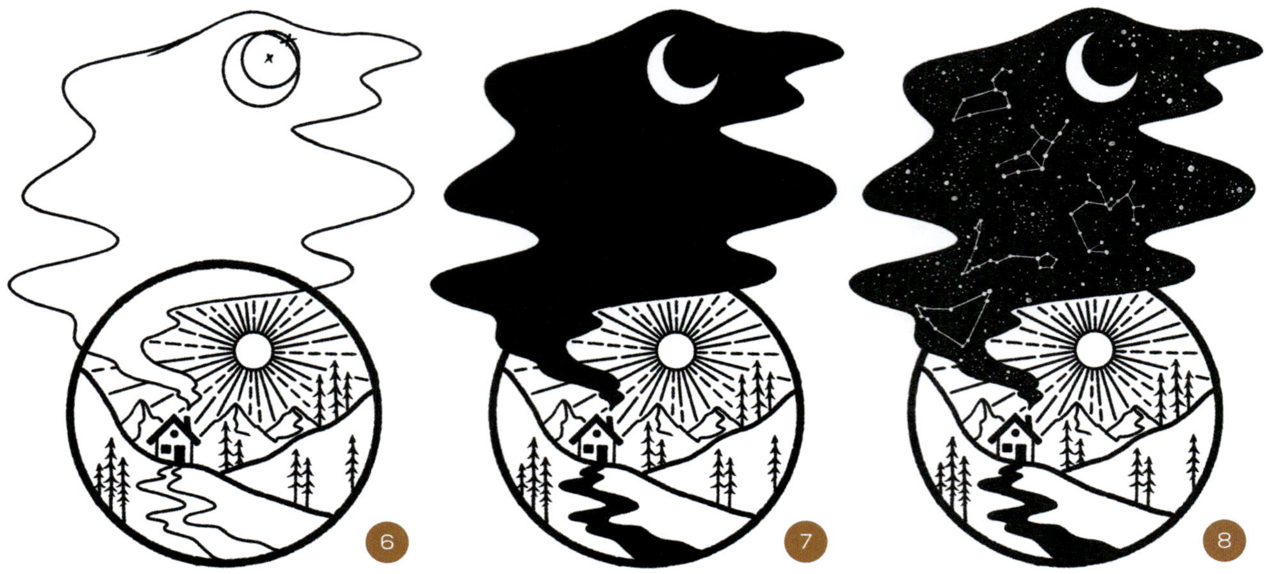

PART TWO: NIGHT DRAWING

STEP 6

Starting from where the cabin smoke meets the circle frame, draw a curvy line to complete a nice cloud of smoke. Then, draw the crescent moon using the trick I explain in the Van Life Night Scene project on page 22.

STEP 7

Fill in the smoke cloud with black to make the night sky. Also, fill the path leading up to the cabin with black.

STEP 8

It's time to draw the constellations you want to see in the sky. For the finish, add stars in white pen around them by drawing big and small dots all over the sky. (Note on gel pens: Sometimes the pens do not draw nice dots when you just touch them to the paper. You need to do a tiny circle to achieve that, as you then rotate the ball in the pen tip, distributing the ink. So, sometimes I simply embrace that my stars aren't perfect round dots. They aren't in space either.) You could also draw some stars on the pathway to the cabin if you wanted.

You have completed a big project now—be proud and do a happy dance!

SUN AND MOON REFLECTION OVER THE SEA

These day and night scenes work over any type of landscape really. I chose the sea here because it's easy and quick and creates a calming effect. If you want something with more detail, you can easily do a mountainscape, hills, dunes, sailboats, tents . . . try to draw what you see in your mind. The stacked curved lines you will use to depict the sea are built in the same way as in the Thunderstorm over the Sea project on page 44.

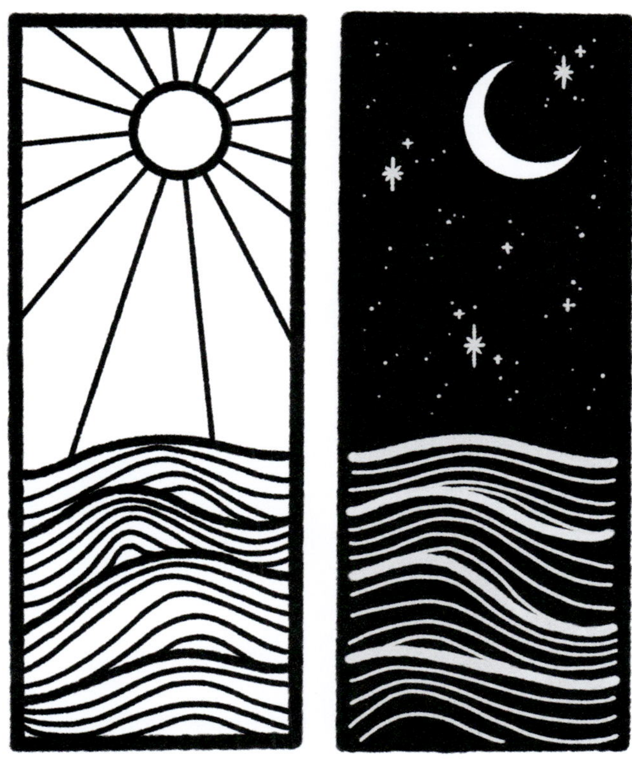

WHAT YOU NEED

Paper of your choice

Black pens in three sizes: 1.5, 0.5 and 01

White pens in two sizes: 10 and 08

Ruler

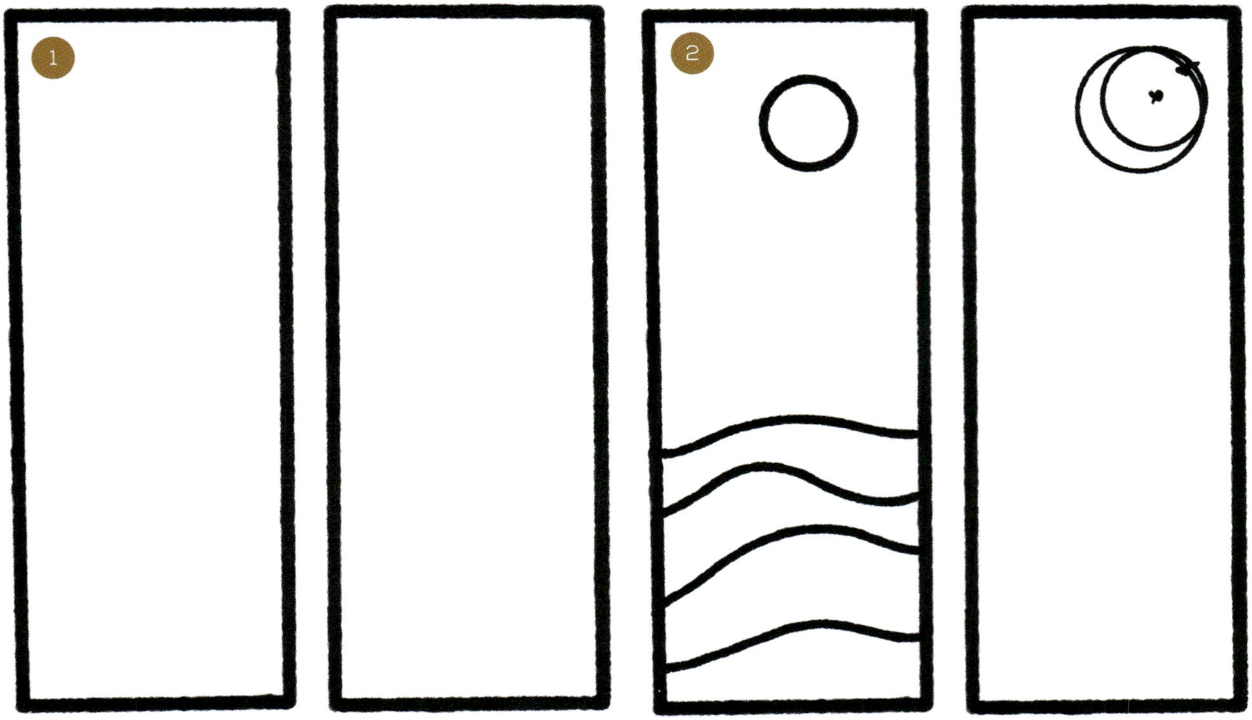

PART ONE: BASIC FORMS

STEP 1

Start by drawing two rectangles of the same size next to each other with the help of your ruler.

STEP 2

In the left rectangle, draw a circle for the sun and curvy lines to create waves for the sea. In the right rectangle, place a crescent moon. You can use the technique described in the Van Life Night Scene project on page 22, as all of that rectangle is going to be black.

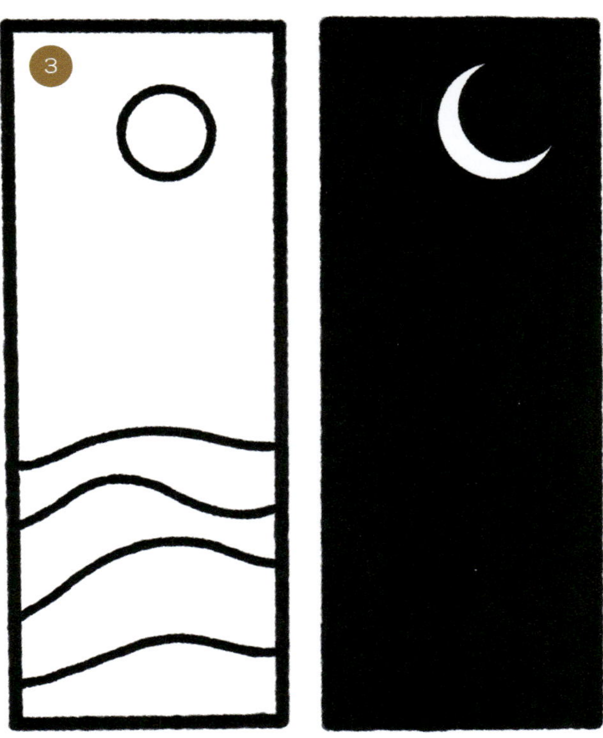

STEP 3

Fill in the night scene (right-hand rectangle) completely with black.

You have reached the halfway point on this project. Feel like taking a break?

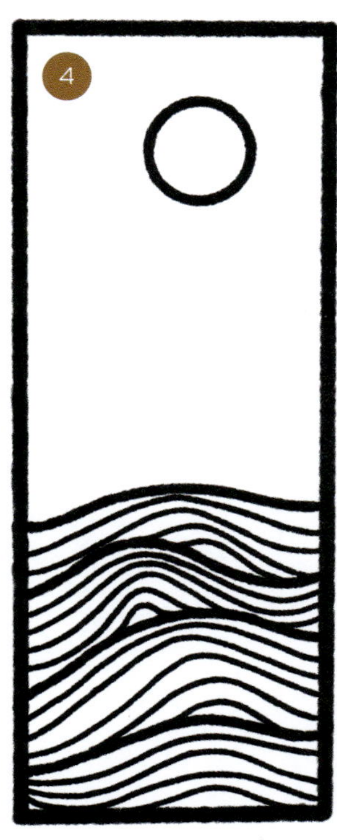

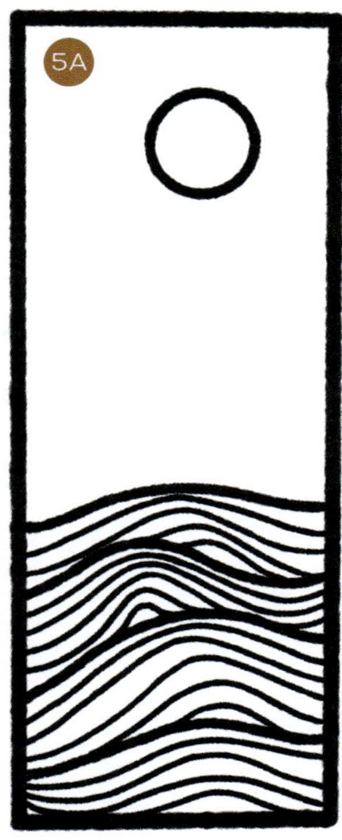

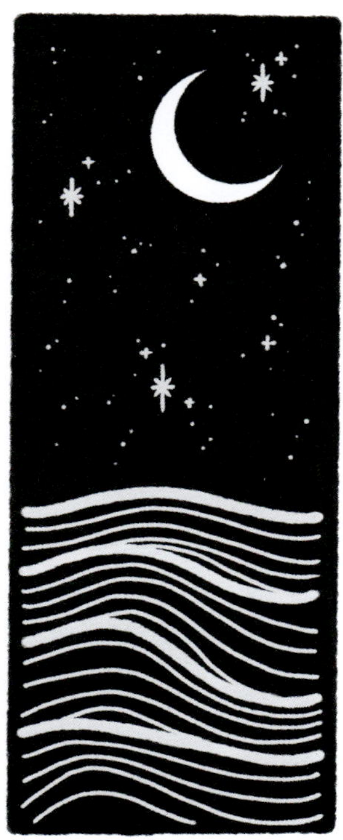

PART TWO: LINEWORK

STEP 4

In the day scene, add thin lines to create movement in the waves using your thick (01) pen.

Repeat the process for the night scene. First, draw lines with your thick (10) white pen and then add thin (08) white lines inside. You should now have scenes similar to the above illustration.

STEP 5

To finalize this project, draw sunrays in the day scene. The night scene gets some stars for the sky.

Nice work with this day and night scene!

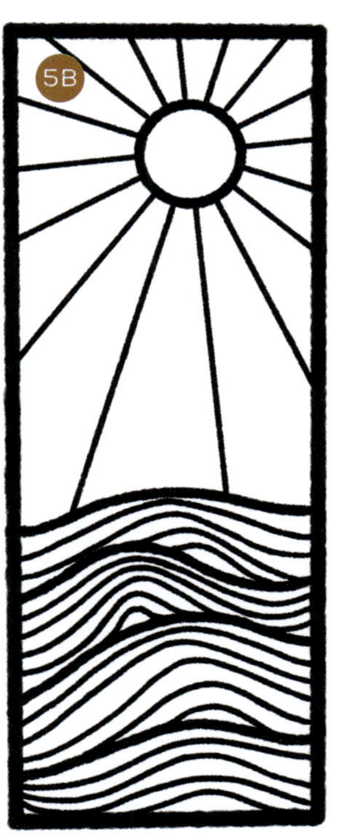

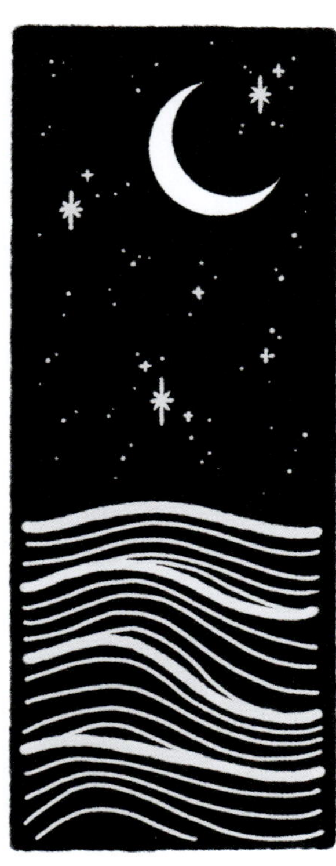

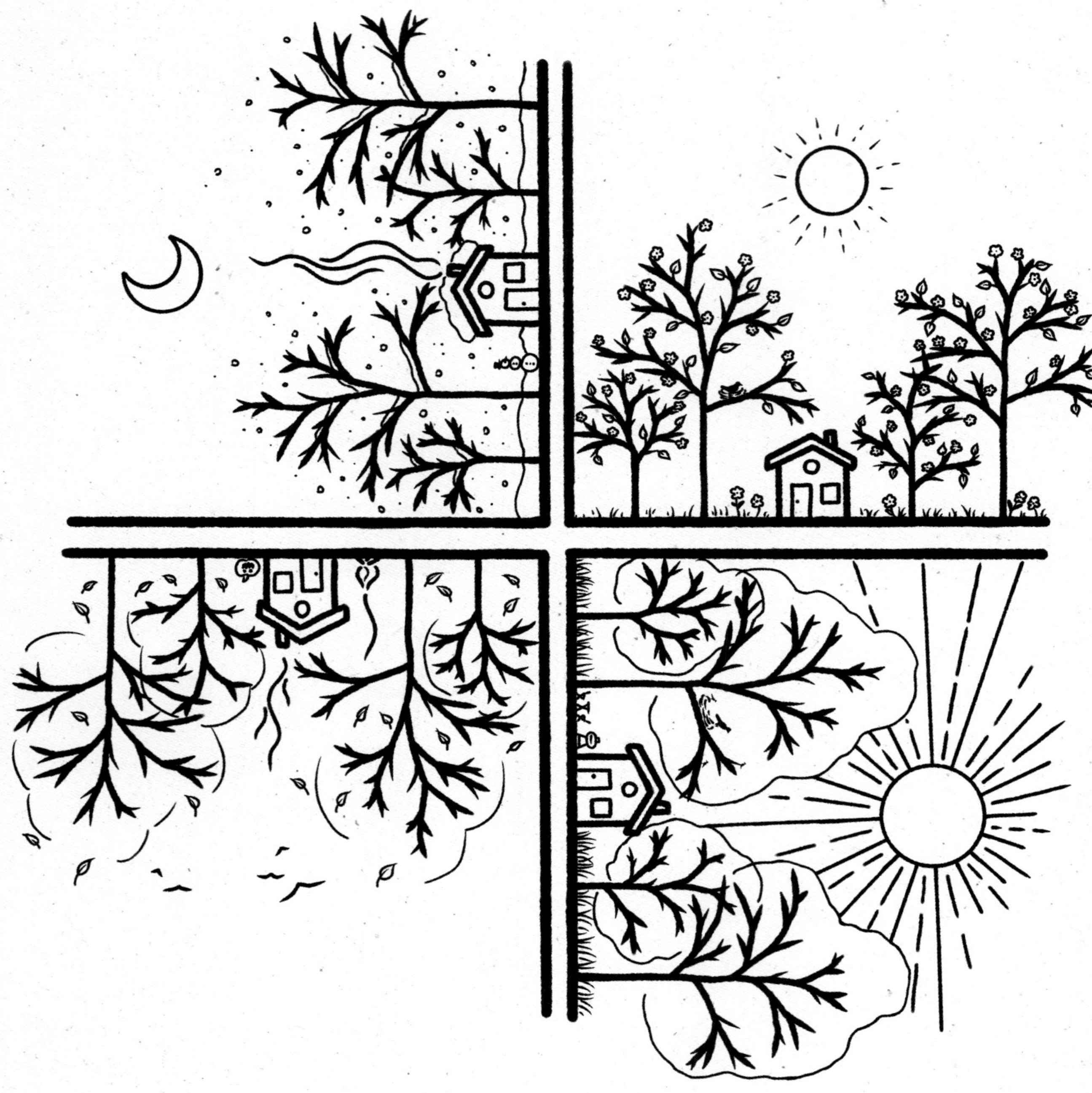

THE SEASONS

Like photographs, drawings capture a moment in time. When you draw the same landscape at different times of day, month or year, your drawing will be different each time, even if the subject of the work will remain the same. This project is based on the idea of change and how to show this to the viewer.

This drawing will challenge your creativity by using the same basic scene and changing it with different elements for each of the seasons. The viewer can turn the paper in any direction. My suggestion is to have the current season the right way up. I cut my sheet of paper into a square for this so it looks nice. It's the last and largest project in the book and it should take between an hour and a half and two hours overall. You can break easily after drawing the base scene and after each segment so the work can be stretched over several drawing sessions.

BASE DRAWING

All seasons are based on the same scene: a cabin surrounded by trees. You will use the base drawing four times, rotated by 90 degrees each time. If you have a light box, this will make the following process a lot easier. A glass table works, too, if you put a light underneath it. Otherwise, bright windows always work.

To get the basis for all seasons as similar as possible, I completed one base drawing on a separate piece of paper and taped it to my window with painter's tape. (This is important—don't use regular sticky tape! It damages your paper when you pull it off, even if you are super careful. Washi tape works, though.) Then, I taped my drawing paper on top, aligning it so that I could draw the spring quadrant first with enough space for the others. Then, I copied the scene. Peel off the paper, rotate it by 90 degrees and align it neatly, then tape it back on. Copy the base scene again. Rinse and repeat twice more.

You then have the basis for adding the seasonal details.

Of course, you don't need to go through that trouble. If you prefer to have more variation in your scenes, just draw a new base for each season and you spare yourself the copywork.

WHAT YOU NEED

Paper of your choice

Black pens in three sizes: 1.5, 05, 01 and 005 (optional)

Ruler

Painter's tape

Light box or window

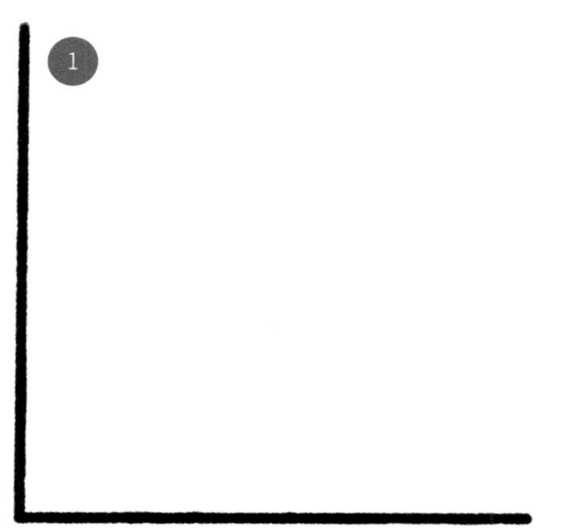

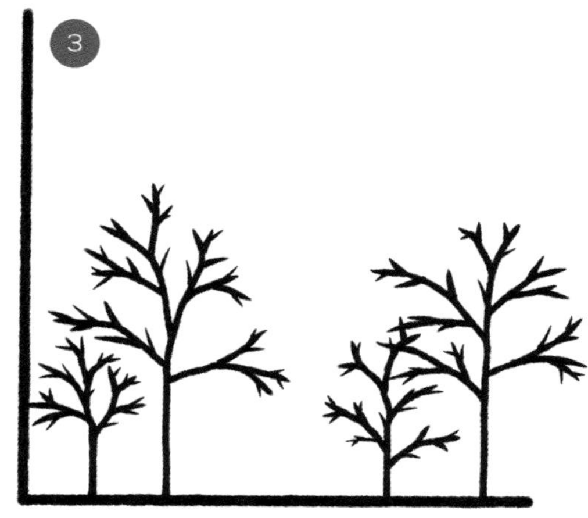

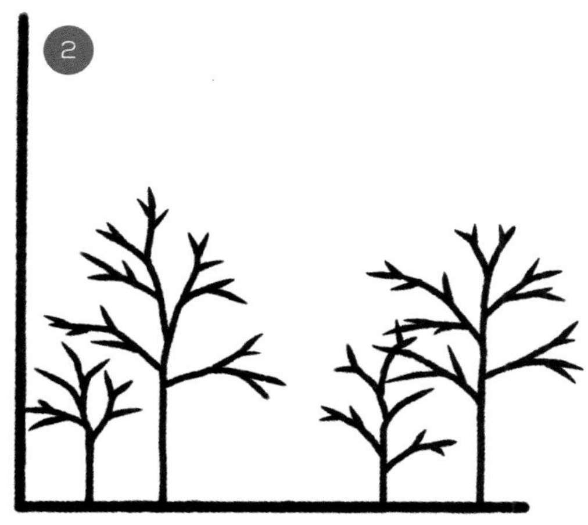

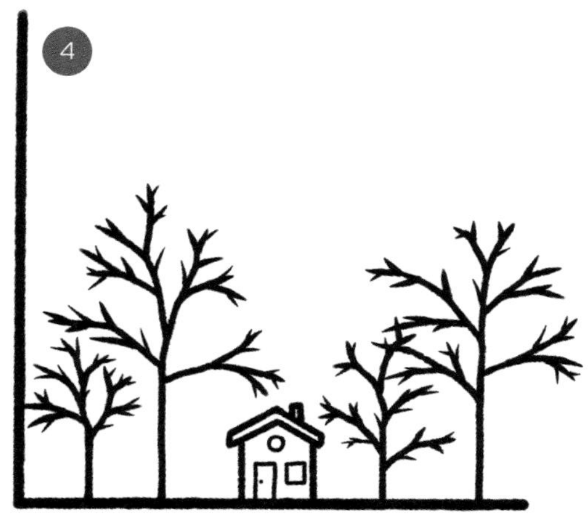

STEP 1

Draw half of a square in your (1.5) pen.

STEP 2

On the baseline, place four trees but leave some space in the middle in your (05) pen.

STEP 3

Add more detail to the tree branches in your (01) pen.

STEP 4

Place the cabin in the middle. Draw the outlines in your (05) pen, and use the (01) pen for the door and windows.

Overall, you don't need to add a lot of detail yet. The elements for each season will fix that slightly bland look the drawing has right now.

SPRING: CABIN SURROUNDED BY BLOOMING TREES

It's time to add details to our spring scene (all steps will be done with our [01] pen). Take a few moments to think about the small things that always give you a hopeful feeling after a cold winter, and show you that nature is waking up again. For me, it's young leaves and grass stalks, blooming trees, birds singing again and the first sunlight. Let's get started!

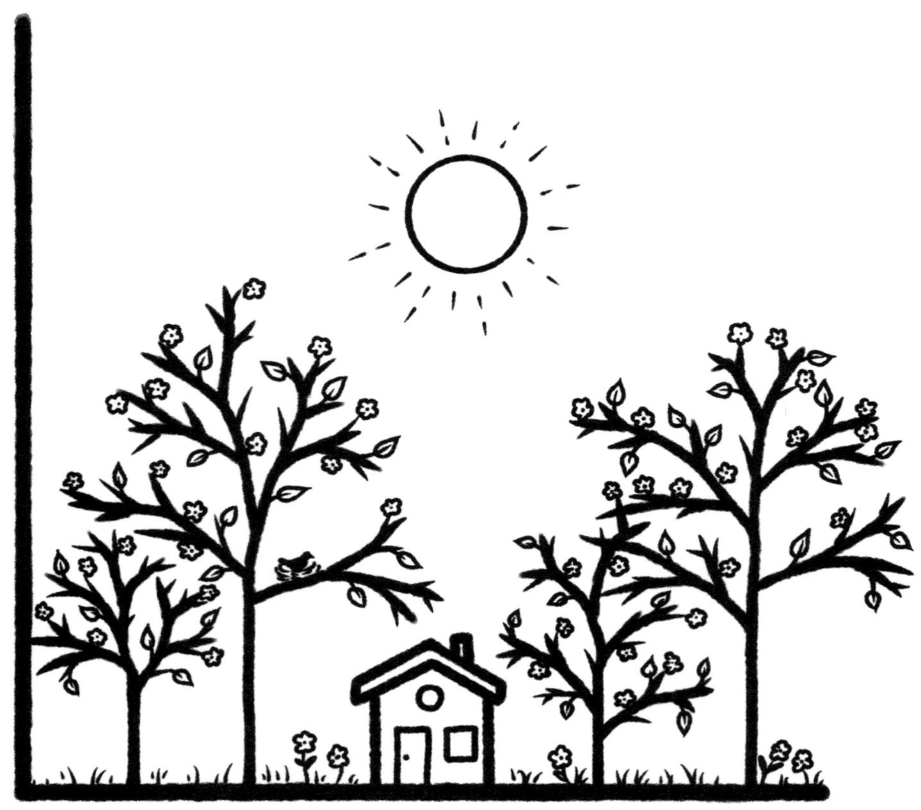

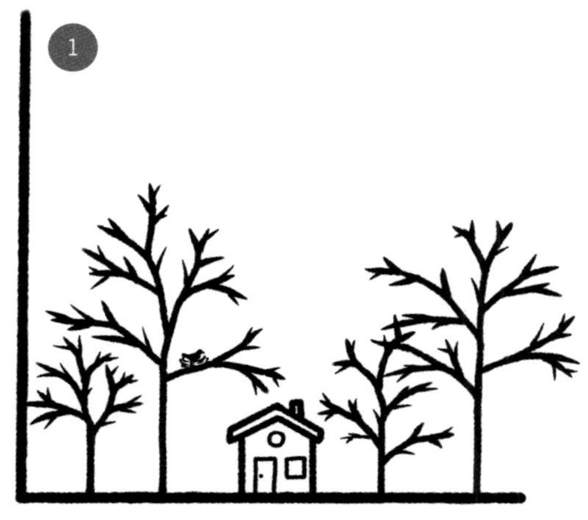

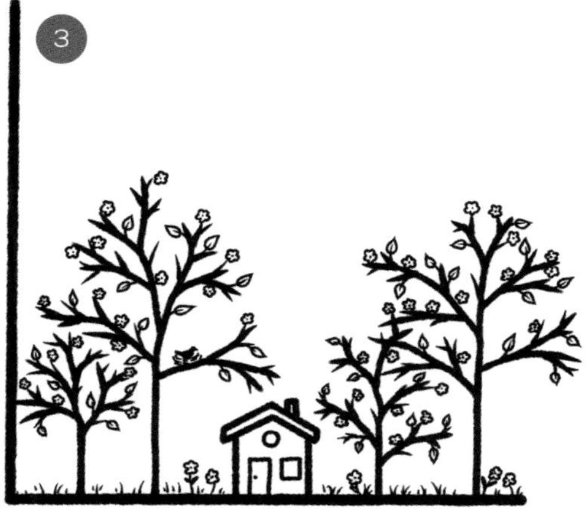

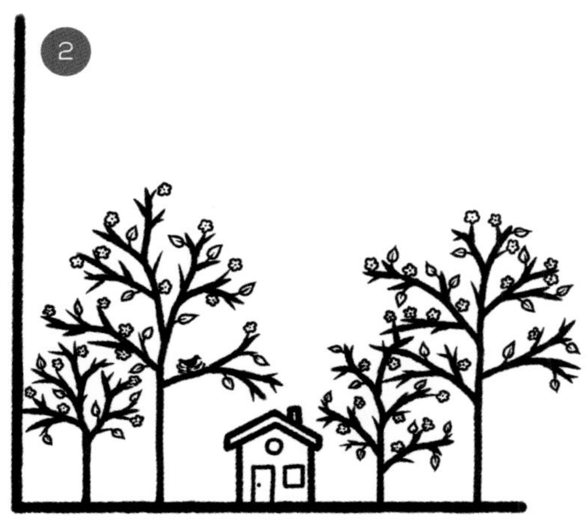

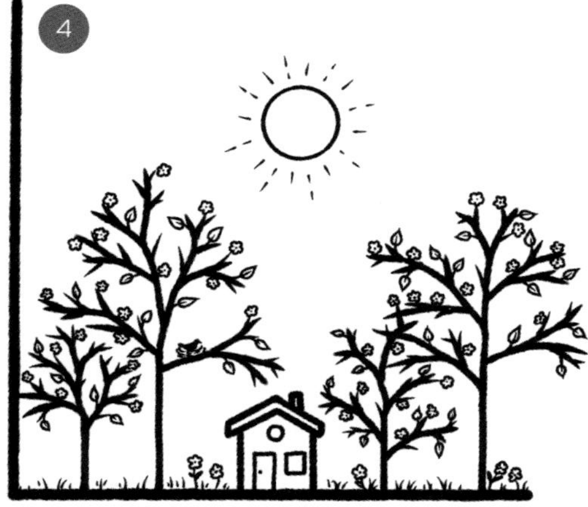

STEP 1

In the largest tree, draw a bird's nest. As it's spring, the bird mama is brooding. Add her sitting in the nest.

STEP 2

In the next step, add small leaves all over the trees. Then, repeat the process with tiny blooms.

STEP 3

Below the trees, draw short lines for grass and put some tiny flowers in the grass.

STEP 4

As a last element, draw a circle for the sun and some fine sunrays around it. Because the sun is not strong yet, I used a thin (01) pen for the rays to bring that across.

SUMMER: SUNNY PATCH OF LEAFY TREES

Moving on to summer. It's the best season for a lot of people. Use the details you added in spring and consider how they might develop from season to season. Think of your favorite summer activities and add them to the drawing. Who wants to join me for an afternoon barbecue?

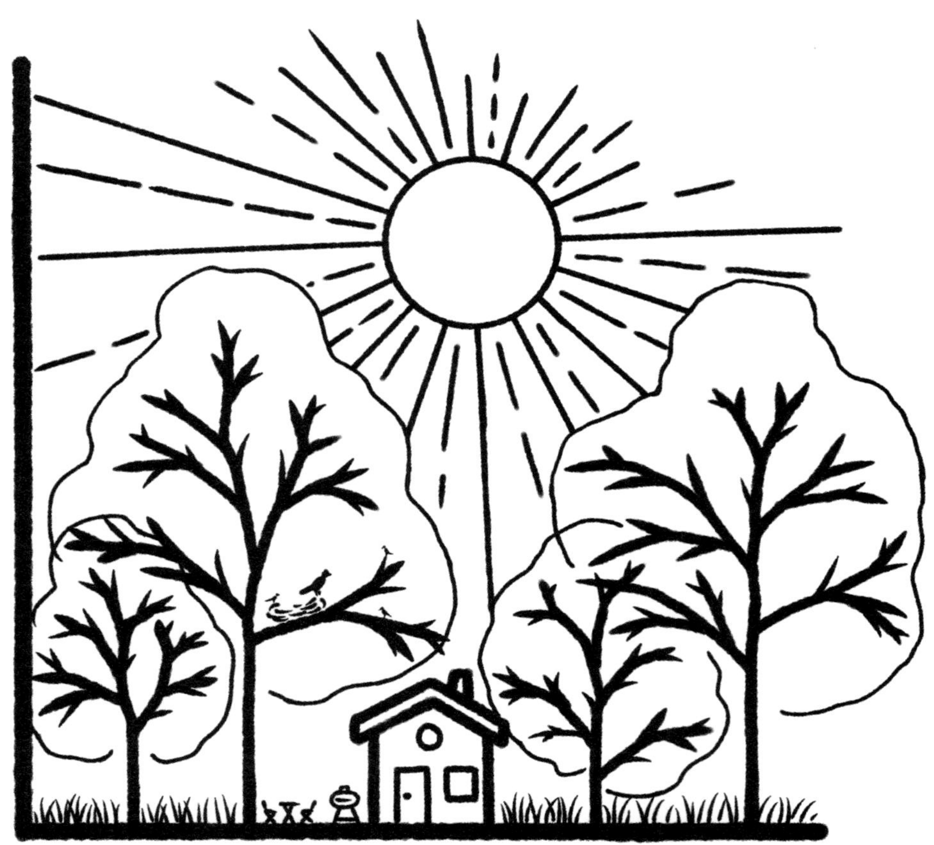

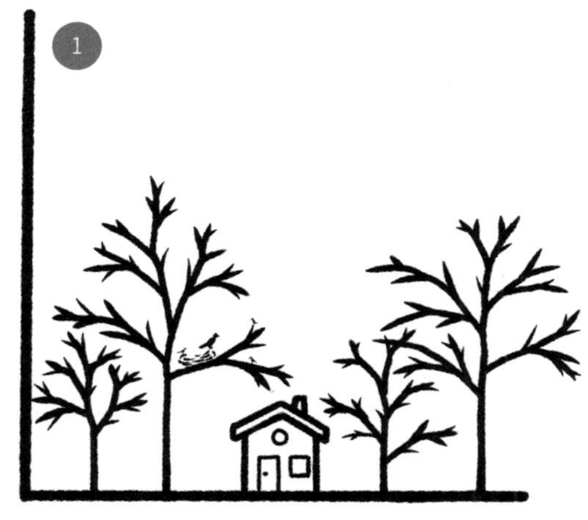

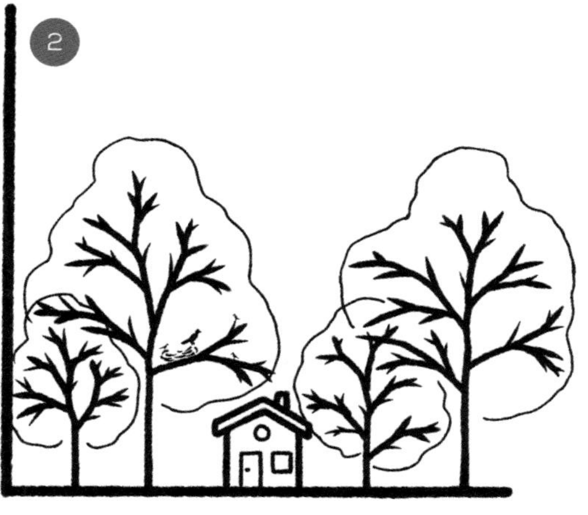

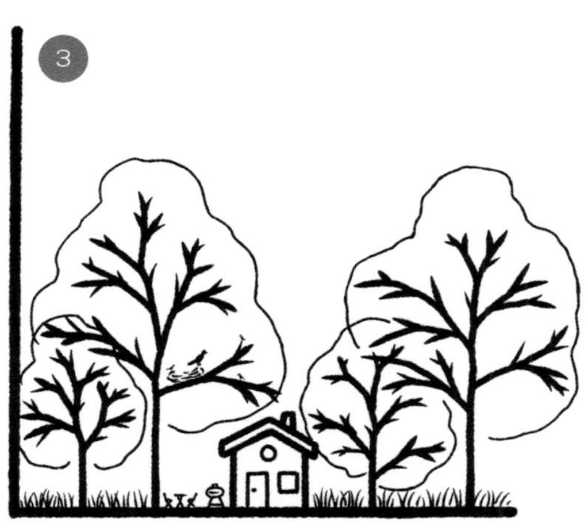

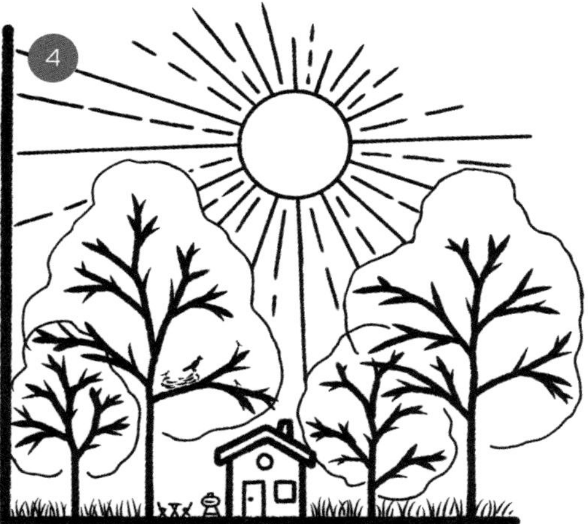

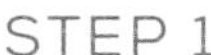

STEP 1

It's summer and the little birdies are ready to leave the nest. That's why I added them on the rim of the nest and on nearby branches together with their watchful mama. If the (01) pen feels too big for the baby birds and you have a (005) pen, this is the perfect time to bring it out. If not, you could also use a very sharp pencil.

STEP 2

Draw the canopy for each of the trees with a thin (01) line that surrounds the branches.

STEP 3

The spring grass has grown and is now much longer and denser. The cabin inhabitants have placed a picnic table and a barbecue outside in the garden. I think they forgot the fairy lights.

STEP 4

In summer, the sun is much stronger. A larger circle and clear sunrays showcase that.

AUTUMN: TREES AND FALLING LEAVES

Time to cozy up with hot tea or hot chocolate—autumn is here!

There are a lot of details to play with when you think about the changes in nature and autumn traditions.

Birds gathering to fly South is one of my favorite things about autumn, so of course I included this into the scene.

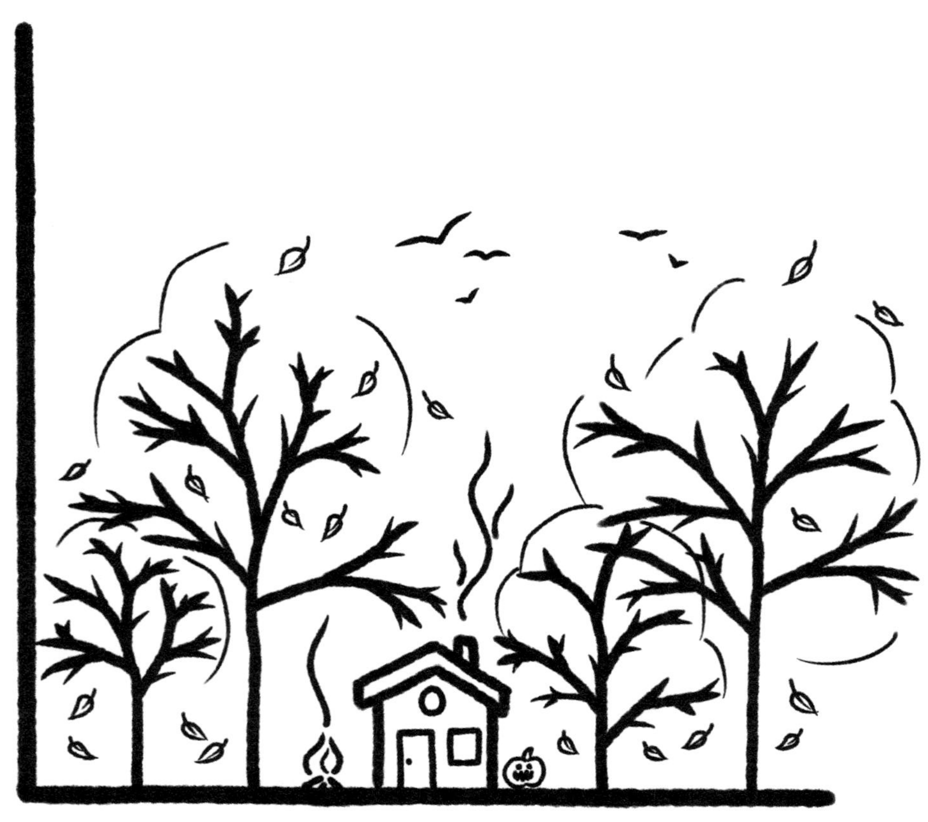

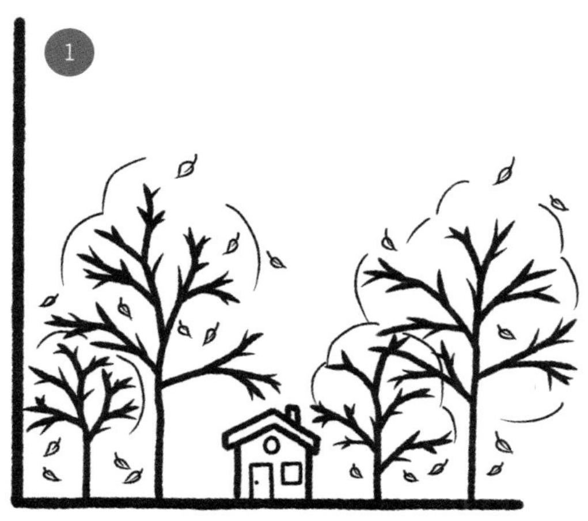

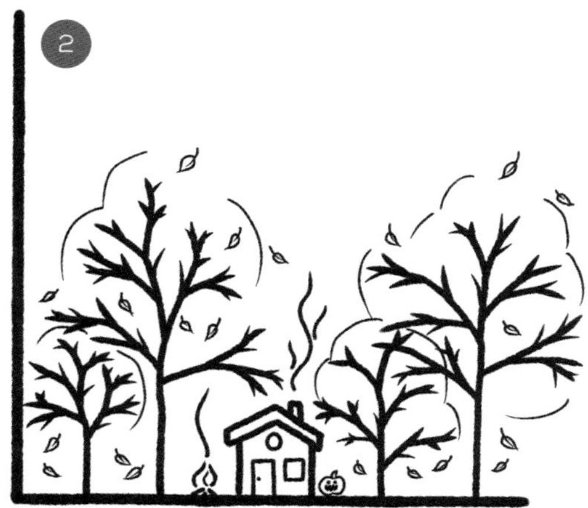

STEP 1

It's fall. And not a golden fall day but a windy one. Draw broken lines for the tree canopies to show that the foliage is not as dense as it was in summer. Add leaves flying in the air and falling toward the ground. Here is a small tutorial:

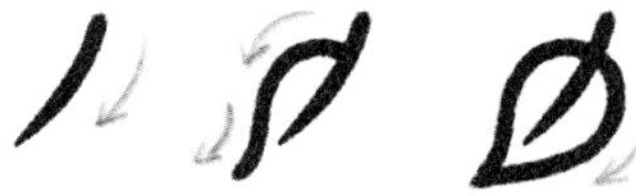

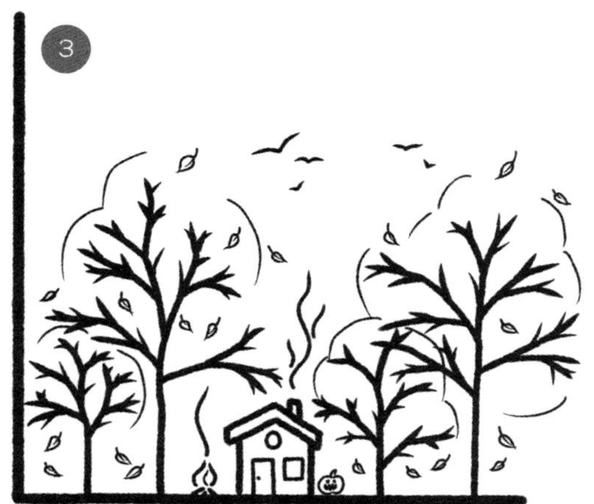

STEP 2

Our cabin inhabitants have a fire going and the Halloween pumpkin is in place too. Trick or treat!

STEP 3

Our bird family flies south before the first snow. Add them in the sky above the trees using curved V shapes.

WINTER: SNOWY TREESCAPE

The year is coming to an end—let's add winter details to our cabin scene! Snow is mandatory here, and you can play with other small details—holiday traditions and decor can feature in this scene for a very personal touch. And for the outdoor lovers: winter activities make a great addition to the scene.

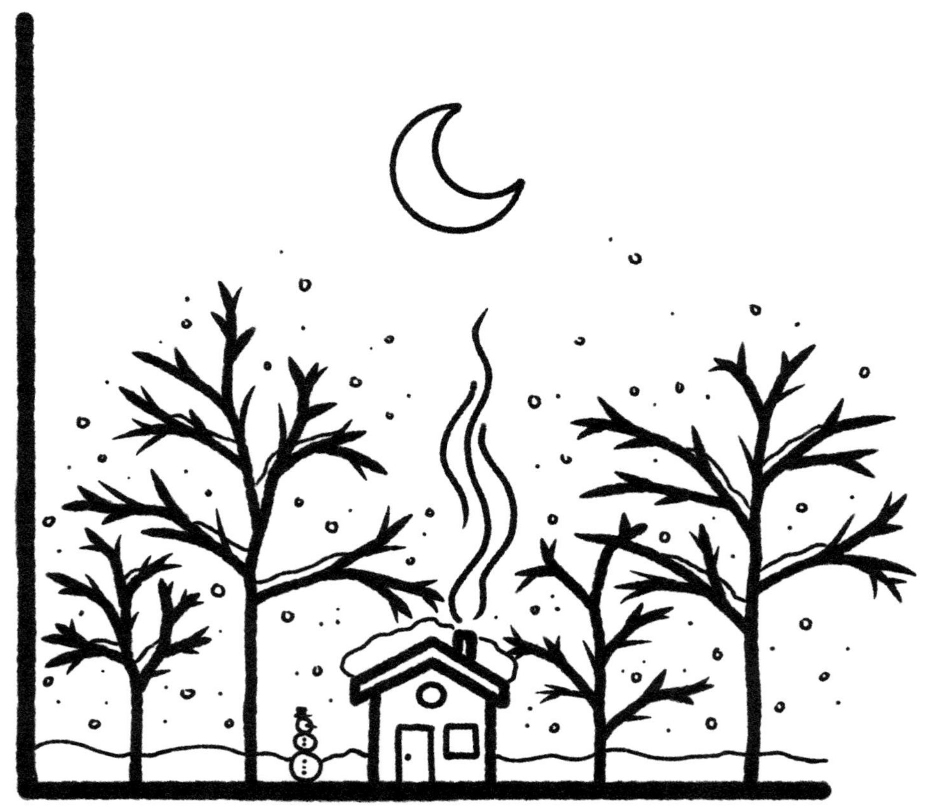

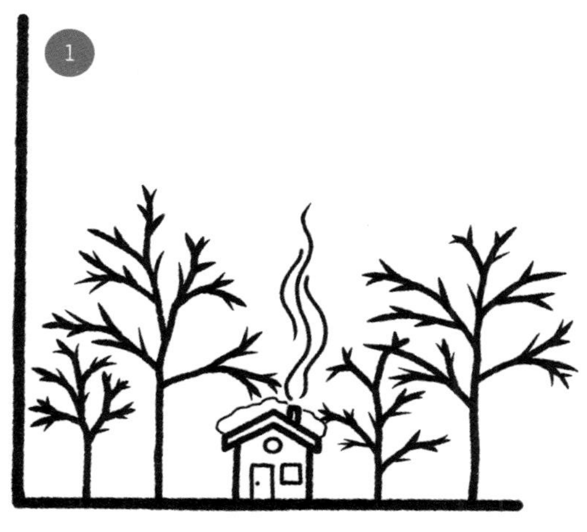

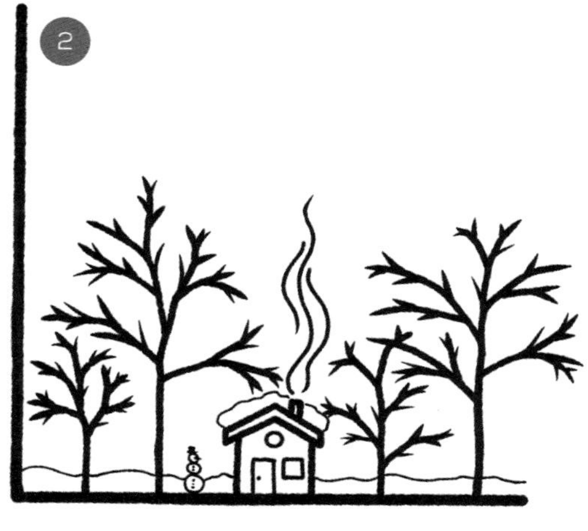

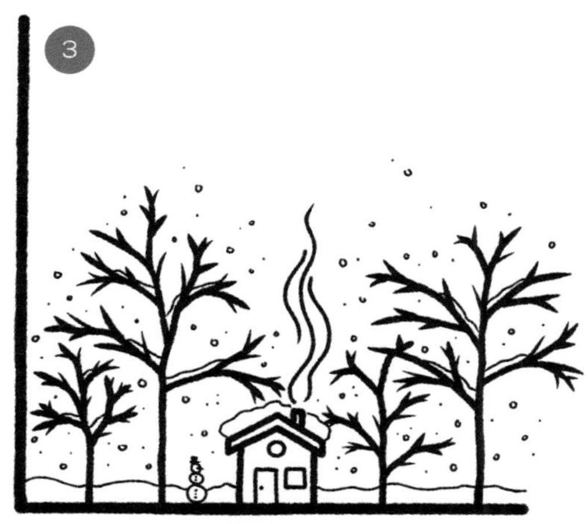

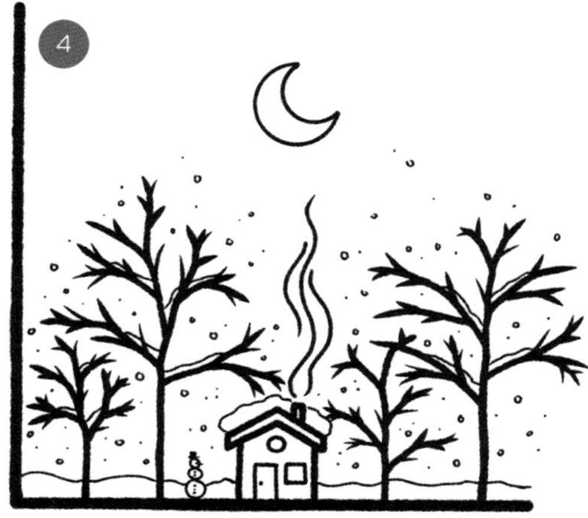

STEP 1

Winter is here! Put a blanket of snow on the cabin roof. Smoke is coming from the chimney from the cozy fireplace inside. Draw the smoke using curved lines that stretch towards the sky.

STEP 2

Our cabin inhabitants build a snowman by stacking three circles that get smaller as they go up, some dots for buttons and a tiny black square for a hat. Place it beside the cabin. Then, draw a blanket of snow over the grass.

STEP 3

It started snowing again. Draw tiny circles and dots as snowflakes. Also, some snow is accumulating on the bigger tree branches, which you can draw as a curving white line, parallel to the branch.

STEP 4

This is the last detail for this project: Draw a crescent moon outline in the sky.

You finished the last project—congratulations! I hope you had fun.

WRAP-UP: DESIGN YOUR OWN MINI LANDSCAPES

After you have done some of the projects in this book, I'm sure you want to design your own landscapes. (*Psst*: They make great gifts!)

It's a lot easier than you think!

In five simple steps, you will have your own designs in no time and some beautiful work to show off:

1. Define your main subject.
2. Select other drawing elements.
3. Collect reference pictures.
4. Decide on the composition.
5. Highlight your center of interest.

Let's use the Cabin in the Woods drawing (page 104) to run through the steps.

MAIN SUBJECT AND DRAWING ELEMENTS

Your main subject is what your drawing is about and the rest of the elements set the scene. Figure out a combination that is not too overwhelming with details. For our example, the main subject is the cabin. As other elements, I picked trees in different sizes and decided on a circle frame, for the overall drawing as well as for the clearing for the cabin. I could have included deer, grass, bushes, bunnies and about 20 other things that you can find in a forest. I didn't, though, because neither of those things would have supported the idea of my drawing: to show a cabin in a wood clearing. Be selective, and, if in doubt, start with fewer elements. You can always add more.

REFERENCES

Now, where to find reference pictures of all your elements? The easiest and fastest way is to search the Internet. You could check different picture-sharing sites, look through a variety of social media channels and, my personal favorite, search travel blogs for amazing pictures.

There are, of course, offline alternatives: take your own pictures or collect magazine scraps or travel catalogs. (*Psst*: Don't tell anyone, but I usually keep the junk mail from outdoor gear companies. They often include great landscape photography or pictures of people doing outdoor activities like camping.)

I recommend setting up a system to collect reference pictures, even when you don't have a specific drawing in mind yet. I have a folder on my phone and computer where I put anything I come across in daily life that sparks my interest, and I try to record notes for any ideas I have for the picture. It's organized in categories, and I access it first when I look for a specific reference.

Now, with our example drawing, I had both pictures I needed (a cabin and a pine tree) on file already as they are elements I draw quite often.

COMPOSITION

The way you combine the elements in your drawing and highlight the main point of interest is the composition. Composition is your friend. It helps to make your drawings more interesting.

Here is an overview of a few standard compositions:

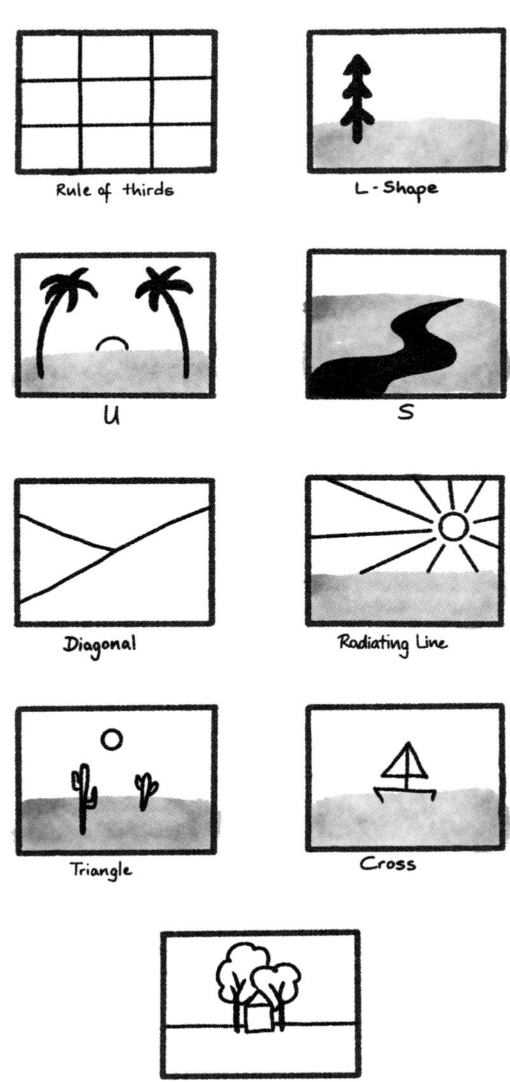

I find that the rule of thirds is a good basis for almost any drawing. Place your main subject where the imaginary gridlines cross. You can also combine different compositions; they are not mutually exclusive.

The next time you see a drawing or painting, check if you can find one of the composition principles. I'm sure you will be successful.

Going back to our example: the cabin in the woods. Imagine the grid for the rule of thirds and you will find the cabin on the lower right intersection.

HIGHLIGHT YOUR CENTER OF INTEREST

After deciding where to place your main subject, let's move on to how you can bring it even more front and center by emphasizing it.

Here are techniques you can use, independently or in combination: light and shade, details, contrast and color.

Light and shade means that you give your main subject a three-dimensional look by leaving the areas where the light directly hits it in white and create gradients, for example, with a stronger texture, where it's a little darker. I use this technique often when I want to give a three-dimensional look to mountains. The texture on the slopes is light on one side and creates a darker effect on the other. Refer to the project Secret Planet Landscape on page 116 to see what I mean.

If you add more details to your main subject, it will also appear more interesting. This is why the cabin has windows, a door, a chimney and very tiny shingles on the roof. As I did not want to add more details to the cabin, this also meant the trees had to be very, very simple. Hence the overly simplified style.

Contrast means that a black area against a white background or the opposite combination will lead the eye to that area. The cabin has quite a few solid black areas to make it look mostly black. As a contrast, I left the surrounding clearing completely white—no details at all—to achieve maximum contrast.

Color is optional in this book and it wasn't part of the original cabin drawing, so I added some to show what it can do. The green in the clearing is much lighter than the rest of the forest, therefore it enforces the focus on the cabin.

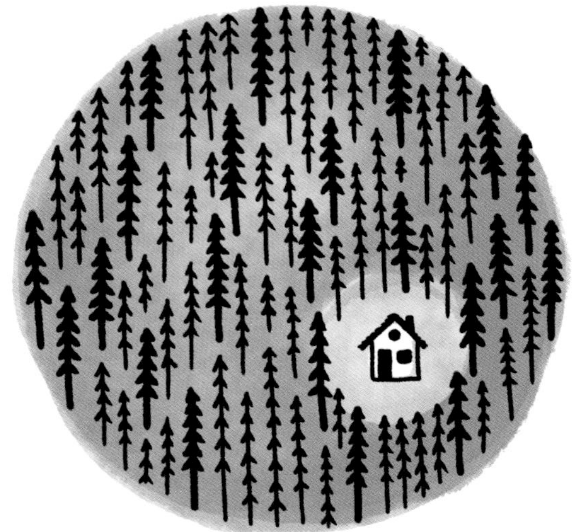

I also use this technique often by highlighting the fire or the sun. See the Circle Scene of a Forest Campground project (page 29) for an example of this. Now, you have all the tools to create your own landscape drawing. Grab your pens and go for it!

DISPLAYING AND DIGITIZING YOUR WORK

After you've put in all the drawing work, you will want to show off the final result to friends and family. We all like to share our hobbies with other people after all. Bonus points if you have friends who like to draw too.

You can display your work in your house. I usually have one wall where I can easily change out drawings to display my current favorites. I've used anything—from blu tack to a clothesline and binder clips or a pinboard—for this and I'm pretty sure I'll keep switching it up in the future. Pinterest is a great source for ideas here.

For a more permanent display, frame your drawings. There are a lot of nicely priced frame options, and if you go for plain black, you can't go wrong. I usually buy them from IKEA® and hang a lot of them in different sizes close together to create a gallery wall. Once the frames are on the wall and the work inside is the main focus, you don't even realize that the frames were only a buck apiece.

A very personal way to use your drawings is as cards or gift tags. Just cut them to the correct size. Use a ruler and a cutting blade for straight edges or use a plain card for your drawing. For gift tags, use a hole punch to make a hole for the ribbon.

If you're looking to share digitally, you will want to scan or photograph your work. I could probably write another book about this, but here is the short version:

Scans have a better quality, and I recommend them if you want to print out your work later on. Most print shops offer scans as well, and you can ask the team there for setting recommendations too.

For home scanning, I recommend using a flatbed scanner. I have two tips for you: Clean and dust the scanner glass diligently before you place your drawing on there and put a couple of books on top of the scanner lid. Why? Little dust pieces will be visible on the scans, especially if you scan at a high resolution. They are a pain to remove with editing software, so it's better not to have any. And the books make sure that the paper is pressed down properly by the lid so no stray light can get in. The pressure by the books keeps out more light than with just the lid itself.

Also, if you plan on scanning your artwork later on, smooth paper will get you a more precise scan. Beware that the texture of rougher paper will be visible on a scan too.

If you don't have a scanner, you can also photograph your work with your smartphone or a digital camera. Place your work on a flat surface in front of a window and make sure you angle it and your camera in a way that no shadows fall on the paper. Try to line up the edge of your paper nicely with the edge of the camera view. Hold your camera parallel to the top of the paper, otherwise your picture might be distorted. A tripod is helpful to get a steady picture but not absolutely necessary.

I recommend taking the picture on a bright but not too sunny day when the light is soft. After you've done a couple of pictures with different weather conditions, you will recognize what I mean when you compare the results.

Pictures for sharing on social media are a different process again. Start out by searching the web for "artwork flat lays" and take it from there.

I would love to see how your projects turned out. If you share them on Instagram, tag me @linesandmountains or write me a message. Of course, if you have questions about any of the projects, get in touch too. Keep drawing!

ACKNOWLEDGMENTS

A huge and heartfelt thank you to all of you. Yes, that includes you! Thank you to every single reader of this book and every single follower on my social media channels. For reading, drawing along, liking, sharing, commenting, recommending to friends and just generally making this book possible at all. You wouldn't be reading this without the support you have given me, and it means the world to me.

Thank you to my partner, Dennis, for believing in @linesandmountains from the very early stages, even when I didn't myself. And for spending all this time doing sports so I could have some peace and quiet to finish this book.

Thank you to my parents Uschi and Walter for simultaneously supporting every creative pursuit I ever tried as a teenager and displaying my early and more recent creations in your house.

Thank you to my sisters for being my sisters and supporting me in their own ways. Paula for giving me time to work on the book, Ursi for being her cheery self and always asking about progress and Johanna for reading every word I wrote repeatedly and all the constructive criticism.

Thank you to my editor, Aïcha. There would be no book without you!

And, of course, thank you to everyone at Page Street who helped to make and sell this book. I felt I was in professional and supportive hands during the whole process, you rock!

ABOUT THE AUTHOR

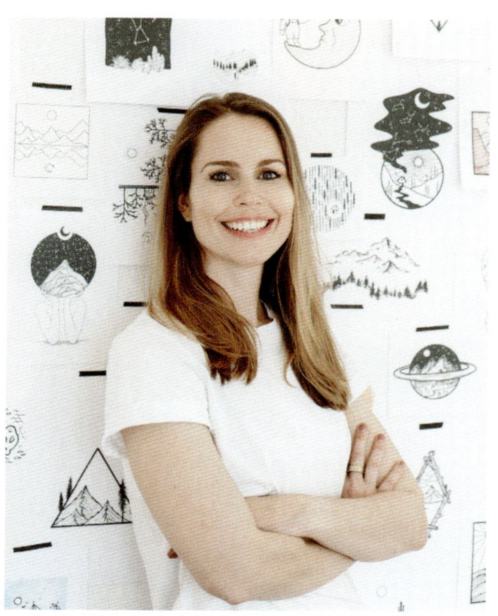

Rosa Hoehn is the creator behind @linesandmountains on Instagram. She uses the inspiration of nature and outdoor adventures in her drawings and is passionate about showing others that drawing can be very relaxing and that small landscape drawings do not have to be realistic or very detailed to be beautiful.

After starting to draw seriously in high school and completing many classes on the subject, Rosa abandoned the idea to pursue a graphic design degree and now holds a tourism management degree. During a particularly busy stage in her career, she turned back to drawing as relaxation.

When the coronavirus pandemic put her career on hold, Rosa used the time to complete a wide range of custom projects for a multitude of clients and get her Etsy shop up and running. You can find her designs on apparel, wall art and more in her shop. By now, there are also more than 100 people with tattoos of her artwork on their bodies!

INDEX

A

Adobe Houses and a Snake, 78–80
Astronaut and the Moon, The, 127–129
Astronaut Floating Through Outer Space, 125–126
autumn, 166–167

B

Baby Seals Playing in the Waves, 56–57
birds, how to, 39
boats, how to, 48
Bridge Over a Small Forest Stream, 98–101

C

Cabin in the Woods, 104–105
Cabin Surrounded by Blooming Trees, 162–163
Cable Car Over the Mountains, 19–21
Cacti in the Desert, 75–77
Canoeing Along the River, 93–94
Chill-Out Hammock Between Palm Trees, 50–53
Circle Scene of a Forest Campground, 29–31
Cloud of Planets, A, 119–121
composition, 171–172
coral, how to, 65

D

Deer Family in a Forest Meadow, 109–111
Desert Night Sky, 81–83
design of landscapes, how to, 170–172
display of artwork, 173
Diver Swimming Through a School of Fish, 61–63

E

eyes, how to, 129

F

fall (season), 166–167
fish, how to, 66
Fishing on a Mountain Lake, 91–92
Flock of Birds Sitting on Power Lines, 138–141

G

Galaxy in a Jar, 122–124

H

High Waterfall, 95–97
Hilly Landscape with Mushrooms, 142–143

I

ink wash/watercolor, 31

J

jar, 122–124
Jellyfish Swarm, 58–60

L

leaves, how to, 51, 167
Lighthouse in the Dunes, The, 40–43
line weight, 10, 13
linework basics, 8–9
Linework Canyons, 84–85

M

materials, about, 7
mistakes, 12–13
Misty Winter Forest, 112–113
moon, how to, 24
Mountain Scene in Day and Night, 146–150
movement control, 17
mushrooms, how to, 143

O

outlines, 10

P

practice, 8–9, 11

R

references, 171
Rock Formation Landscape, 72–74

S

Sailing Around Tropical Islands, 47–49
Seagulls Flying Over the Dock, 37–39
seals, 56–57
Seasons, The
  autumn, 166–167
  base drawing, 160–161
  spring, 162–163
  summer, 164–165
  winter, 168–169
Secret Planet Landscape, 116–118
shadows, 77
ski tracks, 26–28
Small Farm Scene, 135–137
Small Wood Cabin on the Lake, 88–90
Snowy Treescape, 168–169
spring, 162–163
stars, how to, 121
summer, 164–165
Sun and Moon Reflection Over the Sea, 155–157
Sun and Night Sky Over a Cabin, 151–154
sun, how to, 137
Sunny Patch of Leafy Trees, 164–165
supplies, about, 7
Surf Shack, 34–36

T

textures, 10
Thunderstorm Over the Sea, 44–46
Trees and Falling Leaves, 166–167
Turtle Swimming Over Seaweed, 67–69

V

Van Life Night Scene, 22–25

W

warm-up exercises, 8–9
watercolor/ink wash, 31
Way to the Mountaintop, The, 16–18
Whale with Small Fish Friends, 64–66
Windmills in the Country, 132–134
winter, 26–28, 168–169
Winter Mountains with Ski Tracks, 26–28
Wolf Howling at the Moon, 106–108